Taste of Home's
Favorite Brand Name Recipes
2003

Taste of Home Books

Editor: Heidi Reuter Lloyd
Food Editor: Janaan Cunningham
Associate Food Editor: Diane Werner
Senior Recipe Editor: Sue A. Jurack

Front cover photography by Reiman Publications.
Food Photography: Rob Hagen
Senior Food Photography Artist: Stephanie Marchese
Food Photography Artist: Julie Ferron
Photo Studio Manager: Anne Schimmel

Pictured on the front cover *(clockwise from top left):* Classic Lemon Meringue Pie *(page 190),* Green Bean and Potato Salad in Dijon Vinaigrette *(page 36)* and Oriental Barbecued Ribs with Oriental Plum Sauce *(page 142).*

Pictured on the back cover *(clockwise from top left):* Fiesta Chicken Nachos *(page 7),* Southern Barbecue Sandwich *(page 98)* and Chocolate Peanut Butter Parfaits *(page 184).*

ISBN: 0-7853-8374-3

Library of Congress Control Number: 2002116503

Manufactured in China.

8 7 6 5 4 3 2 1

Some of the products listed in this publication may be in limited distribution.

Microwave Cooking: Microwave ovens vary in wattage. Use the cooking times as guidelines and check for doneness before adding more time.

Taste of Home's Favorite Brand Name Recipes 2003

Tried-and-True Favorites Your Family is Sure to Enjoy

THIS IS one of those cookbooks that's hard to put down. We think you'll find that these recipes intrigue you and the photos make you good and hungry! And when that happens you'll surely find yourself thinking about all the wonderful possibilities for lunch tomorrow, that family dinner on Saturday and the bake sale after church on Sunday.

The best part is, you don't have to worry one bit if these recipes will turn out and taste good. You're assured they will, because this book, *Taste of Home's Favorite Brand Name Recipes 2003,* brings together some of the most trusted names in the world of home cooking.

All 327 family-style recipes were hand-selected by the experienced home economists at *Taste of Home,* the most popular cooking magazine in the country. And every one of these recipes features name-brand foods you've used and enjoyed with confidence over the years.

Chosen from the Best

Yes, this book is filled with luscious recipes, and we've spent a year sifting through hundreds of name-brand favorites to create a collection that will make your taste buds tingle and your mouth water.

Biscuit-Topped Hearty Steak Pie (p. 140)

And we went right to the source. For instance:

• When we wanted a refreshing appetizer that wasn't complicated, we chose Hershey's smooth and creamy Chocolate Fruit Dip (see page 11 in the Appetizers & Snacks chapter).

• When we wanted to kick up the flavor of plain tomato soup, we chose the Heinz recipe for Italian Tomato Soup featuring ground beef, onions, garlic, basil and white kidney beans (see page 70 in the Soups chapter).

• And when we decided we needed a sassy salad that combined sweet and tart, we chose a recipe from the National Honey Board, for Ambrosia with Honey Lime Cream Dressing (see page 26 in the Salads chapter).

You'll also find enough desserts to keep your sweet tooth happy for months when you sample the dozens of delicious cakes, cookies, pies, bars and cobblers in a multitude of flavors.

Picture-Perfect Foods

We packed over 300 recipes into the 224 pages of this useful book, and quite a few of those recipes include photos, so you'll be able to see what you're making and how wonderful the finished product will look.

Creamy Chocolate Pie (p. 193)

The photos are large; in fact, a number are full-page in size. You'll count more than 140 color photos, and we hope you enjoy them.

This book will take you from the start of a family meal to the finish, giving you plenty of choices for appealing appetizers, delicious desserts and everything in between—soups, salads, entrees, side dishes and breads.

You won't have to worry about running out of clever combinations. You can mix and match to your heart's content. And your family will be happy, too, because every single recipe has been kitchen-tested and approved by *Taste of Home* food editors.

How to Find a Recipe

This cookbook is indexed in two helpful ways. The general index, beginning on page 213, lists every recipe by food category, major ingredient and/or cooking style.

For example, if you know you want to serve chicken tonight, turn to "chicken" in the general index and ponder the many tasty options. You can also look under general categories such as "oven entrees," "skillet & stovetop suppers" and "grilled & broiled."

The alphabetical index starts on page 221, so once you and your family have discovered a few favorites, it's a snap to find them by name when you're ready to make them again.

We hope you enjoy using *Taste of Home's Favorite Brand Name Recipes 2003* as much as we enjoyed making it. Happy cooking!

Appetizers & Snacks

Fiesta Chicken Nachos

(Pictured at left and on back cover)

1 tablespoon BERTOLLI® Olive Oil
1 pound boneless, skinless chicken breasts
1 jar (16 ounces) RAGÚ® Cheese Creations!® Double
    Cheddar Sauce
1 bag (9 ounces) tortilla chips
2 green and/or red bell peppers, diced
1 small onion, chopped
1 large tomato, diced

In 12-inch skillet, heat oil over medium-high heat and cook chicken, stirring occasionally, 8 minutes or until no longer pink. Remove from skillet; cut into strips.

In same skillet, combine chicken and Ragú® Cheese Creations! Sauce; heat through.

On serving platter, arrange layer of tortilla chips, then 1/2 of the sauce mixture, bell peppers, onion and tomato; repeat, ending with tomato. Garnish, if desired, with chopped fresh cilantro and shredded lettuce. *Makes 4 servings*

Helpful Hint

The most familiar sweet pepper is the green pepper, also known as the bell pepper for its bell-like shape. Green peppers are picked before they ripen. When ripe, a bell pepper is red, yellow, orange, white or purple, depending on the variety.

Clockwise from top left: *Roasted Red Pepper Dip (p. 16), Cheddar Tomato Bacon Toasts (p. 8), Savory Stuffed Mushrooms (p. 18) and Fiesta Chicken Nachos*

Pesto Dijon Pizzas

(Pictured at right)

1/2 cup chopped parsley*
1/3 cup GREY POUPON® Dijon Mustard
1/4 cup PLANTERS® Walnuts, chopped*
1 tablespoon olive oil*
2 tablespoons grated Parmesan cheese,* divided
1-1/2 teaspoons dried basil leaves,* divided
2 (8-ounce) packages small prepared pizza crusts
4 ounces thinly sliced deli baked ham
3 plum tomatoes, sliced
1 cup shredded mozzarella cheese (4 ounces)

1 (7-ounce) container prepared pesto sauce may be substituted for parsley, walnuts, olive oil, 1 tablespoon Parmesan cheese and 1 teaspoon basil. Stir mustard into prepared pesto sauce.

1. Blend parsley, mustard, walnuts, oil, 1 tablespoon Parmesan cheese and 1 teaspoon basil in small bowl. Divide mixture and spread evenly onto each pizza crust. Top each crust with 2 ounces ham, tomato slices and mozzarella cheese. Sprinkle with remaining Parmesan cheese and basil. Place on baking sheet.

2. Bake at 450°F for 8 to 10 minutes or until cheese melts. Cut into wedges; serve warm.

Makes 4 main-dish or 8 appetizer servings

Beefy Guacamole Dip

1 pound ground beef
1 large onion, minced
1 package (1.0 ounce) LAWRY'S® Spices & Seasonings for Tacos
3/4 cup water
1-1/2 cups guacamole
2 medium tomatoes, chopped
1 cup (4 ounces) shredded cheddar cheese
Tortilla chips

In large skillet, cook ground beef and onion over medium-high heat until beef is browned and crumbly; drain fat. Add Spices & Seasonings for Tacos and water; mix well. Bring to a boil over medium-high heat; reduce heat to low and simmer, uncovered, 10 minutes or until liquid is absorbed. In small bowl, combine guacamole and tomatoes; mix well. In large bowl, layer half of beef mixture, guacamole and cheese; repeat layers.

Makes about 4 cups

Serving Suggestion: Serve immediately with tortilla chips.

Mini Sausage Quiches

1/2 cup butter or margarine, softened
3 ounces cream cheese, softened
1 cup all-purpose flour
1/2 pound BOB EVANS® Italian Roll Sausage
1 cup (4 ounces) shredded Swiss cheese
1 tablespoon snipped fresh chives
2 eggs
1 cup half-and-half
1/4 teaspoon salt
Dash cayenne pepper

Beat butter and cream cheese in medium bowl until creamy. Blend in flour; refrigerate 1 hour. Roll into 24 (1-inch) balls; press each into ungreased mini-muffin cup to form pastry shell. Preheat oven to 375°F. To prepare filling, crumble sausage into small skillet. Cook over medium heat until browned, stirring occasionally. Drain off any drippings. Sprinkle evenly into pastry shells in muffin cups; sprinkle with Swiss cheese and chives. Whisk eggs, half-and-half, salt and cayenne until blended; pour into pastry shells. Bake 20 to 30 minutes or until set. Remove from pans. Serve hot. Refrigerate leftovers.

Makes 24 appetizers

Tip: Pour mixture into 12 standard 2-1/2-inch muffin cups to make larger individual quiches. Serve for breakfast.

Cheddar Tomato Bacon Toasts

(Pictured on page 6)

1 jar (16 ounces) RAGÚ® Cheese Creations!® Double Cheddar Sauce
1 medium tomato, chopped
5 slices bacon, crisp-cooked and crumbled (about 1/3 cup)
2 loaves Italian bread (each about 16 inches long), each cut into 16 slices

1. Preheat oven to 350°F. In medium bowl, combine Ragú® Cheese Creations! Sauce, tomato and bacon.

2. On baking sheet, arrange bread slices. Evenly top with sauce mixture.

3. Bake 10 minutes or until sauce mixture is bubbling. Serve immediately.

Makes 16 servings

Pesto Dijon Pizzas

Top to bottom: Crispy Spiced Nut
Breadsticks and Crispy Ranch
Breadsticks

Crispy Ranch Breadsticks

(Pictured above)

2 tablespoons dry ranch party dip mix
2 tablespoons sour cream
1 package (10 ounces) refrigerated pizza dough
Butter, melted

1. Preheat oven to 400°F. Grease baking sheets or line with parchment paper. Combine dip mix and sour cream in small bowl; set aside.

2. Unroll pizza dough on lightly floured work surface. Shape dough into 16×10-inch rectangle. Brush with melted butter. Spread dip mixture evenly over top of dough; cut into 24 (10-inch) strips. Shape into desired shapes.

3. Place breadsticks 1/2 inch apart on prepared baking sheets. Bake 10 minutes or until golden brown. Serve immediately or place on wire rack to cool.
Makes 24 breadsticks

Crispy Spiced Nut Breadsticks: Place 1 cup finely chopped pecans and 1 tablespoon vegetable oil in plastic bag; toss to coat. Combine 1/4 teaspoon chili powder, 1/4 teaspoon ground cumin, 1/4 teaspoon curry powder, 1/8 teaspoon ground cinnamon and dash of cayenne pepper in small bowl. Add to nuts; toss to coat. Place nuts in small pan over medium heat and stir constantly until nuts are lightly toasted. Sprinkle nut mixture with 1 teaspoon garlic salt; cool to room temperature. Instead of spreading dough with sour cream mixture, sprinkle 1/2 cup spiced nuts over dough (store remaining nuts in tightly covered container). Cut into 24 (10-inch) strips. Shape into desired shapes. Bake as directed.

Party Chicken Tarts

1-1/2 cups chopped cooked chicken
2 tablespoons butter or margarine
1 cup chopped fresh mushrooms
1/4 cup finely chopped celery
1/4 cup finely chopped onion
2 tablespoons all-purpose flour
6 tablespoons sour cream
1/2 teaspoon garlic salt
1 package (10 ounces) flaky refrigerator biscuits (10 to 12 count)
Vegetable cooking spray
1 tablespoon butter or margarine, melted
Grated Parmesan cheese

Melt 2 tablespoons butter in large skillet until hot. Add mushrooms, celery and onion; cook and stir 4 to 5 minutes. Sprinkle with flour; stir in chicken and sour cream. Cook until thoroughly heated. Stir in garlic salt; set aside. Cut each biscuit into quarters; press each piece into miniature muffin tins coated with cooking spray to form tart shell. Brush each piece with melted butter. Bake at 400°F 6 minutes. Remove from oven; reduce oven temperature to 350°F. Fill each tart with 1 teaspoon chicken mixture; sprinkle with cheese. Bake 14 to 15 minutes more. Serve immediately.
Makes 40 to 48 appetizers

Tip: For ease in serving at party time, prepare filling ahead and cook tarts 5 minutes. Fill and bake just before serving for best flavor.

Favorite recipe from **National Chicken Council**

Cheese and Pepper Stuffed Potato Skins

(Pictured below)

- **6 large russet potatoes (about 3/4 pound each), scrubbed**
- **4 tablespoons *Frank's® RedHot®* Cayenne Pepper Sauce, divided**
- **2 tablespoons butter, melted**
- **1 large red bell pepper, seeded and finely chopped**
- **1 cup chopped green onions**
- **1 cup (4 ounces) shredded cheddar cheese**

1. Preheat oven to 450°F. Wrap potatoes in foil; bake about 1 hour 15 minutes or until fork tender. Let stand until cool enough to handle. Cut each potato in half lengthwise; scoop out insides,* leaving a 1/4-inch-thick shell. Cut shells in half widthwise. Place shells on large baking sheet.

2. Preheat broiler. Combine 1 tablespoon *Frank's RedHot* Sauce and butter in small bowl; brush on inside of each potato shell. Broil shells, 6 inches from heat, 8 minutes or until golden brown and crispy.

3. Combine remaining 3 tablespoons *Frank's RedHot* Sauce with remaining ingredients in large bowl. Spoon about 1 tablespoon mixture into each potato shell. Broil 2 minutes or until cheese melts. Cut each piece in half to serve.

Makes 12 servings

*Reserve leftover potato for mashed potatoes, home-fries or soup.

Chocolate Fruit Dip

- **1 container (8 ounces) vanilla yogurt**
- **1/3 cup packed light brown sugar**
- **1 tablespoon HERSHEY'S Cocoa**
- **1/2 teaspoon vanilla extract**
- **Dash ground cinnamon**
- **Assorted fresh fruit, cut up**

1. Combine all ingredients except fruit in small bowl; stir with whisk until smooth. Cover; refrigerate until well chilled. Serve with assorted fresh fruit. Cover and refrigerate leftover dip. *Makes 10 servings*

Cheese and Pepper Stuffed Potato Skins

Nutty Broccoli Spread

(Pictured at right)

1 box (10 ounces) BIRDS EYE® frozen Chopped
   Broccoli
4 ounces cream cheese
1/4 cup grated Parmesan cheese
1 teaspoon dried basil
1/4 cup walnuts
1 loaf frozen garlic bread

• Cook broccoli according to package directions;
drain well.

• Preheat oven to 400°F. Place broccoli, cream
cheese, Parmesan cheese and basil in food
processor or blender; process until ingredients are
mixed. (Do not overmix.) Add walnuts; process 3 to
5 seconds.

• Split garlic bread lengthwise. Spread broccoli
mixture evenly over bread.

• Bake 10 to 15 minutes or until bread is toasted and
broccoli mixture is heated through.

• Cut bread into slices; serve hot.

Makes about 2 cups spread

Almond Butter Crunch Pop Corn

1/2 cup butter or margarine
1 cup granulated sugar
1/4 cup light corn syrup
1/4 teaspoon salt
1/2 teaspoon vanilla
1/2 teaspoon butter extract
1/4 teaspoon baking soda
2-1/2 quarts popped JOLLY TIME® Pop Corn
1-1/2 cups whole almonds, toasted*

**To toast almonds, spread on large baking sheet and bake at 325°F
15 to 20 minutes.*

Melt butter in medium saucepan. Stir in sugar, corn
syrup and salt. Bring to a boil, stirring constantly.
Boil 8 minutes, stirring once, over lowest heat
possible to maintain a boil. Remove from heat; stir
in vanilla, butter extract and baking soda. Gradually
pour over popped pop corn and nuts, mixing well.
Turn into large shallow baking pan. Bake at 250°F
30 minutes, mixing well after 15 minutes. Allow to
cool completely. Break apart and store in tightly
covered container. *Makes about 3 quarts*

Open-Faced Reubens

1 box (6 ounces) rye melba toast rounds
1/4 pound thinly sliced cooked corned beef, cut
   into 1/2-inch squares
1 can (8 ounces) sauerkraut, rinsed, drained and
   chopped
1 cup (4 ounces) finely shredded Wisconsin
   Swiss cheese
2 teaspoons prepared mustard
Caraway seeds

Preheat oven to 350°F. Arrange toast rounds on
baking sheets. Top each with 1 beef square and
1 teaspoon sauerkraut. Mix cheese and mustard in
small bowl; spoon about 1 teaspoon cheese mixture
on top of sauerkraut. Sprinkle with caraway seeds.
Bake about 5 minutes or until cheese is melted.

Makes about 48 appetizer servings

Microwave Directions: Arrange 8 toast rounds
around edge of microwave-safe plate lined with
paper towel. Place 2 rounds in center. Top as
directed. Microwave, uncovered, on MEDIUM
(50% power) 1 to 2 minutes until cheese is melted,
turning plate once. Repeat with remaining
ingredients.

Favorite recipe from **Wisconsin Milk Marketing
Board**

Italian Pineapple Salsa

3 cups DOLE® Fresh Pineapple Chunks
1/2 cup chopped DOLE® Red Bell Pepper
3 tablespoons chopped red onion
3 tablespoons chopped fresh basil
4 teaspoons white wine vinegar
1 tablespoon balsamic vinegar
1/4 teaspoon red pepper flakes
1/8 teaspoon salt

• Combine pineapple chunks, bell pepper, onion,
basil, vinegars, red pepper flakes and salt in medium
serving bowl. Cover; chill at least 1 hour to blend
flavors.

• Serve over grilled turkey or beef hamburgers, with
chips. Salsa can also be served as a dip with tortilla
chips or spooned over quesadillas or tacos.

Makes 10 servings

Nutty Broccoli Spread

Chile 'n' Cheese Spirals

(Pictured at right)

4 ounces cream cheese, softened
1 cup (4 ounces) shredded cheddar cheese
1 can (4 ounces) ORTEGA® Diced Green Chiles
3 green onions, sliced
1/2 cup chopped red bell pepper
1 can (2.25 ounces) chopped ripe olives
4 (8-inch) taco-size flour tortillas
ORTEGA® SALSA (any flavor)

COMBINE cream cheese, cheddar cheese, chiles, green onions, pepper and olives in medium bowl.

SPREAD 1/2 cup cheese mixture on each tortilla; roll up. Wrap each roll in plastic wrap; chill for 1 hour.

REMOVE plastic wrap; slice each roll into six 3/4-inch pieces. Serve with salsa for dipping.

Makes 24 appetizers

Tip: Chili 'n' Cheese Spirals can be made ahead and kept in the refrigerator for 1 to 2 days.

Maple Baked Ribs

1/4 cup I CAN'T BELIEVE IT'S NOT BUTTER!®
Spread
2 cloves garlic, finely chopped
1/2 cup ketchup
1/3 cup pure maple syrup or pancake syrup
2 tablespoons firmly packed brown sugar
2 tablespoons white vinegar
2 teaspoons hot pepper sauce
2-1/2 to 3 pounds baby back ribs or spareribs

Preheat oven to 400°F.

In small saucepan, melt I Can't Believe It's Not Butter!® Spread over medium heat and cook garlic, stirring occasionally, 1 minute. Stir in ketchup, syrup, brown sugar, vinegar and hot pepper sauce. Bring to a boil over high heat. Reduce heat to low and simmer 2 minutes.

In bottom of broiler pan, without rack, arrange ribs. Pour maple sauce over ribs. Cover with aluminum foil and bake 45 minutes. Remove foil and bake an additional 10 minutes or until meat juices run clear, basting once with sauce. With knife, slice between ribs and toss with sauce in bottom of pan.

Makes 4 servings

Sweet & Sour Cocktail Meatballs

1 pound ground turkey
3/4 cup plain dry bread crumbs
1/2 cup GREY POUPON® Dijon Mustard, divided
1/2 cup chopped green onions, divided
1 egg, beaten
1/2 teaspoon ground ginger
1/2 teaspoon ground black pepper
1 (8-ounce) can pineapple chunks, undrained
1/3 cup firmly packed light brown sugar
1/4 cup apple cider vinegar
1/4 cup diced red bell pepper
1 teaspoon cornstarch

Combine turkey, bread crumbs, 1/4 cup mustard, 1/4 cup green onions, egg, ginger and black pepper in large bowl. Shape into 32 (1-inch) balls. Place in greased 13×9×2-inch baking dish. Bake at 350°F for 20 minutes.

Combine pineapple chunks with juice, sugar, vinegar, red bell pepper, cornstarch and remaining mustard and green onions in medium saucepan. Cook over medium heat until sauce thickens and begins to boil. Spoon pineapple sauce over meatballs. Bake 5 to 7 minutes more or until meatballs are done. Spoon into serving dish and serve with toothpicks. *Makes 32 appetizers*

Creamy Fruit Blend

1 cup milk
1/2 cup white grape juice
1/2 cup fresh or frozen unsweetened strawberries
1 small ripe peach, peeled, pitted and quartered
1 ripe banana, peeled and quartered
2 tablespoons brown sugar
1 tablespoon lemon juice
1/2 teaspoon almond extract
Fresh fruit (optional)

Process all ingredients in blender or food processor until smooth. Serve immediately. Garnish with fresh fruit, if desired. *Makes 2 to 3 servings*

Chile 'n' Cheese Spirals

Viennese Coffee

Viennese Coffee

(Pictured above)

1 cup heavy cream, divided
1 teaspoon powdered sugar
1 bar (3 ounces) bittersweet or semisweet
**   chocolate**
3 cups strong freshly brewed hot coffee

Chill bowl, beaters and cream before whipping. Place 2/3 cup cream and sugar into chilled bowl. Beat with electric mixer at high speed until soft peaks form. Cover and refrigerate up to 8 hours. If mixture has separated slightly after refrigeration, whisk lightly with wire whisk before using.

For garnish, place waxed paper under chocolate. Holding chocolate in one hand, make short, quick strokes across chocolate with vegetable peeler; set aside. Break remaining chocolate into pieces.

Place remaining 1/3 cup cream in small saucepan. Bring to a simmer over medium-low heat. Add chocolate pieces; cover and remove from heat. Let stand 5 minutes or until chocolate is melted; stir until smooth.

Add hot coffee to chocolate mixture. Heat over low heat just until bubbles form around edge of pan and coffee is heated through, stirring often. Remove from heat. Pour into 4 warmed mugs. Top with whipped cream. Garnish with chocolate shavings.

Makes about 4 servings

Roasted Red Pepper Dip

(Pictured on page 6)

1 (8-ounce) container BREAKSTONE'S® or
**   KNUDSEN® Sour Cream**
1 (7-ounce) jar roasted red peppers, drained
4 ounces PHILADELPHIA® Cream Cheese
1/2 teaspoon chopped fresh or frozen chives
**   Fresh chives and red bell pepper, for garnish**
**   WHEAT THINS® Snack Crackers and fresh**
**   vegetables**

1. Blend sour cream, peppers, cream cheese and chopped chives with electric mixer until well mixed.

2. Spoon into bowl; refrigerate for at least 1 hour.

3. Garnish with chives and red bell pepper if desired. Serve as dip with snack crackers and fresh vegetables.

Makes 2 cups

Ham and Cheese Muffin Rolls

1 (1-pound) loaf frozen bread dough, thawed
3 tablespoons prepared mustard
1 tablespoon honey
2 cups shredded Swiss cheese
3/4 pound very thinly sliced CURE 81® ham
**   Mango chutney, if desired**

On floured surface, roll dough into 21×12-inch rectangle. In small bowl, combine mustard and honey. Spread mustard mixture over dough. Sprinkle dough with cheese. Lay ham slices over cheese. Starting with long side, roll dough up tightly. Cut dough into 12 equal slices. Place slices, cut sides up, in greased muffin cups, pressing slightly. Cover. Let rise in warm place 45 minutes or until doubled in size. Heat oven to 375°F. Bake 30 minutes or until golden. Cover with foil if rolls become too brown. Serve with chutney, if desired.

Makes 12 appetizer servings

Campbell's® Shrimp Dip

(Pictured below)

1 package (8 ounces) cream cheese, softened
1 can (10-3/4 ounces) CAMPBELL'S® Condensed
   Cream of Shrimp Soup
1/2 teaspoon Louisiana-style hot sauce
1/4 cup finely chopped celery
1 tablespoon finely chopped onion

Stir cream cheese until smooth. Stir in soup, hot sauce, celery and onion. Refrigerate at least 4 hours. Serve with crackers, chips or fresh vegetables for dipping.   *Makes 2-1/4 cups*

Helpful Hint

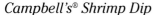

Keep celery fresh for up to two weeks by storing it in a plastic bag in the refrigerator. If celery becomes limp or wilted, freshen it by soaking trimmed ribs in a bowl of ice water for about one hour.

Cashew & Pretzel Toffee Clusters

3/4 cup packed brown sugar
3/4 cup light corn syrup
1/2 cup butter
  2 teaspoons vanilla
  4 cups tiny pretzel twists (not sticks)
  4 cups bite-sized toasted wheat squares cereal
  1 can (9-1/4 ounces) salted cashew halves and
    pieces

1. Preheat oven to 300°F. Spray large baking sheet with nonstick cooking spray.

2. Place brown sugar, corn syrup and butter in heavy small saucepan. Heat over medium heat until mixture boils and sugar dissolves, stirring frequently. Remove from heat; stir in vanilla.

3. Combine pretzels, cereal and cashews in large bowl. Pour sugar mixture over pretzel mixture; toss to coat evenly. Spread on prepared baking sheet. Bake 30 minutes, stirring after 15 minutes. Spread onto greased waxed paper. Cool completely; break into clusters. Store in airtight container at room temperature.   *Makes about 8 cups clusters*

Campbell's® Shrimp Dip

Tortilla Crunch Chicken Fingers

(Pictured at right)

1 envelope LIPTON® RECIPE SECRETS® Savory Herb with Garlic Soup Mix
1 cup finely crushed plain tortilla chips or cornflakes (about 3 ounces)
1-1/2 pounds boneless, skinless chicken breasts, cut into strips
1 egg
2 tablespoons water
2 tablespoons margarine or butter, melted

Preheat oven to 400°F.

In medium bowl, combine savory herb with garlic soup mix and tortilla chips. In large plastic bag or bowl, combine chicken and egg beaten with water until evenly coated. Remove chicken and dip in tortilla mixture until evenly coated; discard bag. On 15-1/2×10-1/2×1-inch jelly-roll pan sprayed with nonstick cooking spray, arrange chicken; drizzle with margarine. Bake, uncovered, 12 minutes or until chicken juices run clear. Serve with chunky salsa, if desired. *Makes about 24 chicken fingers*

Savory Stuffed Mushrooms

(Pictured on page 6)

20 medium mushrooms
2 tablespoons finely chopped onion
2 tablespoons finely chopped red bell pepper
3 tablespoons FLEISCHMANN'S® Original Margarine
1/2 cup dry seasoned bread crumbs
1/2 teaspoon dried basil leaves

1. Remove stems from mushrooms; finely chop 1/4 cup stems.

2. Cook and stir chopped stems, onion and pepper in margarine in skillet over medium heat until tender. Remove from heat; stir in crumbs and basil.

3. Spoon crumb mixture loosely into mushroom caps; place on baking sheet. Bake at 400°F for 15 minutes or until hot. *Makes 20 appetizers*

Italian-Topped Garlic Bread

1 pound BOB EVANS® Italian Roll Sausage
1 (1-pound) loaf crusty Italian bread
1/2 cup butter, melted
2 teaspoons minced garlic
2 cups (8 ounces) shredded mozzarella cheese
2 cups diced tomatoes
8 ounces fresh mushrooms, sliced
3 tablespoons grated Parmesan cheese

Preheat oven to 325°F. Crumble and cook sausage in medium skillet until browned. Drain off any drippings. Cut bread into 1-inch slices. Combine butter and garlic in small bowl; brush bread slices with mixture. Arrange on ungreased baking sheet. Combine mozzarella cheese, tomatoes, mushrooms, Parmesan cheese and sausage; spread on bread slices. Bake 10 to 12 minutes or until cheese is melted and golden brown. Serve warm. Refrigerate leftovers. *Makes about 10 appetizer servings*

Cheesy Barbecued Bean Dip

1/2 cup canned vegetarian baked beans
3 tablespoons pasteurized process cheese spread
2 tablespoons regular or hickory smoke barbecue sauce
1 green onion (optional)
2 large carrots, cut into diagonal slices
1 medium red or green bell pepper, cut into chunks

1. Place beans in small microwavable bowl; mash slightly with fork. Stir in process cheese spread and barbecue sauce. Cover with vented plastic wrap.

2. Microwave at HIGH 1 minute; stir. Microwave 30 seconds or until hot. Garnish with green onion, if desired. Serve with carrot slices and bell pepper chunks. *Makes 4 servings*

Chicken Parmesan Stromboli

(Pictured at right)

    1 pound boneless, skinless chicken breast halves
1/2 teaspoon salt
1/4 teaspoon ground black pepper
    2 teaspoons olive or vegetable oil
    2 cups shredded mozzarella cheese (about
        8 ounces)
    1 jar (28 ounces) RAGÚ® Chunky Gardenstyle
        Pasta Sauce, divided
    2 tablespoons grated Parmesan cheese
    1 tablespoon finely chopped fresh parsley
    1 pound fresh or thawed frozen bread dough

Preheat oven to 400°F. Season chicken with salt and
pepper. In 12-inch skillet, heat oil over medium-high
heat and cook chicken until juices run clear.
Remove chicken from skillet and let cool; pull into
large shreds.

In medium bowl, combine chicken, mozzarella
cheese, 1/2 cup Ragú® Chunky Gardenstyle Pasta
Sauce, Parmesan cheese and parsley; set aside.

On greased jelly-roll pan, press dough to form
12×10-inch rectangle. Arrange chicken mixture
down center of dough. Cover filling bringing one
long side into center, then overlap with the other
long side; pinch seam to seal. Fold in ends and
pinch to seal. Arrange on pan, seam-side down.
Gently press in sides to form 12×4-inch loaf. Bake
35 minutes or until dough is cooked and golden. Cut
stromboli into slices. Heat remaining pasta sauce
and serve with stromboli.   *Makes 6 servings*

Pepperidge Farm® Two Cheese Party Pastries

1/2 package (17-1/4-ounce size) PEPPERIDGE
        FARM® Frozen Puff Pastry Sheets (1 sheet)
1-1/2 cups crumbled blue cheese (about 6 ounces)
1/2 package (8-ounce size) cream cheese, softened
1/4 cup heavy cream
    1 teaspoon lemon juice
1/4 cup walnuts, chopped
        Chopped fresh parsley
    1 medium Granny Smith apple, thinly sliced

1. Thaw pastry sheet at room temperature
30 minutes. Preheat oven to 400°F.

2. Unfold pastry on lightly floured surface. Cut
into 3 strips along fold marks. Cut each strip into
6 rectangles. Place 2 inches apart on baking sheet.
Bake 15 minutes or until golden. Remove from
baking sheet. Cool on wire rack.

3. In medium bowl with electric mixer at low speed,
beat blue cheese, cream cheese, cream and lemon
juice until smooth.

4. Split pastries into 2 layers. Spread 18 halves with
1 tablespoon cheese mixture. Top with remaining
halves and spread with remaining cheese mixture.
Sprinkle with walnuts and parsley. Top each pastry
with **1** apple slice. Chill before serving.
                                    Makes 18 pastries

Savory Sausage Mushroom Turnovers

    1 (12-ounce) package frozen bulk pork sausage,
        thawed
    1 cup chopped mushrooms
1/3 cup chopped onion
1/2 cup shredded Swiss cheese (2 ounces)
1/3 cup GREY POUPON® COUNTRY DIJON®
        Mustard
    2 tablespoons diced red bell pepper
1/2 teaspoon dried thyme leaves
    2 (8-ounce) packages refrigerated crescent rolls
    1 egg, beaten
        Sesame or poppy seed

1. Cook sausage, mushrooms and onion in large
skillet over medium heat until sausage is cooked,
stirring occasionally to break up sausage. Remove
from heat; drain if necessary. Stir in cheese,
mustard, bell pepper and thyme.

2. Separate each package of crescent rolls into
4 rectangles; press perforations together to seal.
On floured surface, roll each rectangle into 6-inch
square. Cut each square into quarters, making
32 squares total. Place 1 scant tablespoon sausage
mixture on each square; fold dough over filling on
the diagonal to form triangle. Press edges with fork
to seal. Place on greased baking sheets.

3. Brush triangles with beaten egg and sprinkle with
sesame or poppy seed. Bake at 375°F for 10 to
12 minutes or until golden brown. Serve warm.
                                    Makes 32 appetizers

Chicken Parmesan Stromboli

Salads

Antipasto Salad Stack

(Pictured at left)

8 ounces uncooked rotini
2 medium tomatoes, halved lengthwise and thinly sliced
3 ounces sliced pepperoni, divided
1 can (15 to 16 ounces) red kidney or black beans, rinsed
   and drained
1/2 cup pimiento-stuffed green olives
3/4 cup grated Parmesan cheese
1/2 bottle (8 ounces) purchased Italian salad dressing
6 to 8 large Romaine lettuce leaves, thinly sliced

1. Cook pasta according to package directions; drain. Cool slightly.

2. While pasta is cooking, arrange tomatoes and half of pepperoni around bottom edge of 3-quart glass serving bowl.

3. Layer cooked pasta, remaining pepperoni, beans, olives and cheese in bowl; drizzle with salad dressing.

4. Top with lettuce; cover and chill at least 1 hour or up to 24 hours.

5. To complete recipe, toss salad gently just before serving.
Makes 6 main-dish servings

Helpful Hint

Romaine lettuce has elongated heads with dark green outer leaves and lighter, more tender hearts. The leaves are very crisp and sturdy. When choosing lettuce, remember the dark green varieties have more nutrients than the lighter ones.

Clockwise from top left: *Juicy Layered Orange Pineapple Mold (p. 32), Antipasto Salad Stack, Mexican Taco Salad (p. 34) and Green Bean and Potato Salad in Dijon Vinaigrette (p. 36)*

Tangy Rice, Apple and Cabbage Slaw

(Pictured at right)

2/3 cup Celery Seed Vinaigrette (recipe follows)
2 cups water
2 teaspoons butter
1/4 teaspoon salt
3/4 cup uncooked long-grain white rice
2 cups shredded red and green cabbage or prepared coleslaw mix
1-1/2 cups chopped, unpeeled tart red apples
1/2 cup chopped green onions with tops
1/2 cup grated carrots
1/2 cup slivered almonds

1. Prepare Celery Seed Vinaigrette; set aside.

2. Bring water, butter and salt to a boil in 2-quart saucepan over medium-high heat. Stir in rice. Reduce heat to low; simmer, covered, 20 minutes. Remove from heat. Let stand 5 minutes or until water is absorbed; set aside.

3. Combine cabbage, apples, green onions, carrots and almonds in large bowl. Add rice; mix well.

4. Stir in Celery Seed Vinaigrette; toss until well combined. Cover; refrigerate until ready to serve.

Makes 6 to 8 servings

Celery Seed Vinaigrette

1/2 cup vegetable oil
3 tablespoons honey
2 tablespoons white wine vinegar
1 teaspoon celery seed
3/4 teaspoon dry mustard
Salt to taste

Combine oil, honey, vinegar, celery seed and mustard in small bowl. Stir with wire whisk until well blended. Add salt; stir to blend.

Makes 3/4 cup vinaigrette

Helpful Hint

For quick preparation of this salad, the Celery Seed Vinaigrette can be prepared in advance. Cover it and store it in the refrigerator for up to two days. Whisk the vinaigrette thoroughly before tossing it with the remaining ingredients.

Red Snapper in Pineapple-Citrus Escabeche

1 DOLE® Fresh Pineapple
1-1/4 pounds red snapper fillets, cut into 1-inch pieces
Salt and black pepper, to taste
4 tablespoons plus 1/3 cup olive or vegetable oil, divided
1 cup thinly sliced red onion
1/2 cup thinly sliced green bell pepper
1/2 cup thinly sliced red bell pepper
2 teaspoons finely chopped garlic
2 teaspoons dried oregano leaves, crushed
1/2 cup orange juice
1/3 cup lime juice
Mixed salad greens

• Twist off crown from pineapple. Cut pineapple in half lengthwise. Refrigerate one half for later use. Cut remaining half in half. Core and skin fruit. Coarsely chop fruit; set aside.

• Season fish with salt and black pepper.

• Fry fish in large, non-stick skillet in 2 tablespoons hot oil over medium-high heat until brown on bottom. Turn fish over and brown other side. Remove fish to large, shallow, non-metallic dish. Set aside.

• Heat 2 tablespoons oil in skillet over medium-high heat. Add onion, bell peppers, garlic and oregano. Cook and stir 1 minute. Add pineapple; cook and stir 2 minutes or until onion is tender-crisp. Remove from heat and let cool.

• Stir orange juice, lime juice and remaining 1/3 cup oil into cooled pepper mixture. Pour mixture over fish. Cover and marinate 2 hours in refrigerator before serving. Arrange, mixed greens over individual plates. Spoon escabeche over greens.

Makes 6 servings

Note: Escabeche is a dish made with cooked fish and a spicy marinade, which is chilled before serving.

Tangy Rice, Apple and Cabbage Slaw

Fajita Steak Salad

(Pictured at right)

3/4 cup A.1.® **THICK & HEARTY Steak Sauce**
1/2 cup mild thick and chunky salsa
3 tablespoons vegetable oil, divided
2 tablespoons red wine vinegar
2 cups thinly sliced red, yellow and/or green bell peppers
1 cup thin onion wedges
2 cloves garlic, minced
1 pound cooked beef steak, cut into julienne strips (about 2 cups)
4 cups torn mixed salad greens
1 cup shredded cheddar cheese (4 ounces)
1/2 cup sliced pitted ripe olives
Tortilla chips

In small bowl, blend steak sauce, salsa, 2 tablespoons oil and vinegar; set aside.

In large skillet, over medium-high heat, sauté peppers, onion and garlic in remaining 1 tablespoon oil until tender. In large nonmetal bowl, combine pepper mixture, steak and steak sauce mixture. Cover; refrigerate until serving time.

To serve, toss chilled steak mixture with salad greens, cheese and olives. Serve with tortilla chips.
Makes 6 servings

Hot German Potato Salad

1-1/2 pounds new or boiling-type potatoes, cut into 3/4-inch cubes
1-1/3 cups water, divided
1/2 teaspoon salt
1/2 pound bacon, cut widthwise into thin strips
2 tablespoons cider vinegar
4 teaspoons sugar
1 tablespoon *French's*® Worcestershire Sauce
2 teaspoons cornstarch
1/4 teaspoon ground black pepper
1-1/3 cups *French's*® French Fried Onions, divided
1 cup chopped green bell pepper
1 cup chopped celery
1/4 cup chopped pimientos

Place potatoes, 1 cup water and salt in 3-quart microwave-safe dish. Cover and microwave on HIGH 15 minutes or until potatoes are tender, stirring once. Drain in colander; set aside.

Place bacon in same dish. Microwave, uncovered, on HIGH 5 minutes or until bacon is crisp, stirring once. Remove bacon with slotted spoon; set aside. Pour off all but 1/4 cup bacon drippings. Stir in remaining 1/3 cup water, vinegar, sugar, Worcestershire, cornstarch and black pepper. Microwave, uncovered, on HIGH 1 to 2 minutes or until dressing has thickened, stirring once.

Return potatoes to dish. Add *2/3 cup* French Fried Onions, bell pepper, celery, pimientos and reserved bacon; toss well to coat evenly. Microwave, uncovered, on HIGH 2 minutes. Stir. Sprinkle with remaining *2/3 cup* onions. Microwave on HIGH 1 minute or until onions are golden. Serve warm.
Makes 6 side-dish servings

Ambrosia with Honey Lime Cream Dressing

1/4 cup honey
2 tablespoons fresh lime juice
3 oranges, peeled and sectioned
2 bananas, peeled and sliced
1 green apple, cored and cubed
1 red apple, cored and cubed
1 cup flaked coconut
Honey Lime Cream Dressing (recipe follows)

1. Combine honey and juice in large bowl; add fruit and toss until coated with honey mixture.

2. Layer fruit alternately with coconut in serving bowl. Top with Honey Lime Cream Dressing.
Makes 4 servings

Honey Lime Cream Dressing

1/2 cup cold whipping cream
2 tablespoons honey
1 teaspoon grated lime peel

1. Beat cream in large bowl with electric mixer at high speed until fluffy.

2. Drizzle honey into cream; beat until stiff peaks form. Fold in lime peel. *Makes 1 cup dressing*

Favorite recipe from **National Honey Board**

Tuna Pasta Primavera Salad

(Pictured below)

2 cups cooked and chilled small shell pasta
1-1/2 cups halved cherry tomatoes
1/2 cup thinly sliced carrots
1/2 cup sliced celery
1/2 cup chopped seeded peeled cucumber
1/2 cup thinly sliced radishes
1/2 cup thawed frozen peas
1/4 cup slivered red bell pepper
2 tablespoons minced green onion, including
    tops
1 (7-ounce) pouch of STARKIST® Premium
    Albacore or Chunk Light Tuna
1 cup salad dressing of choice
    Bibb or red leaf lettuce
    Fresh herbs, for garnish

In large bowl, combine all ingredients except lettuce and herbs. Chill several hours. If using oil and vinegar dressing, stir salad mixture occasionally to evenly marinate ingredients. Place lettuce leaves on each plate; spoon salad over lettuce. Garnish with fresh herbs, if desired.   *Makes 6 servings*

Tuna Pasta Primavera Salad

Chicken Potato Salad Olé

2 large ripe tomatoes, seeded and chopped
3/4 cup chopped green onions
1/4 cup fresh cilantro leaves, chopped
1 to 2 tablespoons chopped, seeded, pickled
    jalapeño peppers
1-1/2 teaspoons salt, divided
1 cup HELLMANN'S® or BEST FOODS® Real or
    Light Mayonnaise or Low Fat Mayonnaise
    Dressing
3 tablespoons lime juice
1 teaspoon chili powder
1 teaspoon ground cumin
2 pounds small red potatoes, cooked and sliced
    1/4 inch thick
2 cups shredded cooked chicken
1 large yellow or red bell pepper, diced
    Lettuce leaves
    Tortilla chips, lime slices, whole chili peppers
    and cilantro sprigs for garnish (optional)

1. In medium bowl, combine tomatoes, onions, chopped cilantro, jalapeño peppers and 1 teaspoon salt; set aside.

2. In large bowl, combine mayonnaise, lime juice, chili powder, cumin and remaining 1/2 teaspoon salt. Add potatoes, chicken, bell pepper and half of tomato mixture; toss to coat well. Cover; chill.

3. To serve, spoon salad onto lettuce-lined platter. Spoon remaining tomato mixture over salad. If desired, garnish with tortilla chips, lime slices, whole chili peppers and cilantro sprigs.
                            Makes 6 servings

Orange Roughy and Orzo Salad

1-1/2 cups uncooked orzo pasta
1/4 cup extra virgin olive oil
1/4 cup cider vinegar
1/2 teaspoon dried tarragon leaves, crushed *or*
        2 teaspoons chopped fresh tarragon
1/4 teaspoon salt
1/4 teaspoon white pepper
2 carrots, cut into julienne strips
1/2 green bell pepper, chopped
1/3 cup cornmeal
1 tablespoon Cajun seasoning
3/4 pound orange roughy fillets
    Vegetable oil for frying
1 cup chopped fresh parsley
    Fresh parsley sprigs for garnish

Veg•All® Vinaigrette Salad

1. Cook orzo according to package directions. Drain; place in large bowl.

2. Combine olive oil, vinegar, tarragon, salt and white pepper in small bowl; toss with orzo. Top with carrots and bell pepper; refrigerate.

3. Mix cornmeal and Cajun seasoning in shallow dish. Rinse orange roughy and pat dry with paper towels. Cut into 2×1-inch strips. Coat with cornmeal mixture.

4. Pour enough vegetable oil into large skillet to coat bottom; heat over medium-high heat until hot. Add half the fish strips; cook 4 minutes or until golden brown, turning halfway through cooking time to brown other side. Remove cooked fish and drain on paper towels. Repeat with remaining fish.

5. To serve, toss orzo mixture with chopped parsley. Transfer to serving platter. Arrange warm fish strips over top of salad. Garnish, if desired.

Makes 4 servings

Veg•All® Vinaigrette Salad

(Pictured above)

 1 can (15 ounces) VEG•ALL® Original Mixed
   Vegetables, drained
 1 can (15 ounces) black beans, drained and
   rinsed
 1-1/2 cups cherry tomatoes, halved
 4 green onions, minced
 1/2 cup minced fresh parsley
 1 bottle (8 ounces) Italian salad dressing
   Lettuce

In large mixing bowl, combine Veg•All, beans, tomatoes, green onions, and parsley. Pour dressing over vegetables; toss to blend. Cover; refrigerate for at least 2 hours or until chilled. Serve on bed of lettuce.

Makes 4 servings

Creamy Fruited Mold

(Pictured at right)

1 cup boiling water
1 package (4-serving size) JELL-O® Brand Gelatin
    Dessert, any flavor
1 cup cold water or apple juice
1-1/2 cups thawed COOL WHIP® Whipped Topping
1 cup diced fruit

STIR boiling water into gelatin in medium bowl at least 2 minutes until completely dissolved. Stir in cold water. Refrigerate about 1-1/4 hours or until slightly thickened (consistency of unbeaten egg whites). Gently stir in whipped topping. Refrigerate about 15 minutes or until thickened (spoon drawn through leaves definite impression). Stir in fruit. Pour into 5-cup mold.

REFRIGERATE 4 hours or until firm. Unmold. Garnish as desired.

Makes 8 servings

Black Bean Turkey Pepper Salad

3/4 pound fully cooked honey-roasted turkey
    breast, cut into 1/4-inch cubes
1 small red bell pepper, cut into 1/4-inch cubes
1 small yellow bell pepper, cut into 1/4-inch
    cubes
1 can (15 ounces) black beans, rinsed and
    drained
1 cup thinly sliced green onions
3/4 cup chopped fresh cilantro
2 tablespoons olive oil
1 tablespoon red wine vinegar
1 teaspoon ground cumin
1/4 teaspoon cayenne pepper

1. In large bowl, combine turkey, red and yellow peppers, black beans, onions and cilantro.

2. In small bowl, whisk together oil, vinegar, cumin and cayenne pepper. Fold dressing into turkey mixture. Cover and refrigerate 1 hour.

Makes 6 servings

Favorite recipe from **National Turkey Federation**

Mediterranean Rice Salad

2 tablespoons vegetable oil, divided
1 pound large shrimp, peeled and deveined
1 large clove garlic, minced
2 green onions, sliced
2 cups water
1 cup long-grain rice
1 teaspoon salt
1 medium cucumber, diced
1/2 cup crumbled feta cheese

SPICY VINAIGRETTE
1/4 cup olive oil
3 tablespoons cider vinegar
1 tablespoon Dijon mustard
1 teaspoon salt
1 teaspoon TABASCO® brand Pepper Sauce

Heat 1 tablespoon vegetable oil in 3-quart saucepan over medium-high heat. Cook half the shrimp until pink and tender. With slotted spoon, remove to large bowl. Repeat with remaining shrimp and oil. Reduce heat to medium. Cook garlic and green onions about 2 minutes in drippings remaining in saucepan; stir frequently.

Add water, rice and salt to saucepan. Over high heat, heat to boiling. Reduce heat to low; cover and simmer 20 minutes or until rice is tender. Meanwhile, add cucumber and feta cheese to bowl containing shrimp.

To prepare Spicy Vinaigrette, combine all vinaigrette ingredients in a small bowl. Add rice and vinaigrette to shrimp mixture and toss to mix well.

Makes 6 servings

Family French Dressing

1/2 cup HEINZ® Tomato Ketchup
1/2 cup vegetable oil
1/4 cup HEINZ® Apple Cider Vinegar
1 tablespoon confectioners' sugar
1 clove garlic, split
1/4 teaspoon salt
    Dash pepper

Combine all ingredients in jar; cover and shake vigorously. Refrigerate to blend flavors. Remove garlic; shake again before serving over tossed green salads.

Makes 1-1/4 cups

Tangy Garlic Tortellini Salad

(Pictured at right)

1/4 cup mayonnaise
1/4 cup plain yogurt
1 tablespoon plus 1-1/2 teaspoons lemon juice
1 tablespoon olive oil
2 teaspoons chopped fresh chives or 1/4 cup chopped green onion
1 teaspoon LAWRY'S® Seasoned Pepper
1 to 1-1/4 teaspoons LAWRY'S® Garlic Salt
9 ounces fresh cheese-filled tortellini or 8 ounces spiral pasta, cooked and drained
1 medium-sized red bell pepper, cut into thin strips
1 medium zucchini, cut into julienne strips
2 medium carrots, cut into julienne strips

In small bowl, combine all ingredients except pasta and vegetables. In medium bowl, combine pasta and vegetables; mix lightly. Add dressing; toss lightly to coat. Refrigerate at least 30 minutes. Garnish as desired. *Makes 4 to 6 servings*

Serving Suggestion: Serve with crusty French or sourdough bread.

Juicy Layered Orange Pineapple Mold

(Pictured on page 22)

1 can (20 ounces) crushed pineapple in juice, undrained
Cold orange juice
1-1/2 cups boiling water
1 package (8-serving size) or 2 packages (4-serving size each) JELL-O® Brand Orange Flavor Gelatin
1 package (8 ounces) PHILADELPHIA® Cream Cheese, softened

DRAIN pineapple, reserving juice. Add cold orange juice to pineapple juice to make 1-1/2 cups. Stir boiling water into gelatin in large bowl at least 2 minutes until completely dissolved. Stir in measured juice. Reserve 1 cup gelatin at room temperature.

STIR 1/2 of the crushed pineapple into remaining gelatin. Pour into 6-cup mold which has been sprayed with no stick cooking spray. Refrigerate about 2 hours or until set but not firm (should stick to finger when touched and should mound).

STIR reserved gelatin gradually into cream cheese in medium bowl with wire whisk until smooth. Stir in remaining crushed pineapple. Spoon over gelatin layer in mold.

REFRIGERATE 4 hours or until firm. Unmold. Garnish as desired. *Makes 10 servings*

Springtime Wild Rice & Orange Salad

1 can (11 ounces) mandarin orange segments in light syrup, undrained
1-1/4 cups white and wild rice specialty blend
1/4 pound sugar snap or snow peas, cut in half widthwise
1/2 cup light Italian salad dressing
1/3 cup orange juice
1/4 cup slivered almonds, toasted*
1/4 cup chopped fresh basil or parsley
1 teaspoon fresh grated orange peel
1-1/3 cups *French's*® French Fried Onions
Lettuce leaves (optional)

*To toast almonds, spread on baking sheet. Bake at 350°F 8 minutes or until lightly golden.

Drain syrup from mandarin oranges into 4-cup measuring cup; reserve mandarin segments. Add enough water to syrup to equal 2-1/2 cups liquid. Pour into medium saucepan. Bring to a boil over high heat. Stir in rice. Reduce heat to medium-low. Cook, covered, 20 minutes or until rice is tender. Stir in sugar snap peas during last minute of cooking. Drain; rinse under cold running water. Transfer to large bowl; refrigerate 30 minutes or until well chilled.

Add salad dressing, orange juice, almonds, basil, grated peel and reserved mandarin segments to rice mixture; toss well to coat evenly.

Place French Fried Onions on microwavable dish. Microwave on HIGH 1 minute. Stir onions into rice mixture. Serve on lettuce leaves, if desired.
Makes 6 to 8 servings

Tangy Garlic Tortellini Salad

Crunchy Onion Layered Salad with Dilly Dijon Dressing

(Pictured at right)

LAYERED SALAD

    4 cups washed and torn salad greens
    8 ounces boiled ham, cut into cubes
    4 hard cooked eggs, chopped
    2 ripe tomatoes, chopped
    1 bell pepper (green, red or yellow), seeded and chopped
    1 bunch radishes, sliced
    1 package (10 ounces) frozen peas, thawed and drained
1-1/3 cups *French's®* French Fried Onions

DILLY DIJON DRESSING

    1 cup regular or reduced-fat mayonnaise
    1 cup buttermilk or whole milk
1/4 cup *French's®* Napa Valley Style Dijon Mustard
    1 package (1 ounce) ranch salad dressing mix
1/2 teaspoon dried dill weed

Layer salad ingredients in 3-quart straight-sided glass bowl. Combine Dilly Dijon Dressing ingredients in small bowl; mix well. Spoon over salad just before serving. Garnish as desired.

Makes 4 main-dish or 6 side-dish servings
(about 2 cups dressing)

Tip: For extra-crispy flavor, place French Fried Onions on a microwave-safe plate. Microwave on HIGH 1 to 2 minutes until golden.

Fabulous Fruit & Feta Salad

    1 package (10 ounces) mixed salad greens
    1 can (11 ounces) mandarin orange segments, drained
1/2 cup thinly sliced red onion
    1 cup coarsely chopped walnuts, toasted
    1 package (4 ounces) ATHENOS® Traditional Crumbled Feta Cheese
3/4 cup KRAFT LIGHT DONE RIGHT!® Raspberry Vinaigrette Dressing

TOSS greens, orange segments, onion, walnuts and feta cheese in large bowl. Add dressing; toss to coat.

Makes 6 servings

Tip: To toast nuts, spread walnuts in single layer on cookie sheet. Bake at 350°F for 7 minutes or until lightly toasted, stirring occasionally.

Mexican Taco Salad

(Pictured on page 22)

    1 pound ground beef or turkey
    1 cup (1 small) chopped onion
    1 cup ORTEGA® Salsa Prima-Thick & Chunky Mild
3/4 cup water
    1 package (1-1/4 ounces) ORTEGA® Taco Seasoning Mix
1-3/4 cups (16-ounce can) kidney or pinto beans, rinsed and drained
1/2 cup (4-ounce can) ORTEGA® Diced Green Chiles
    6 tortilla shells or 3 cups (3 ounces) tortilla chips
    6 cups shredded lettuce, *divided*
    Chopped tomatoes (optional)
3/4 cup (3 ounces) shredded Nacho & Taco blend cheese, *divided*
    Sour cream (optional)
    Guacamole (optional)
    ORTEGA® Thick & Smooth Taco Sauce

COOK beef and onion until beef is brown; drain. Stir in salsa, water and seasoning mix. Bring to a boil. Reduce heat to low; cook for 2 to 3 minutes. Stir in beans and chiles.

LAYER ingredients as follows in *each* shell: *1 cup* lettuce, *3/4 cup* meat mixture, tomatoes *2 tablespoons* cheese and sour cream. Serve with guacamole and taco sauce. *Makes 6 servings*

Wild Rice Summer Salad

    3 cups cooked wild rice
3/4 cup diced zucchini
3/4 cup diced yellow squash
    2 plum tomatoes, seeded and diced
    3 green onions, thinly sliced
    1 cup cubed mozzarella cheese
1/4 cup chopped fresh basil leaves
1/2 cup bottled creamy Parmesan dressing

In large bowl, toss salad ingredients. Add dressing and toss. *Makes 6 servings*

Favorite recipe from **Minnesota Cultivated Wild Rice Council**

Crunchy Onion Layered Salad
with Dilly Dijon Dressing

Cool Summer Gazpacho Salad

Cool Summer Gazpacho Salad

(Pictured above)

3 cups DOLE® Fresh Pineapple, cut into chunks
2 cups chopped tomatoes, drained
1 large cucumber, halved lengthwise and thinly
    sliced
1/4 cup chopped green onions
1/4 cup red wine vinegar
4 teaspoons olive or vegetable oil
1/2 teaspoon dried basil leaves, crushed

• Stir together pineapple and remaining ingredients
in large bowl. Cover; chill 1 hour or overnight to
blend flavors. Stir before serving.

Makes 10 servings

Tip: Cider vinegar can be substituted for the red
wine vinegar, if desired.

Green Bean and Potato Salad in Dijon Vinaigrette

(Pictured on page 22 and on front cover)

Dijon Vinaigrette (recipe follows)
1-1/2 pounds small red-skin potatoes, unpeeled
10 ounces fresh green beans
1 cup halved or quartered cherry tomatoes
1/2 cup chopped onion
1/8 teaspoon salt
1/8 teaspoon black pepper

1. Prepare Dijon Vinaigrette; set aside.

2. Place potatoes in 3-quart saucepan; cover with
water. Bring to a boil over medium-high heat.
Reduce heat to low; simmer, covered, 10 to
15 minutes until fork-tender.

3. Drain potatoes in colander. Rinse under cold
running water; drain. Cut potatoes lengthwise into
halves with large utility knife; set aside.

4. Stem and cut beans into 2-inch pieces. Place
beans in 2-quart saucepan; cover with water. Bring
to a boil over medium-high heat. Reduce heat to
low; simmer, covered, 5 to 6 minutes until beans are
crisp-tender.

5. Transfer beans to colander; rinse under cold
running water. Drain; set aside.

6. Combine potatoes, beans, tomatoes and onion in
large bowl. Add Dijon Vinaigrette, salt and pepper;
toss well. Cover tightly with plastic wrap.
Refrigerate 2 to 3 hours. *Makes 6 servings*

Dijon Vinaigrette

1/2 fresh lemon
3 tablespoons honey-Dijon mustard
2 tablespoons red wine vinegar
1 clove garlic, minced
1/2 teaspoon Worcestershire sauce
1/3 cup extra-virgin olive oil

1. To juice lemon, remove any visible seeds with tip
of utility knife. Using citrus reamer or squeezing
tightly with hand, squeeze juice from lemon into
small bowl. Remove any remaining seeds from bowl;
discard.

2. Add mustard, vinegar, garlic and Worcestershire;
whisk to blend. Gradually whisk in oil.

Makes 2/3 cup

Bob Evans Honey Mustard Steak Salad

(Pictured below)

1 pound boneless beef sirloin steak (1 inch thick)
1 (15-ounce) jar BOB EVANS® Honey Mustard
   Salad Dressing, divided
6 cups bite-size salad greens
1 cup fresh button mushrooms, quartered
2 medium carrots, cut into 1/4-inch slices
1 large fresh tomato, cut into wedges
1/2 medium red onion, thinly sliced
1/2 green bell pepper, cut into 1-inch pieces

Combine steak and 1 cup dressing in large sealed freezer bag; marinate in refrigerator at least 1 hour. Toss remaining salad ingredients except dressing in large bowl; arrange on 4 large plates. Preheat broiler. Remove steak from bag and discard marinade. Place on broiler pan; broil 5 to 6 minutes on each side for medium-rare. Thinly slice steak and arrange over salads; drizzle with remaining dressing. Serve immediately.

Makes 4 main-dish servings

Crunchy Layered Beef & Bean Salad

1 pound ground beef or turkey
2 cans (15 to 19 ounces *each*) black beans or
   pinto beans, rinsed and drained
1 can (14-1/2 ounces) stewed tomatoes,
   undrained
1-1/2 cups *French's*® French Fried Onions, divided
1 tablespoon *Frank's*® *RedHot*® Cayenne Pepper
   Sauce
1 package (1-1/4 ounces) taco seasoning mix
6 cups shredded lettuce
1 cup (4 ounces) shredded Cheddar or Monterey
   Jack cheese

1. Cook beef in large nonstick skillet over medium heat until thoroughly browned; drain well. Stir in beans, tomatoes, *2/3 cup* French Fried Onions, **Frank's RedHot** Sauce and taco seasoning. Heat to boiling. Cook over medium heat 5 minutes, stirring occasionally.

2. Spoon beef mixture over lettuce on serving platter. Top with cheese.

3. Microwave remaining *1 cup* onions 1 minute on HIGH. Sprinkle over salad.

Makes 6 servings

Bob Evans Honey Mustard Steak Salad

Thai Peanut Salad

(Pictured at right)

1 cup picante sauce
1/4 cup chunky-style peanut butter
2 tablespoons honey
2 tablespoons orange juice
1 teaspoon soy sauce
1/2 teaspoon ground ginger
2 cups (12 ounces) chopped CURE 81® ham
1 (7-ounce) package spaghetti, cooked
1/4 cup dry roasted unsalted peanuts
1/4 cup red bell pepper, cut into julienne strips
2 tablespoons chopped cilantro

In small saucepan, combine picante sauce, peanut butter, honey, orange juice, soy sauce and ginger. Cook, stirring over low heat until mixture is smooth. Add 1/4 cup sauce mixture to ham. Gently toss remaining sauce mixture with hot cooked pasta. Toss pasta mixture with ham mixture, peanuts and pepper strips. Cover and chill 1 to 2 hours. Before serving, sprinkle with cilantro.   *Makes 4 servings*

Pecan-Pork Salad with Honey-Balsamic Dressing

4 boneless pork chops
    Salt and black pepper
2 teaspoons vegetable oil
2 cloves garlic, minced
1/4 cup honey
3 tablespoons balsamic vinegar
4 cups torn iceberg lettuce, Boston lettuce or
    Bibb lettuce
1 cup sliced fresh strawberries
1/2 cup sliced celery
1/4 cup chopped pecans

Heat large skillet over medium-high heat. Season chops with salt and pepper; brush with a little oil. Cook, turning occasionally to brown evenly, until chops are just done. Remove chops from skillet and reserve. Add any remaining oil to pan; quickly sauté garlic until tender, about 1 to 2 minutes, stirring constantly. Stir in honey and vinegar; cook and stir 1 minute or until heated through. In large bowl, toss together lettuce, strawberries, celery and honey mixture. Divide lettuce mixture among individual plates. Slice each pork chop and fan over salads. Sprinkle with pecans.   *Makes 4 servings*

Favorite recipe from **National Pork Board**

Confetti Apple Salad

1 Washington Golden Delicious apple (about
    6 ounces), cored and chopped
1/2 cup flaked coconut
1/2 cup chopped carrot
1/2 cup raisins
1/2 cup lemon-flavored yogurt
1/3 cup coarsely chopped cashews or peanuts
    Curly lettuce leaves

Combine all ingredients except nuts and lettuce and allow flavors to blend for 1 hour. Stir in nuts. Arrange salad on lettuce-lined plates.
    Makes 2 to 3 servings

Favorite recipe from **Washington Apple Commission**

Juice 'n Fruit Salad

2 cups boiling water, divided
1 package (4-serving size) JELL-O® Brand
    Gelatin, any red flavor
1 cup cold orange juice, divided
1 can (8 ounces) sliced peaches, drained,
    chopped
1 package (4-serving size) JELL-O® Brand Orange
    Flavor Gelatin
1 can (8 ounces) crushed pineapple, drained

STIR 1 cup of the boiling water into red gelatin in medium bowl at least 2 minutes until completely dissolved. Stir in 1/2 cup of the cold juice. Refrigerate about 45 minutes or until slightly thickened (consistency of unbeaten egg whites). Stir in peaches. Spoon into 5-cup mold which has been sprayed with no stick cooking spray. Refrigerate about 20 minutes or until set but not firm (should stick to finger when touched and should mound).

MEANWHILE, stir remaining 1 cup boiling water into orange gelatin in medium bowl at least 2 minutes until completely dissolved. Stir in remaining 1/2 cup cold juice. Refrigerate about 45 minutes or until slightly thickened. Stir in pineapple. Spoon over red gelatin in mold.

REFRIGERATE 4 hours or until firm. Unmold. Garnish as desired.   *Makes 10 servings*

Thai Peanut Salad

Southwest Caesar Salad

(Pictured at right)

1 package (10 ounces) DOLE® Complete Caesar
    Salad
2 cups cubed cooked chicken breast
1 can (14 to 16 ounces) kidney, black or pinto
    beans, drained
1 can (8 ounces) whole kernel corn, drained
1 medium tomato, cut into wedges
1 medium DOLE® Red, Yellow or Green Bell
    Pepper, thinly sliced
1/2 medium onion, thinly sliced

• Combine romaine, croutons and Parmesan cheese
from salad bag with chicken, beans, corn, tomato,
bell pepper and onion in large serving bowl.

• Pour dressing from packet over salad; toss to coat
evenly. Serve with crusty bread, if desired.

Makes 4 servings

Note: Refrigerate salad blends, complete salads and
vegetable combinations in their original bags as
soon as you get them home. Since the bags have
been designed with a special material to keep
vegetables at their freshest, you can store any
leftovers in the same bags, tightly closed, in your
refrigerator crisper.

Old-Fashioned Corn Relish

1/3 cup cider vinegar
2 tablespoons sugar
1 tablespoon cornstarch
3 tablespoons *French's*® Classic Yellow® Mustard
1/4 teaspoon seasoned salt
1 package (10 ounces) frozen corn, thawed and
    drained
1/2 cup chopped celery
1/2 cup chopped red bell pepper
1/4 cup finely chopped red onion
3 tablespoons sweet pickle relish

Combine vinegar, sugar and cornstarch in large
microwave-safe bowl; mix well. Stir in mustard and
salt. Microwave, uncovered, on HIGH 1 to 2 minutes
or until thickened, stirring once. Add corn, celery,
pepper, onion and pickle relish; toss well to coat
evenly. Cover and refrigerate 30 minutes before
serving. Serve as a relish on hamburgers or hot
dogs, or serve on the side with grilled meats.

Makes about 3 cups

Cucumber Wild Rice Salad

1/2 cup sour cream
2 tablespoons plus 1-1/2 teaspoons lemon juice
1 tablespoon sugar
1/2 teaspoon salt
1/2 teaspoon dill weed
1 small onion
2 cups cooked wild rice
1 cucumber, sliced

In medium bowl, combine sour cream, lemon juice,
sugar, salt and dill. Thinly slice onion and separate
into rings. Add wild rice, onion and cucumber to
sour cream mixture. Cover; chill.

Makes 4 servings

Favorite recipe from **Minnesota Cultivated Wild
Rice Council**

Gazpacho Salad

1 cup diced tomato
1/2 cup diced peeled cucumber
1/4 cup diced green bell pepper
2 tablespoons diced red bell pepper
2 tablespoons thinly sliced green onion
2 tablespoons vinegar
1/4 teaspoon black pepper
1/8 teaspoon garlic powder (optional)
1-1/2 cups tomato juice
1 package (4-serving size) JELL-O® Brand Lemon
    Flavor Gelatin Dessert
Crackers (optional)

MIX vegetables, vinegar, black pepper and garlic
powder in medium bowl; set aside. Bring tomato
juice to boil in small saucepan. Stir into gelatin in
large bowl at least 2 minutes until completely
dissolved. Refrigerate about 1-1/4 hours or until
slightly thickened (consistency of unbeaten egg
whites).

STIR in vegetable mixture. Pour into 4-cup mold.

REFRIGERATE 3 hours or until firm. Unmold. Serve
with crackers if desired. Garnish as desired.

Makes 6 servings

Southwest Caesar Salad

Seafood Pea-Ista Salad

(Pictured at right)

    8 ounces corkscrew pasta
    1 cup broccoli florets
    1/2 cup mayonnaise or salad dressing
    1/4 cup zesty Italian salad dressing
    2 tablespoons grated Parmesan cheese
    2 cups canned green or yellow black-eyed peas,
        rinsed and drained
    1-1/2 cups (about 8 ounces) chopped imitation
        crabmeat
    1/2 cup chopped green bell pepper
    1/2 cup chopped tomato
    1/4 cup sliced green onions

1. Cook pasta according to package directions; drain.

2. Heat 1 quart lightly salted water in 2-quart saucepan over high heat to a boil. Add broccoli. Return to a boil; boil 3 minutes until crisp-tender. Drain broccoli, then immediately plunge into cold water to stop cooking. Drain and cool.

3. Combine mayonnaise, Italian salad dressing and cheese in large bowl until well blended.

4. Add pasta, broccoli, peas, crabmeat, bell pepper, tomato and onions; toss gently to coat. Cover; refrigerate at least 2 hours before serving.

Makes 4 to 6 servings

Thousand Island Dressing

    1 cup mayonnaise or salad dressing
    1 tablespoon HEINZ® Apple Cider Vinegar
    1 to 2 teaspoons granulated sugar
    1/4 cup HEINZ® Tomato Ketchup
    2 tablespoons HEINZ® Sweet Relish
    1 hard-cooked egg, finely chopped

In medium bowl, blend mayonnaise with vinegar, sugar and ketchup. Fold in relish and egg. Cover; refrigerate. Serve over head lettuce, salad greens or sliced tomatoes. *Makes about 1-3/4 cups*

Ensalada Simplese

    5 cups torn lettuce (combination of romaine and
        iceberg)
    1/2 cup chopped zucchini
    1 can (7 ounces) whole kernel corn, drained
    1/2 cup chopped red bell pepper
    1/4 cup sliced green onions
    1/3 cup dairy sour cream
    2 tablespoons mayonnaise
    1 teaspoon lemon juice
    3/4 teaspoon dry mustard
    1/2 teaspoon LAWRY'S® Seasoned Salt
    1/2 teaspoon LAWRY'S® Garlic Powder with
        Parsley

In large bowl, combine lettuce, zucchini, corn, bell pepper and green onions. Refrigerate. In separate small bowl, combine remaining ingredients; mix well. Refrigerate. To serve, gently toss greens and dressing. *Makes 4 to 6 servings*

Tip: Adding shredded, cooked chicken or cooked shrimp turns this salad into a main dish.

Chinese Pork Salad

    1 pound pork strips
    1/2 cup Oriental stir-fry sauce
    1/2 red onion, peeled and thinly sliced
    2 packages (10 ounces each) frozen snow peas,
        thawed and drained
    1 can (11 ounces) mandarin oranges, drained
    1 can (3 ounces) chow mein noodles

Marinate pork in stir-fry sauce. In large nonstick skillet, stir-fry pork and onion over medium-high heat 4 to 5 minutes. In large bowl, toss pork mixture together with remaining ingredients.

Makes 4 servings

Favorite recipe from **National Pork Board**

Side Dishes

Southwest Stuffed Potatoes

(Pictured at left)

      4 large (or 8 small) baking potatoes
  1/2 cup milk
  1/4 cup butter, softened
      2 teaspoons chili powder
  1/4 teaspoon salt
  1/4 teaspoon pepper
      1 can (15 ounce) VEG•ALL® Original Mixed Vegetables, drained
  1/4 cup shredded cheddar cheese

1. Preheat oven to 400°F.

2. Bake potatoes in oven 50 to 60 minutes or until tender.

3. Slice off top of each potato lengthwise.

4. Scoop out potato pulp, leaving a thin shell.

5. Mash potato pulp until smooth; add milk, butter, chili powder, salt, and pepper; beat until fluffy.

6. Fold in Veg•All.

7. Divide mixture among potato shells; sprinkle with cheese.

8. Place on baking sheet.

9. Bake 10 minutes or until cheese has melted and tops are golden brown.

10. Serve hot.   *Makes 4 to 8 servings*

Clockwise from top left: *Honey Nut Squash (p. 46), Sombrero Vegetable Bake (p. 54), Southwest Stuffed Potatoes and 1-2-3 Cheddar Broccoli Casserole (p. 48)*

Creamy Mashed Potato Bake

(Pictured at right)

3 cups mashed potatoes
1 cup sour cream
1/4 cup milk
1/4 teaspoon garlic powder
1-1/3 cups *French's*® French Fried Onions, divided
1 cup (4 ounces) shredded cheddar cheese, divided

1. Preheat oven to 350°F. Combine mashed potatoes, sour cream, milk and garlic powder.

2. Spoon half of mixture into 2-quart casserole. Sprinkle with *2/3 cup* French Fried Onions and *1/2 cup* cheese. Top with remaining potato mixture.

3. Bake, uncovered, 30 minutes or until hot. Top with remaining *2/3 cup* onions and *1/2 cup* cheese. Bake 5 minutes or until onions are golden.

Makes 6 servings

Frenched Beans with Celery

3/4 pound fresh green beans
2 ribs celery
2 tablespoons butter, melted
2 tablespoons toasted sunflower kernels*
Celery leaves and carrot slices for garnish

*To toast sunflower kernels, heat 1/2 teaspoon oil in small skillet over medium heat. Add sunflower kernels; cook and stir 3 minutes or until lightly browned, shaking pan constantly. Remove to paper towels.

1. Place beans in colander; rinse well. To prepare beans, snap off stem end from each bean, pulling strings down to remove if present. (Young tender beans may have no strings.)

2. Slice beans lengthwise; set aside.

3. To prepare celery, trim stem end and leaves from ribs. Reserve leaves for garnish, if desired. Slice ribs thin on the diagonal.

4. Bring 1 inch of water in 2-quart saucepan to a boil over high heat. Add beans and celery. Cover; reduce heat to medium-low. Simmer 8 minutes or until beans are crisp-tender; drain.

5. Toss beans and celery with butter. Transfer to warm serving dish. Sprinkle with sunflower kernels. Garnish, if desired. Serve immediately.

Makes 6 side-dish servings

Honey Nut Squash

(Pictured on page 44)

2 acorn squash (about 6 ounces each)
1/4 cup honey
2 tablespoons butter or margarine, melted
2 tablespoons chopped walnuts
2 tablespoons raisins
2 teaspoons Worcestershire sauce

Cut acorn squash lengthwise into halves; do not remove seeds. Place cut sides up in baking pan or on baking sheet. Bake at 400°F 30 to 45 minutes or until soft. Remove seeds and fibers.

Combine honey, butter, walnuts, raisins and Worcestershire sauce; spoon into squash. Bake 5 to 10 minutes more or until lightly glazed.

Makes 4 servings

Microwave Directions: Cut acorn squash lengthwise into halves and remove seeds. Microwave according to manufacturer's directions. Combine honey, butter, walnuts, raisins and Worcestershire sauce; spoon into squash. Microwave at HIGH (100%) 30 seconds or until thoroughly heated and lightly glazed.

Favorite recipe from **National Honey Board**

Summer Vegetable Medley

2 medium carrots
2 medium yellow squash
2 medium zucchini
1 tablespoon olive oil
1 tablespoon butter
2 teaspoons dried Italian seasoning
Fresh basil (optional)

Slice vegetables into 3×1/8-inch strips. Heat oil and butter in large skillet over medium-high heat. Add carrots; cook and stir 1 minute. Add yellow squash, zucchini and Italian seasoning; cook and stir until vegetables are crisp-tender. Place vegetables in serving bowl. Garnish with fresh basil, if desired.

Makes 4 to 6 side-dish servings

1-2-3 Cheddar Broccoli Casserole

(Pictured on page 44)

1 jar (16 ounces) RAGÚ® Cheese Creations!®
    Double Cheddar Sauce
2 boxes (10 ounces each) frozen broccoli florets,
    thawed
1/4 cup plain or Italian seasoned dry bread crumbs
1 tablespoon margarine or butter, melted

1. Preheat oven to 350°F. In 1-1/2-quart casserole, combine Ragú Cheese Creations! Sauce and broccoli.

2. Evenly top with bread crumbs combined with margarine.

3. Bake, uncovered, 20 minutes or until bread crumbs are golden and broccoli is tender.

Makes 6 servings

Tip: Substitute your favorite frozen vegetables for broccoli florets.

Mexican-Style Stuffed Peppers

Mexican-Style Stuffed Peppers

(Pictured below left)

6 medium red or green bell peppers, halved,
    seeded
3 tablespoons water
2 cups cooked long-grain white rice
1-3/4 cups (1-pound jar) ORTEGA® Salsa
    Prima-Garden Style Mild, *divided*
1-1/2 cups (6 ounces) shredded cheddar cheese,
    divided
3/4 cup frozen peas and carrots
3/4 cup whole-kernel corn
1/2 cup (about 3) chopped green onions
1/2 teaspoon garlic salt

PREHEAT oven to 375°F.

PLACE bell peppers and water in microwave-safe dish; cover with plastic wrap. Microwave on HIGH (100%) power for 4 to 5 minutes or until slightly tender; drain.

COMBINE rice, *3/4 cup* salsa, *1 cup* cheese, peas and carrots, corn, green onions and garlic salt in large bowl. Fill peppers with mixture, mounding slightly. Place peppers in ungreased 13×9-inch baking pan; top with *remaining 1 cup* salsa and *remaining 1/2 cup* cheese. Cover.

BAKE for 35 to 40 minutes. Uncover; bake for additional 5 minutes or until heated through and cheese is melted. *Makes 6 servings*

To Freeze Ahead: PREPARE as above; do not bake. Cover; freeze for up to 2 months. Thaw overnight in refrigerator. **PREHEAT** oven to 375°F. **BAKE** for 40 to 45 minutes. Uncover, bake for additional 5 minutes or until heated through and cheese is melted.

Manwich Baked Noodles

4 cups cooked pasta
3 cups *prepared* HUNT'S® Original Manwich
1-1/2 cups shredded cheddar cheese, divided
    PAM® No-Stick Cooking Spray

In large bowl, combine pasta, prepared Manwich and 1 cup cheese. Pour into baking dish sprayed with cooking spray; sprinkle remaining 1/2 cup cheese over top. Bake, covered, at 350°F 30 minutes. Remove cover; bake, uncovered, 10 minutes or until hot and bubbling. *Makes 4 to 6 servings*

Nutty Vegetable Pilaf

Nutty Vegetable Pilaf

(Pictured above)

1 tablespoon vegetable oil
2 cups coarsely chopped broccoli
2 medium carrots, julienned
1 medium onion, chopped
1 cup sliced fresh mushrooms
2 cloves garlic, minced
1/2 teaspoon dried thyme leaves
1/2 teaspoon dried basil leaves
1/2 teaspoon salt
1/4 teaspoon ground black pepper
3 cups cooked brown rice
1/2 cup chopped pecans, toasted*
1/2 cup shredded Parmesan cheese (optional)

To toast pecans, place on baking sheet; bake 5 to 7 minutes in 350°F oven, or until nuts are just beginning to darken and are fragrant.

Heat oil in large skillet over medium-high heat until hot. Add broccoli, carrots and onion. Cook and stir 5 to 7 minutes or until broccoli and carrots are tender and onion begins to brown. Add mushrooms, garlic, thyme, basil, salt and pepper. Cook and stir 2 to 3 minutes or until mushrooms are tender. Add rice and pecans; cook 1 to 2 minutes, stirring, until well blended and thoroughly heated. Sprinkle with cheese, if desired. *Makes 6 servings*

Favorite recipe from **USA Rice Federation**

Helpful Hint

Because brown rice contains the bran and the germ, it is more nutritious than white rice. It also takes longer to cook. Light tan in color, it has a chewy texture and nutty flavor. Quick brown rice (cooks in 15 minutes) and instant brown rice (cooks in 10 minutes) are also available.

Baked Spiced Squash

(Pictured at right)

2 boxes (10 ounces each) BIRDS EYE® frozen
    Cooked Winter Squash, thawed
2 egg whites, lightly beaten
1/4 cup brown sugar
2 teaspoons butter or margarine, melted
1 teaspoon ground cinnamon
1/2 cup herbed croutons, coarsely crushed

• Preheat oven to 400°F. Combine squash, egg whites, sugar, butter and cinnamon; mix well.

• Pour into 1-quart baking dish sprayed with nonstick cooking spray.

• Bake, uncovered, 20 to 25 minutes or until center is set.

• Remove from oven; sprinkle crushed croutons on top. Bake 5 to 7 minutes longer or until croutons are browned. Garnish as desired.

Makes 6 to 8 servings

Cornmeal Squares with Salsa

1 cup yellow cornmeal
1 teaspoon chili powder
4 cups water
1 teaspoon salt
1 cup (4 ounces) grated Monterey Jack cheese
1 (4-ounce) can chopped green chilis, drained
    and patted dry
1/4 cup chopped fresh cilantro
6 tablespoons vegetable oil, divided
1 (11-ounce) jar NEWMAN'S OWN® All Natural
    Salsa

In small bowl, combine cornmeal and chili powder; set aside. In large saucepan, heat water and salt over medium heat to boiling. Sprinkle cornmeal mixture 1/4 cup at a time into water, whisking constantly. Cook, stirring constantly with wooden spoon, until thickened, about 10 minutes. Stir in cheese, chilis and cilantro. Spread evenly in oiled 15×10×1-inch baking pan. Refrigerate to cool completely. Cut cooked cornmeal into fifteen 3×3-1/4-inch squares.

In large, nonstick saucepan, heat 2 tablespoons oil over medium-high heat. Add five squares and cook, turning once, until golden brown, 8 to 10 minutes. Repeat with remaining oil and squares. Serve with Newman's Own® All Natural Salsa.

Makes 4 to 6 servings

Pepperidge Farm® Vegetable Stuffing Bake

4 cups PEPPERIDGE FARM® Herb Seasoned
    Stuffing
2 tablespoons margarine *or* butter, melted
1 can (10-3/4 ounces) CAMPBELL'S® Condensed
    Cream of Mushroom Soup *or* 98% Fat Free
    Cream of Mushroom Soup
1/2 cup sour cream
2 small zucchini, shredded (about 2 cups)
2 medium carrots, shredded (about 1 cup)
1 small onion, finely chopped (about 1/4 cup)

1. Mix *1 cup* stuffing and margarine. Set aside.

2. Mix soup, sour cream, zucchini, carrots and onion. Add remaining stuffing. Mix lightly. Spoon into 1-1/2-quart casserole. Sprinkle with reserved stuffing mixture.

3. Bake at 350°F. for 35 minutes or until hot.

Makes 6 servings

Campbell's® Cheddary Pouch Potatoes

1 can (10-3/4 ounces) CAMPBELL'S® Condensed
    Cheddar Cheese Soup
1/4 cup milk
1/2 teaspoon garlic powder
1/4 teaspoon onion powder
4 cups frozen steak fries
    Paprika

1. In large bowl mix soup, milk, garlic powder and onion powder. Stir in potatoes.

2. Cut four 14-inch squares of heavy-duty aluminum foil. Spoon *1 cup* soup mixture onto each square, arranging potatoes to make a single layer. Sprinkle with paprika. Bring up sides of foil and double fold. Double fold ends to make packet.

3. Place potato packets on grill rack over medium-hot coals. Grill 25 minutes or until potatoes are tender.

Makes 4 servings

Baked Spiced Squash

Rosemary Garlic Potatoes

(Pictured at right)

4 large red skin potatoes, cut into wedges (about 2 pounds)
1-1/2 teaspoons dried rosemary leaves
1 teaspoon garlic powder
2 tablespoons FLEISCHMANN'S® Original Margarine, melted

1. Toss potatoes with rosemary and garlic in large bowl; arrange on lightly greased baking dish in single layer. Drizzle with melted margarine.

2. Broil 4 inches from heat source for 25 to 30 minutes or until tender, turning potatoes over once. Garnish as desired. *Makes 4 servings*

Apple Brown Rice Stuffing

1 pound BOB EVANS® Savory Sage or Original Recipe Roll Sausage
3 cups cooked brown rice
2 tablespoons olive oil
1 medium apple, peeled, cored and sliced
1 medium onion, chopped
2 ribs celery, chopped
4 medium mushrooms, sliced
1/3 cup raisins
1/2 teaspoon poultry seasoning
1/4 teaspoon dried thyme leaves
1/4 teaspoon black pepper
1/4 cup apple juice
1/3 cup sliced almonds
1/3 cup crushed wheat cereal squares or other dry cereal

Preheat oven to 350°F. Crumble and cook sausage in large skillet until browned. Drain off any drippings and transfer sausage to large bowl. Stir in rice. Add olive oil to same skillet with apple, onion, celery, mushrooms, raisins, poultry seasoning, thyme and pepper; cook and stir until vegetables are crisp-tender. Stir into sausage mixture. Add apple juice to moisten. Spread almonds and crushed cereal on baking sheet; bake 10 minutes. Add to sausage mixture and toss lightly. Place in greased 2-quart casserole dish and bake, covered, 30 minutes or until heated through. Refrigerate leftovers. *Makes 6 servings*

Vegetables Italiano

1 cup Italian seasoned bread crumbs
1/3 cup grated Parmesan cheese
2/3 cup HELLMANN'S® or BEST FOODS® Real or Light Mayonnaise or Low Fat Mayonnaise Dressing
6 cups assorted vegetables: broccoli florets, carrot slices, cauliflower florets, small mushrooms, green and/or red bell pepper strips, yellow squash slices and/or zucchini strips

1. Preheat oven to 425°F.

2. In plastic food bag combine crumbs and Parmesan; shake to blend well. In another bag combine mayonnaise and vegetables; shake to coat well. Add mayonnaise-coated vegetables, half at a time, to crumb mixture; shake to coat well.

3. Arrange in single layer on ungreased cookie sheet so that pieces do not touch.

4. Bake in 425°F oven 10 minutes or until golden. *Makes about 8 servings*

Broccoli & Red Pepper Sauté

2 tablespoons olive or vegetable oil
4 cups small broccoli florets
1 large red bell pepper, cut into thin strips
1 medium onion, sliced
1 clove garlic, finely chopped
1 envelope LIPTON® RECIPE SECRETS® Golden Herb with Lemon Soup Mix*
1 cup water
1/4 cup sliced almonds, toasted (optional)

Also terrific with Lipton Recipe Secrets Savory Herb with Garlic Soup Mix.

In 12-inch skillet, heat oil over medium heat and cook broccoli, red pepper, onion and garlic, stirring occasionally, 5 minutes or until onion is tender. Add Golden Herb with Lemon Soup Mix with water. Simmer covered 5 minutes or until broccoli is tender. Sprinkle with almonds.

Makes about 6 servings

Rosemary Garlic Potatoes

Grilled Asparagus and New Potatoes

Grilled Asparagus and New Potatoes

(Pictured at left)

1 pound small red potatoes, scrubbed and
   quartered
1/4 cup *French's*® Classic Yellow® Mustard or Napa
   Valley Style Dijon Mustard
3 tablespoons minced fresh dill *or* 2 teaspoons
   dried dill weed
3 tablespoons olive oil
3 tablespoons lemon juice
1 tablespoon grated lemon peel
1/8 teaspoon black pepper
1 pound asparagus, washed and trimmed

1. Place potatoes and 1/4 cup water in shallow
microwavable dish. Cover and microwave on HIGH
(100%) 8 minutes or until potatoes are crisp-tender,
turning once. Drain.

2. Combine mustard, dill, oil, lemon juice, lemon
peel and pepper in small bowl. Brush mixture on
potatoes and asparagus. Place vegetables in grilling
basket. Grill over medium-high heat 8 minutes
or until potatoes and asparagus are fork-tender,
turning and basting often with mustard mixture.

Makes 4 servings

Sombrero Vegetable Bake

(Pictured on page 44)

1 tablespoon olive oil
1 clove garlic, minced
1/4 teaspoon ground cumin
1 can (14-1/2 ounces) stewed tomatoes
1 package (10 ounces) frozen corn, thawed
2 small zucchini, cut into 3/4-inch chunks
2 tablespoons *Frank's*® *RedHot*® Cayenne Pepper
   Sauce
1/4 teaspoon salt
1-1/3 cups *French's*® French Fried Onions

Whisk together oil, garlic and cumin in 2-quart
microwavable bowl. Microwave, uncovered, on
HIGH 1 minute.

Stir in tomatoes with liquid, corn, zucchini, *Frank's*
RedHot Sauce and salt. Cover tightly with plastic
wrap. Microwave on HIGH 8 to 10 minutes or until
zucchini is crisp-tender, stirring twice. Uncover;
sprinkle with French Fried Onions. Microwave on
HIGH 1 minute or until onions are golden.

Makes 6 side-dish servings

Captain's Choice Baked Beans

1 pound ground beef
1 can (16 ounces) baked beans
1 can (16 ounces) dark red kidney beans,
   drained
1 can (15 ounces) butter beans, drained
1 onion, chopped
1/2 cup packed brown sugar
1/2 cup MISSISSIPPI® Barbecue Sauce
2 tablespoons prepared mustard
1 tablespoon Worcestershire sauce
3 to 4 strips bacon (optional)

1. Preheat oven to 350°F. Brown ground beef;
drain fat.

2. In 2-quart casserole, combine ground beef and
remaining ingredients except bacon. Place bacon
strips on top.

3. Bake, uncovered, at 350°F for 1-1/4 hours.

Makes 6 servings

Cabbage Wedges with Tangy Hot Dressing

(Pictured below)

1 slice bacon, cut widthwise into 1/4-inch strips
2 teaspoons cornstarch
2/3 cup unsweetened apple juice
1/4 cup cider or red wine vinegar
1 tablespoon brown sugar
1/2 teaspoon caraway seeds
1 green onion, thinly sliced
1/2 head red or green cabbage (about 1 pound),
 cut into 4 wedges

1. Cook bacon in large skillet over medium heat until crisp. Remove bacon with slotted spoon to paper towel; set aside. Meanwhile, dissolve cornstarch in apple juice in small bowl. Stir in vinegar, brown sugar and caraway seeds; set aside. Add onion to hot drippings. Cook and stir until onion is soft but not brown.

2. Place cabbage wedges, on flat side, in drippings mixture. Pour cornstarch mixture over cabbage wedges. Cook over medium heat 4 minutes. Carefully turn cabbage wedges over with spatula.

Cook 6 minutes more or until cabbage is fork-tender and dressing is thickened.

3. Remove cabbage to cutting board with spatula; carefully cut core away with utility knife. Transfer to warm serving plates. Pour hot dressing over cabbage wedges. Sprinkle with reserved bacon pieces. Garnish as desired. Serve immediately.

Makes 4 side-dish servings

Helpful Hint

When buying green and red cabbage, look for well-trimmed, compact heads that feel heavy for their size. They should have a bright color and be free of withered leaves. When cooking red cabbage, add a little lemon juice or vinegar to the cooking liquid to maintain its bright color.

*Cabbage Wedges with Tangy
Hot Dressing*

Barley and Wild Rice Pilaf

(Pictured at right)

1/2 cup uncooked wild rice
  2 tablespoons olive oil, divided
  1 medium onion, chopped
  1 cup uncooked pearl barley
  3 cloves garlic, minced
  4 cups chicken broth
  1 large red bell pepper, cut into 1/4-inch pieces
  3 ounces fresh mushrooms, thinly sliced
1/2 cup frozen green peas, thawed
1/2 cup shredded carrot
  1 teaspoon dried oregano leaves *or* 1 tablespoon
     chopped fresh oregano

1. Rinse rice in fine strainer under cold running water. Drain; set aside.

2. Heat 1 tablespoon oil in 3-quart saucepan over medium-high heat. Add onion; cook and stir about 10 minutes or until tender. Add barley, rice and garlic; cook and stir over medium heat 1 minute.

3. Stir in chicken broth. Bring to a boil over medium-high heat. Reduce heat to low; simmer, covered, about 1 hour or until barley and rice are tender.

4. Heat remaining 1 tablespoon oil in large skillet over medium-high heat. Add bell pepper, mushrooms, peas, carrot and dried oregano; cook and stir 5 to 6 minutes until vegetables are tender.

5. Stir bell pepper mixture into rice mixture. Garnish with fresh oregano, if desired.

Makes 6 to 8 servings

Parsnip Patties

  1 pound fresh parsnips, peeled and cut into
     3/4-inch chunks
  4 tablespoons butter or margarine, divided
1/4 cup chopped onion
1/4 cup all-purpose flour
1/3 cup milk
  2 teaspoons chopped chives
    Salt and pepper
3/4 cup fresh bread crumbs
  2 tablespoons vegetable oil

1. Pour 1 inch water into medium saucepan. Bring to a boil over high heat; add parsnip chunks. Cover; boil 10 minutes or until parsnips are fork-tender. Drain. Place in large bowl. Coarsely mash with fork; set aside.

2. Heat 2 tablespoons butter in small skillet over medium-high heat until melted and bubbly. Add onion; cook and stir until transparent. Stir in flour with wire whisk; heat until bubbly and lightly browned. Whisk in milk; heat until thickened. Stir flour mixture into mashed parsnips. Add chives and season with salt and pepper to taste.

3. Form parsnip mixture into four patties. Spread bread crumbs on plate. Dip patties in bread crumbs to coat all sides evenly. Press crumbs firmly into patties. Place on waxed paper and refrigerate 2 hours.

4. Heat remaining 2 tablespoons butter and oil in 12-inch skillet over medium-high heat until butter is melted and bubbly. Add patties; cook about 5 minutes on each side or until browned. Transfer to warm dish. Garnish as desired.

Makes 4 side-dish servings

Hush Puppies

    CRISCO® Oil* for deep frying
  1 cup yellow cornmeal
1/2 cup all-purpose flour
1-1/2 teaspoons baking soda
1/2 teaspoon salt
  1 cup buttermilk
  1 egg, beaten
1/4 cup finely chopped onion

Use your favorite Crisco Oil product.

1. Heat 2 to 3 inches oil to 365°F in deep fryer or deep saucepan.

2. Combine cornmeal, flour, baking soda and salt in large bowl. Stir in buttermilk, egg and onion. Mix well.

3. Drop by teaspoonfuls, a few at a time, into oil. Fry 2 minutes or until dark golden brown. Turn as needed for even browning. Remove with slotted metal spoon. Drain on paper towels. Serve immediately. *Makes 4 servings*

Note: The batter can be prepared up to 3 hours in advance and refrigerated, tightly covered. Fry hush puppies just prior to serving.

Barley and Wild Rice Pilaf

Ratatouille Stuffed Zucchini

(Pictured at right)

2 medium zucchini
1/2 cup chopped onion
1 clove garlic, minced
1 tablespoon FLEISCHMANN'S® Original
    Margarine, divided
1/2 cup chopped green bell pepper
1/2 cup chopped peeled eggplant
1/2 cup chopped tomato
1/4 cup EGG BEATERS® Healthy Real Egg Product
1 teaspoon dried basil leaves
19 club crackers, divided
1 tablespoon grated Parmesan cheese

Halve each zucchini lengthwise; scoop out center portions, leaving 1/4-inch shell. Chop 1 cup scooped out zucchini filling; reserve.

In large nonstick skillet, over medium heat, sauté onion and garlic in 2 teaspoons margarine until tender. Stir in bell pepper, eggplant, tomato and reserved chopped zucchini; cook until tender-crisp, about 5 minutes. Remove from heat; stir in Egg Beaters® and basil.

Coarsely break 15 crackers; stir into vegetable mixture. Spoon vegetable mixture into zucchini shells. Place zucchini shells in 11×7×2-inch baking dish.

Melt remaining margarine. Crush remaining crackers; in small bowl, toss with melted margarine until well coated. Stir in cheese; sprinkle over vegetable mixture. Bake, uncovered, at 375°F for 20 to 25 minutes or until hot.   *Makes 4 servings*

Baked Spanish Rice and Barley

1/2 cup chopped onion
1/2 cup chopped green bell pepper
2 cloves garlic, minced
2 teaspoons vegetable oil
1 cup coarsely chopped seeded tomatoes
1 cup chicken broth
1/2 cup uncooked white rice
1/2 cup water
3 tablespoons quick-cooking barley
1/4 teaspoon black pepper
1/8 teaspoon salt

1. Preheat oven to 350°F. Coat 1-1/2-quart casserole with nonstick cooking spray. Cook and stir onion,

bell pepper and garlic in oil in medium saucepan over medium heat until vegetables are tender. Stir in tomatoes, broth, rice, water, barley, black pepper and salt. Bring to a boil over high heat.

2. Pour mixture into prepared casserole. Cover; bake 25 to 30 minutes or until rice and barley are tender and liquid is absorbed. Fluff rice mixture with fork.   *Makes 4 servings*

Campbell's® Creamed Onion Bake

4 tablespoons margarine *or* butter
1-1/2 cups PEPPERIDGE FARM® Corn Bread Stuffing
2 tablespoons chopped fresh parsley *or*
    2 teaspoons dried parsley flakes
3 large onions, cut in half and sliced (about
    3 cups)
1 can (10-3/4 ounces) CAMPBELL'S® Condensed
    Cream of Mushroom Soup *or* 98% Fat Free
    Cream of Mushroom Soup
1/4 cup milk
1 cup frozen peas
1 cup shredded Cheddar cheese (4 ounces)

1. Melt **2 tablespoons** margarine and mix with stuffing and parsley. Set aside.

2. In medium skillet over medium heat, heat remaining margarine. Add onions and cook until tender.

3. Stir in soup, milk and peas. Spoon into 2-quart shallow baking dish. Sprinkle cheese and stuffing mixture over soup mixture.

4. Bake at 350°F. for 30 minutes or until hot.
    Makes 6 servings

Helpful Hint

When onions are cut, they release sulfur compounds that bring tears to the eyes. Believe it or not, chewing a piece of bread while peeling and chopping may help to minimize the tears.

Ratatouille Stuffed Zucchini

Cheesy Corn Bake

(Pictured at right)

3 eggs, well beaten
1 can (14-3/4 ounces) creamed corn
3/4 cup unseasoned dry bread crumbs
3/4 cup (3 ounces) shredded cheddar cheese
1/2 medium green bell pepper, chopped
1/2 cup hot milk
1 tablespoon chopped onion
1 teaspoon LAWRY'S® Seasoned Salt
3/4 teaspoon LAWRY'S® Seasoned Pepper
1/4 teaspoon LAWRY'S® Garlic Powder with
Parsley

In large bowl, combine all ingredients. Pour into ungreased 2-quart casserole. Bake in 350°F oven 1 hour. Let stand 10 minutes before serving.

Makes 6 servings

Serving Suggestions: Serve with meat loaf, baked chicken or fried fish. Or, serve topped with prepared LAWRY'S® Original Style Spaghetti Sauce for extra flavor.

Broth-Braised Brussels Sprouts

1 pound fresh brussels sprouts
1/2 cup condensed beef broth *or* 1/2 cup water
plus 2 teaspoons instant beef bouillon
granules
1 tablespoon butter or margarine, softened
1/4 cup freshly grated Parmesan cheese
Paprika

1. Trim stems from brussels sprouts and pull off outer discolored leaves.

2. Use large enough saucepan to allow sprouts to fit in single layer. Place sprouts and broth in saucepan. Bring to a boil; reduce heat. Cover; simmer about 5 minutes or just until sprouts turn bright green and are crisp-tender.

3. Uncover; simmer until liquid is almost evaporated. Toss cooked sprouts with butter, then cheese. Sprinkle with paprika to taste. Garnish as desired. *Makes 4 side-dish servings*

Tip: For faster, more even cooking, cut an "X" deep into the stem end of each brussels sprout.

Mushroom Casserole Florentine

1 bag UNCLE BEN'S® Boil-In-Bag Rice
2 tablespoons butter or margarine
1/4 cup chopped onion
1 pound fresh mushrooms, cut into quarters
1/4 teaspoon crushed dried thyme or rosemary
leaves
1 can (10-3/4 ounces) condensed cream of
celery soup
1 package (10 ounces) frozen chopped spinach,
thawed and drained
3/4 cup shredded sharp Cheddar cheese

COOK: CLEAN: Wash hands. Prepare rice according to package directions. Preheat oven to 350°F. Meanwhile, in medium skillet, melt butter over medium heat; cook onion in butter until tender, stirring occasionally. Add mushrooms and thyme; cook until liquid is evaporated, stirring occasionally. Add rice; reduce heat to low. Cook 3 minutes, stirring frequently. Remove from heat. Stir in soup, spinach and cheese. Pour mixture into 1-1/2-quart casserole. Bake, uncovered, 10 minutes or until cheese melts and rice is hot. Stir before serving.

SERVE: Garnish with additional cheese, if desired.

CHILL: Refrigerate leftovers immediately.

Makes 6 servings

Mostaccioli with Spinach and Feta

8 ounces mostaccioli or penne
2 tablespoons olive oil
3 cups chopped tomatoes
1 package (10 ounces) frozen chopped spinach,
thawed, well drained
1/2 cup chopped green onions
1 package (8 ounces) ATHENOS® Feta Cheese
with Basil & Tomato, crumbled

• Cook pasta as directed on package; drain. Return to pan; toss with oil.

• Add tomatoes, spinach and onions; toss lightly. Cook and stir 2 minutes or until thoroughly heated.

• Add cheese; cook 1 minute. *Makes 8 servings*

Saucy Garden Patch Vegetables

(Pictured at right)

1 can (10-3/4 ounces) condensed cheddar
cheese soup
1/2 cup sour cream
1/4 cup milk
1 bag (16 ounces) frozen vegetable combination,
such as broccoli, corn and red bell pepper,
thawed and drained
1 bag (16 ounces) frozen vegetable combination,
such as brussels sprouts, carrots and
cauliflower, thawed and drained
1 cup (4 ounces) shredded cheddar cheese
1-1/3 cups *French's®* French Fried Onions, divided

MICROWAVE DIRECTIONS
Combine soup, sour cream and milk in large bowl.
Stir in vegetables, cheese and *2/3 cup* French Fried
Onions. Spoon into microwavable 2-quart oblong
baking dish.

Cover loosely with plastic wrap. Microwave on
HIGH 10 minutes or until vegetables are tender and
mixture is heated through, stirring halfway through
cooking time. Uncover; sprinkle with remaining
2/3 cup onions. Microwave on HIGH 1 minute or
until onions are golden.   *Makes 8 to 10 servings*

Oven Directions: Prepare vegetable mixture as
above. Bake, covered, in 400°F oven 45 minutes or
until tender and mixture is heated through. Stir;
sprinkle with remaining onions. Bake, uncovered,
1 minute.

Carrots Amandine

1 pound carrots, peeled and cut into 1/2-inch
diagonal slices
1/4 cup golden raisins (optional)
1/4 cup I CAN'T BELIEVE IT'S NOT BUTTER!®
Spread
3 tablespoons honey
1 teaspoon lemon juice
1/4 teaspoon ground ginger (optional)
1/4 cup sliced almonds, toasted

On stovetop or in microwave oven, steam carrots
and raisins until tender; drain. Stir in I Can't Believe
It's Not Butter! Spread, honey, lemon juice and
ginger. Spoon into serving bowl and sprinkle with
almonds.   *Makes 4 servings*

Moroccan Couscous

1 cup low-sodium chicken broth
1/2 teaspoon ground cinnamon
1/8 teaspoon ground nutmeg
2/3 cup uncooked couscous
2/3 cup DOLE® Pitted Dates or Pitted Prunes,
chopped
1/2 cup chopped green onions
1/3 cup DOLE® Golden or Seedless Raisins
3 tablespoons sliced almonds, toasted

• Combine broth, cinnamon and nutmeg in medium
saucepan. Bring to boil.

• Stir in couscous, dates, green onions and raisins.
Remove from heat; cover. Let stand 5 minutes.

• Stir couscous mixture with fork; spoon into
serving dish. Sprinkle with almonds.

Makes 6 servings

Simply Green Beans

1 pound fresh green beans, ends removed and
cut in half widthwise
1 tablespoon butter, melted
3 tablespoons coarsely grated Romano cheese
1/4 to 1/2 teaspoon LAWRY'S® Seasoned Pepper
1/4 teaspoon LAWRY'S® Garlic Powder with
Parsley

In large saucepan, bring 2 quarts of water to a boil
over medium-high heat; add beans. After water has
returned to a boil, cook beans 4 minutes. Drain;
rinse under cold water. In medium skillet, heat
butter. Add green beans and cook over medium-high
heat 3 minutes or until tender. Add remaining
ingredients; toss well. Serve hot.

Makes 4 servings

Microwave Directions: In microwave-safe shallow
dish, place green beans and 1/4 cup water. Cover
with plastic wrap, venting one corner. Microwave
on HIGH 14 to 16 minutes, stirring after 7 minutes;
drain. Add butter, Seasoned Pepper and Garlic
Powder with Parsley. Stir; let stand covered
1 minute. Sprinkle with cheese.

Serving Suggestion: Great accompaniment to roast
chicken or fresh fish fillets.

Saucy Garden Patch Vegetables

Antipasto Rice

(Pictured at right)

1-1/2 cups water
1/2 cup tomato juice
1 cup uncooked white rice*
1 teaspoon dried basil leaves
1 teaspoon dried oregano leaves
1/2 teaspoon salt (optional)
1 can (14 ounces) artichoke hearts, drained and quartered
1 jar (7 ounces) roasted red peppers, drained and chopped
1 can (2-1/4 ounces) sliced ripe olives, drained
2 tablespoons snipped fresh parsley
2 tablespoons lemon juice
1/2 teaspoon ground black pepper
2 tablespoons grated Parmesan cheese

Recipe is based on regular-milled long grain white rice. For medium grain rice, use 1-1/4 cups water and cook for 15 minutes. For parboiled rice, use 1-3/4 cups water and cook for 20 to 25 minutes.

Mix water, tomato juice, rice, basil, oregano, and salt in 2- to 3-quart saucepan. Bring to a boil; stir once or twice. Reduce heat; cover and simmer 15 minutes or until rice is tender and liquid is absorbed. Stir in artichokes, red peppers, olives, parsley, lemon juice and black pepper. Cook 5 minutes longer or until thoroughly heated. Sprinkle with cheese. Garnish as desired. *Makes 8 servings*

Favorite recipe from **USA Rice Federation**

Sweet Potato Soufflé

3 eggs, separated
3/4 cup sugar
1-1/4 cups mashed sweet potatoes, fresh or canned
1 cup chopped California walnuts, divided
Sugar
Whipped cream (optional)

Preheat oven to 350°F. Beat egg yolks in bowl until frothy. Beat in sugar until lemon-colored. Beat in potatoes and 1/2 cup walnuts until blended. Beat egg whites in separate bowl until stiff peaks form; fold into potato mixture. Turn into buttered and sugared soufflé dish. Sprinkle remaining walnuts on top. Dust with sugar. Bake 15 minutes or until thermometer reads 160°F. Serve immediately with whipped cream, if desired. *Makes 6 servings*

Favorite recipe from **Walnut Marketing Board**

Broccoli-Stuffed Shells

1 tablespoon butter or margarine
1/4 cup chopped onion
1 cup ricotta cheese
1 egg
2 cups chopped cooked broccoli *or* 1 package (10 ounces) frozen chopped broccoli, thawed and well drained
1 cup (4 ounces) shredded Monterey Jack cheese
20 jumbo pasta shells
1 can (28 ounces) crushed tomatoes with added puree
1 packet (1 ounce) HIDDEN VALLEY® The Original Ranch® Salad Dressing & Seasoning Mix
1/4 cup grated Parmesan cheese

Preheat oven to 350°F. In small skillet, melt butter over medium heat. Add onion; cook until onion is tender but not browned. Remove from heat; cool. In large bowl, stir ricotta cheese and egg until well-blended. Add broccoli and Monterey Jack cheese; mix well. In large pot of boiling water, cook pasta shells 8 to 10 minutes or just until tender; drain. Rinse under cold running water; drain again. Stuff each shell with about 2 tablespoons broccoli-cheese mixture.

In medium bowl, combine tomatoes, sautéed onion and salad dressing & seasoning mix; mix well. Pour one third of the tomato mixture into 13×9-inch baking dish. Arrange filled shells in dish. Spoon remaining tomato mixture over top. Sprinkle with Parmesan cheese. Bake, covered, until hot and bubbly, about 30 minutes. *Makes 4 servings*

Helpful Hint

Broccoli is most often steamed, boiled or stir-fried until crisp-tender. Overcooking results in mushy broccoli with a strong flavor. Steam florets 5 to 7 minutes and spears 7 to 9 minutes. Drop florets into a small amount of boiling water in a saucepan and boil 5 to 7 minutes; boil spears 7 to 9 minutes.

Antipasto Rice

Soups

Cheesy Potato Chowder

(Pictured at left)

1-1/2 cups water
   3 medium red potatoes, peeled and cubed
   1 rib celery, sliced
   1 medium carrot, chopped
1/4 cup butter or margarine
   3 green onions, sliced
1/4 cup all-purpose flour
   1 teaspoon salt
1/8 teaspoon black pepper
   4 cups milk
   2 cups (8 ounces) shredded American cheese
   1 cup (4 ounces) shredded Swiss cheese
1/2 teaspoon caraway seeds
   Fresh chervil for garnish
   Oyster crackers (optional)

1. Combine water, potatoes, celery and carrot in medium saucepan. Bring to a boil over high heat. Reduce heat to medium; simmer, uncovered, 10 minutes or until vegetables are tender.

2. Meanwhile, melt butter in large saucepan over medium heat. Cook and stir onions in butter 2 minutes or until tender but not brown. Stir in flour, salt and pepper. Cook and stir about 1 minute.

3. Stir milk and potato mixture into flour mixture; cook and stir over medium heat until bubbly. Cook and stir 1 minute more. Stir in cheeses and caraway seeds. Reduce heat to low; simmer, uncovered, until cheeses are melted and mixture is hot, stirring constantly. Garnish with chervil. Serve with oyster crackers, if desired. *Makes 6 servings*

Clockwise from top left: *Cheesy Potato Chowder, Chicken Gumbo (p. 72), White Bean Soup (p. 68) and Tortilla Soup (p. 88)*

Greek Lemon and Rice Soup

(Pictured at right)

> 2 tablespoons butter
> 1/3 cup minced green onions with tops
> 6 cups canned chicken broth
> 2/3 cup uncooked long grain white rice
> 4 eggs
>   Juice of 1 fresh lemon, or to taste
> 1/8 teaspoon white pepper (optional)

1. Melt butter in 3-quart saucepan over medium heat. Add green onions. Cook and stir about 3 minutes or until green onions are tender.

2. Stir in chicken broth and rice. Bring to a boil over medium-high heat. Reduce heat to low; simmer, covered, 20 to 25 minutes or until rice is tender.

3. Beat eggs in medium bowl with wire whisk until well beaten. Add lemon juice and 1/2 cup broth mixture to bowl. Gradually return lemon juice mixture to broth mixture in saucepan, stirring constantly. Cook and stir over low heat 2 to 3 minutes or until broth mixture thickens enough to lightly coat spoon. *Do not boil.*

4. Stir in pepper, if desired. Garnish with fresh mint and lemon peel, if desired. *Makes 6 to 8 servings*

White Bean Soup

(Pictured on page 66)

> 6 strips (about 6 ounces) bacon, cut into
>   1/2-inch pieces
> 3 cans (15 ounces each) white kidney or
>   cannellini beans, drained and rinsed, divided
> 3 cans (about 14 ounces each) chicken broth
> 1 medium onion, finely chopped
> 3 cloves garlic, minced
> 1-1/2 teaspoons dried thyme leaves
> 1-1/2 teaspoons dried rosemary, crushed

1. Cook and stir bacon in Dutch oven over medium-high heat about 10 minutes or until crisp.

2. While bacon is cooking, blend 1-1/2 cans beans and broth in blender or food processor until smooth.

3. Drain all but 1 tablespoon bacon fat from Dutch oven. Stir in onion, garlic, thyme and rosemary. Reduce heat to medium; cover and cook 3 minutes

or until onion is transparent. Uncover and cook 3 minutes or until onion is tender, stirring frequently.

4. Add puréed bean mixture and remaining 1-1/2 cans beans to bacon mixture. Cover and simmer 5 minutes or until heated through.

Makes 4 servings

Tip: For a special touch, sprinkle chopped fresh thyme over soup just before serving.

Butternut Bisque

> 1 teaspoon margarine or butter
> 1 large onion, coarsely chopped
> 1 medium butternut squash (about
>   1-1/2 pounds), peeled, seeded and cut into
>   1/2-inch pieces
> 2 cans (14-1/2 ounces each) chicken broth,
>   divided
> 1/2 teaspoon ground nutmeg or freshly grated
>   nutmeg
> 1/8 teaspoon white pepper
>   Plain yogurt and chives for garnish (optional)

Melt margarine in large saucepan over medium heat. Add onion; cook and stir 3 minutes.

Add squash and 1 can chicken broth; bring to a boil over high heat. Reduce heat to low; cover and simmer 20 minutes or until squash is very tender.

Process squash mixture, in 2 batches, in food processor until smooth. Return soup to saucepan; add remaining can of broth, nutmeg and pepper. Simmer, uncovered, 5 minutes, stirring occasionally.*

Ladle soup into soup bowls. Place yogurt in pastry bag fitted with round decorating tip. Pipe onto soup in decorative design. Garnish with chives, if desired.

Makes 6 servings (about 5 cups)

At this point, soup may be covered and refrigerated up to 2 days before serving. Reheat over medium heat, stirring occasionally.

Cream of Butternut Soup: Add 1/2 cup whipping cream or half-and-half with second can of broth. Proceed as directed.

Turkey, Corn and Sweet Potato Soup

(Pictured at right)

1/2 cup chopped onion
1 small jalapeño pepper, minced
1 teaspoon margarine
5 cups turkey or chicken broth
1-1/2 pounds sweet potatoes, peeled and cut into
1-inch cubes
2 cups cubed cooked turkey
1/2 teaspoon salt
1-1/2 cups frozen corn
Fresh cilantro (optional)

In 5-quart saucepan over medium-high heat, cook and stir onion and jalapeño pepper in margarine 5 minutes or until onion is soft. Add broth, potatoes, turkey and salt; bring to a boil. Reduce heat to low, cover and simmer 20 to 25 minutes or until potatoes are tender. Stir in corn. Increase heat to medium and cook 5 to 6 minutes.

To serve, spoon 1 cup soup in bowl and garnish with cilantro, if desired. *Makes 8 servings*

Favorite recipe from **National Turkey Federation**

Manhattan Clam Chowder

1/4 cup chopped uncooked bacon
1 cup chopped onion
1/2 cup chopped carrots
1/2 cup chopped celery
2 cans (14.5 ounces each) CONTADINA® Recipe Ready Diced Tomatoes, undrained
1 can (8 ounces) CONTADINA® Tomato Sauce
1 bottle (8 ounces) clam juice
1 large bay leaf
1/2 teaspoon chopped fresh rosemary
1/8 teaspoon pepper
2 cans (6.5 ounces each) chopped clams, undrained

1. Sauté bacon with onion, carrots and celery in large saucepan.

2. Stir in undrained tomatoes with remaining ingredients, except clams. Heat to boiling. Reduce heat; boil gently, uncovered, 15 minutes. Stir in clams and juice.

3. Heat additional 5 minutes. Remove bay leaf before serving. *Makes 6-1/2 cups*

Black-Eyed Pea Soup

2 large potatoes
4 medium onions, thinly sliced
4 carrots, thinly sliced
1/2 pound bacon, diced
8 quarts water
2 pounds dried black-eyed peas, rinsed
2 cups thinly sliced celery
1 meaty ham bone
2 whole jalapeño peppers*
4 bay leaves
1/2 teaspoon dried thyme leaves, crushed
Salt and black pepper to taste

Jalapeño peppers can sting and irritate the skin; wear rubber gloves when handling peppers and do not touch eyes. Wash hands after handling.

Peel and grate potatoes. Place grated potatoes in large bowl of cold water; set aside.

Mix onions, carrots and bacon in stockpot. Cook and stir over medium-high heat until onions are golden. Drain potatoes. Add water, peas, potatoes, celery, ham bone, jalapeño peppers, bay and thyme to onion mixture. Season with salt and black pepper. Reduce heat to low. Simmer, covered, 3 to 4 hours. Remove jalapeño peppers and bay leaves; discard.

Remove ham bone; cool. Cut meat from bone. Chop meat into bite-size pieces; return to stockpot.
Makes 12 to 16 servings

Swanson® Spinach Tortellini Soup

6 cups SWANSON® Chicken Broth
1/4 teaspoon garlic powder *or* 1 clove garlic, minced
1/8 teaspoon pepper
1 cup frozen cheese-filled tortellini
2 cups coarsely chopped fresh spinach leaves *or* 1 cup frozen chopped spinach

MIX broth, garlic and pepper in saucepot. Heat to a boil. Stir in tortellini.

COOK over medium heat 10 minutes. Add spinach. Cook 5 minutes or until tortellini is done.
Makes 6 servings

Turkey, Corn and Sweet Potato Soup

Double Pea Soup

Chicken Gumbo

(Pictured on page 66)

3 tablespoons vegetable oil
1 pound boneless skinless chicken breasts, cut
   into 1-inch pieces
1/2 pound smoked sausage,* cut into 3/4-inch
   slices
1 bag (16 ounces) BIRDS EYE® frozen Farm Fresh
   Mixtures Broccoli, Corn and Red Peppers
1 can (14-1/2 ounces) stewed tomatoes
1-1/2 cups water

*For a spicy gumbo, use andouille sausage. Any type of kielbasa or
turkey kielbasa can also be used.*

• Heat oil in large saucepan over high heat. Add
chicken and sausage; cook until browned, about
8 minutes.

• Add vegetables, tomatoes and water; bring to boil.
Reduce heat to medium; cover and cook 5 to
6 minutes.   *Makes 4 to 6 servings*

Double Pea Soup

(Pictured at left)

1 tablespoon vegetable oil
1 large white onion, finely chopped
3 cloves garlic, finely chopped
2 cups water
2 cups dried split peas
1 bay leaf
1 teaspoon ground mustard
1-1/2 cups frozen green peas
1 teaspoon salt
1/4 teaspoon black pepper
Sour cream (optional)

1. Heat oil in large saucepan or Dutch oven over
medium-high heat until hot. Add onion; cook
5 minutes or until onion is tender, stirring
occasionally. Add garlic; cook and stir 2 minutes.

2. Stir water, split peas, bay leaf and mustard into
saucepan. Bring to a boil over high heat. Cover;
reduce heat to medium-low. Simmer 45 minutes or
until split peas are tender, stirring occasionally.

3. Stir green peas, salt and pepper into saucepan;
cover. Cook 10 minutes or until green peas are
tender. Remove bay leaf; discard. Blend using hand-
held blender until smooth, or process small batches
in blender or food processor until smooth.

4. Top each serving with sour cream before serving.
Garnish as desired.   *Makes 6 servings*

Italian Tomato Soup

1/2 pound lean ground beef
1/2 cup chopped onion
1 clove garlic, minced
1 can (28 ounces) diced tomatoes, undrained
1 can (15 ounces) white kidney beans, drained,
   rinsed
3/4 cup HEINZ® Tomato Ketchup
1/2 cup thinly sliced carrots
1 teaspoon dried basil leaves
1/4 teaspoon salt

In medium saucepan, brown beef, onion and garlic;
drain excess fat. Add tomatoes with juices and
remaining ingredients. Cover; simmer 15 minutes.
           Makes 4 to 6 servings (about 6 cups)

Chicken Tortilla Soup

(Pictured below)

2 large ripe avocados, halved and pitted
4 teaspoons TABASCO® brand Green Pepper
    Sauce, divided
1/2 teaspoon salt *or* to taste
3 (14-1/2-ounce) cans chicken broth
3 boneless, skinless chicken breast halves (about
    1 pound)
2 tablespoons uncooked rice
1 large tomato, seeded and chopped
1/2 cup chopped onion
1/4 cup finely chopped cilantro
    Tortilla chips
1/2 cup (2 ounces) shredded Monterey Jack cheese

Scoop out avocado into medium bowl and mash with fork. Add 1-1/2 teaspoons TABASCO® Green Pepper Sauce and salt; blend gently but thoroughly. Set aside.

Heat chicken broth to boiling in 4-quart saucepan. Add chicken breast halves; reduce heat and cook until chicken is no longer pink. Remove chicken and cut into bite-size pieces. Add rice and cook about 15 minutes or until tender. Return chicken to saucepan. Just before serving, stir in tomato, onion, cilantro and remaining 2-1/2 teaspoons TABASCO® Green Pepper Sauce.

To serve, break small handful of tortilla chips into bottom of each bowl. Ladle soup over tortilla chips. Top with cheese and 1 rounded tablespoon avocado mixture. Serve immediately with additional TABASCO® Green Pepper Sauce, if desired.

Makes 8 servings

Creamy Broccoli Noodle Soup

3-1/2 cups milk
1 package (10 ounces) frozen chopped broccoli
1 pouch LIPTON® Soup Secrets Noodle Soup
    Mix with Real Chicken Broth

In medium saucepan, combine all ingredients; bring to a boil. Reduce heat and simmer, uncovered, stirring occasionally, 5 minutes or until noodles are tender.

Makes 4 (1-cup) servings

Chicken Tortilla Soup

Beefy Broccoli & Cheese Soup

(Pictured at right)

2 cups chicken broth
1 package (10 ounces) frozen chopped broccoli, thawed
1/4 cup chopped onion
1/4 pound ground beef
1 cup milk
2 tablespoons all-purpose flour
1 cup (4 ounces) shredded sharp cheddar cheese
1-1/2 teaspoons chopped fresh oregano *or*
    1/2 teaspoon dried oregano leaves
    Salt and black pepper
    Hot pepper sauce

Bring broth to a boil in medium saucepan. Add broccoli and onion; cook 5 minutes or until broccoli is tender.

Meanwhile, brown ground beef in small skillet; drain. Gradually add milk to flour in small bowl, mixing until well blended. Add with ground beef to broth mixture; cook, stirring constantly, until mixture is thickened and bubbly.

Add cheese and oregano; stir until cheese is melted. Season with salt, pepper and hot pepper sauce to taste. *Makes 4 to 5 servings*

Chicken and Homemade Noodle Soup

3/4 cup all-purpose flour
2 teaspoons finely chopped fresh thyme *or*
    1/2 teaspoon dried thyme leaves, divided
1/4 teaspoon salt
1 egg yolk, beaten
3 tablespoons cold water
1 pound boneless skinless chicken thighs, cut into 1/2- to 3/4-inch pieces
2 cups cold water
5 cups chicken broth
1 medium onion, chopped
1 medium carrot, thinly sliced
3/4 cup frozen peas
    Chopped fresh parsley for garnish

1. To prepare noodles, stir together flour, 1 teaspoon thyme and salt in small bowl. Add egg yolk and 3 tablespoons water. Stir together until mixed. Shape into small ball. Place dough on lightly floured surface; flatten slightly. Knead 5 minutes or until dough is smooth and elastic, adding more flour to prevent sticking if necessary. Cover with plastic wrap. Let stand 15 minutes.

2. Roll out dough to 1/8-inch thickness or thinner on lightly floured surface with lightly floured rolling pin. If dough is too elastic, let rest a few minutes. Let rolled-out dough stand about 30 minutes to dry slightly. Cut into 1/4-inch-wide strips. Cut strips 1-1/2 to 2 inches long; set aside.

3. Combine chicken and 2 cups water in medium saucepan. Bring to a boil over high heat. Reduce heat to medium-low; cover and simmer 5 minutes or until chicken is no longer pink. Drain and rinse chicken; set aside. Combine chicken broth, onion, carrot and remaining 1 teaspoon thyme in 5-quart Dutch oven. Bring to a boil over high heat. Add noodles. Reduce heat to medium-low; simmer, uncovered, 8 minutes or until noodles are tender. Stir in chicken and peas. Bring soup just to a boil. Sprinkle with parsley. *Makes 4 servings*

Wild Rice Steak and Cabbage Soup

4 cups chopped cabbage
2 tablespoons vegetable oil
1 medium onion, chopped
2 cloves garlic, chopped
1 pound beef chuck steak, cut into 1/2-inch cubes
7 cups beef broth
3 cups cooked wild rice
1 box (10 ounces) cut carrots, sliced
1-1/2 teaspoons caraway seeds
1 teaspoon salt
1 teaspoon black pepper
1-1/2 cups shredded Swiss cheese

In large saucepan, sauté cabbage in oil 5 minutes, stirring frequently; do not brown. Add onion and garlic; sauté 3 minutes. Add beef; cook 5 minutes. Add remaining ingredients except cheese; simmer, covered, 1 hour. Ladle into bowls and top with cheese. *Makes 6 to 8 servings*

Favorite recipe from **Minnesota Cultivated Wild Rice Council**

Beefy Broccoli & Cheese Soup

Carrot-Rice Soup

(Pictured at right)

1 pound carrots, peeled and chopped
1 medium onion, chopped
1 tablespoon margarine
4 cups chicken broth, divided
1/4 teaspoon dried tarragon leaves
1/4 teaspoon ground white pepper
2-1/4 cups cooked rice
1/4 cup sour cream
Snipped parsley or mint for garnish

Cook carrots and onion in margarine in large saucepan or Dutch oven over medium-high heat 2 to 3 minutes or until onion is tender. Add 2 cups broth, tarragon, and pepper. Reduce heat; simmer 10 minutes. Combine vegetables and broth in food processor or blender in batches; cover and process until smooth. Return to saucepan. Add remaining 2 cups broth and rice; thoroughly heat. Dollop sour cream on each serving of soup. Garnish with parsley. *Makes 6 servings*

Favorite recipe from **USA Rice Federation**

Savory Potato & Roasted Garlic Soup

2 slices bacon
1 pound all-purpose or red-skinned potatoes, peeled and cubed
1 medium onion, diced
1 small red bell pepper, diced
1 rib celery, chopped
1/4 teaspoon dried thyme leaves, crushed
1/8 teaspoon ground black pepper
1 can (14-1/2 ounces) chicken broth
1/4 cup dry white wine or additional chicken broth
1 jar (16 ounces) RAGÚ® Cheese Creations!® Roasted Garlic Parmesan Sauce

In 3-quart saucepan, cook bacon; remove and crumble. Reserve drippings. Add potatoes, onion, bell pepper, celery, thyme and black pepper to reserved drippings. Cook over medium heat, stirring occasionally, 6 minutes or until onion is tender. Stir in chicken broth and wine. Bring to a boil over high heat. Reduce heat to low and simmer covered 10 minutes or until vegetables are tender. Stir in Ragú Cheese Creations! Sauce; heat through. Garnish with bacon. *Makes 6 (1-cup) servings*

Dijon Ham and Lentil Soup

1 cup finely chopped onion
3/4 cup finely chopped green bell pepper
1/2 cup finely chopped carrot
1 clove garlic, minced
1 bay leaf
2 (14-1/2-ounce) cans chicken broth
1 (14-1/2-ounce) can stewed tomatoes
1-1/4 cups water
1 cup diced ham
3/4 cup dry lentils
1/2 cup GREY POUPON® COUNTRY DIJON® Mustard

Combine all ingredients except mustard in large saucepan. Heat to a boil over medium-high heat. Reduce heat; simmer, uncovered, for 1 hour. Stir in mustard. Discard bay leaf. Serve soup hot.
Makes 6 servings

Corn and Chicken Chowder

3 tablespoons butter *or* margarine, divided
1 pound boneless skinless chicken breasts, cut into chunks
2 medium leeks, sliced (2 cups)
2 medium potatoes, cut into bite-size chunks
1 large green pepper, diced
2 tablespoons paprika
2 tablespoons flour
3 cups chicken broth
2-1/2 cups fresh corn kernels
1-1/2 teaspoons TABASCO® brand Pepper Sauce
1 teaspoon salt
1 cup half-and-half

In 4-quart saucepan over medium-high heat, melt 1 tablespoon butter. Cook chicken chunks until well browned on all sides, stirring frequently. With slotted spoon, remove chicken; set aside.

Add 2 tablespoons butter to drippings remaining in saucepan. Over medium heat, cook leeks, potatoes and green pepper until tender, stirring occasionally. Stir in paprika and flour until well blended; cook for 1 minute. Add chicken broth, corn kernels, TABASCO® Sauce, salt and chicken chunks. Over high heat, heat to boiling. Reduce heat to low; cover and simmer 20 minutes. Stir in half-and-half; heat through. *Makes 8 cups*

Hearty Chicken and Rice Soup

(Pictured at right)

10 cups chicken broth
1 medium onion, chopped
1 cup sliced celery
1 cup sliced carrots
1/4 cup snipped fresh parsley
1/2 teaspoon cracked black pepper
1/2 teaspoon dried thyme leaves
1 bay leaf
1-1/2 cups cubed chicken (about 3/4 pound)
2 cups cooked rice
2 tablespoons lime juice
Lime slices for garnish

Combine broth, onion, celery, carrots, parsley, pepper, thyme and bay leaf in Dutch oven. Bring to a boil, stirring once or twice. Reduce heat; simmer, uncovered, 10 to 15 minutes. Add chicken; simmer, uncovered, 5 to 10 minutes or until chicken is no longer pink in center. Remove and discard bay leaf. Stir in rice and lime juice just before serving. Garnish with lime slices. *Makes 8 servings*

Favorite recipe from **USA Rice Federation**

Shrimp Bisque

1 pound medium shrimp, peeled and deveined
1/2 cup chopped onion
1/2 cup chopped celery
1/2 cup chopped carrot
2 tablespoons butter or margarine
2 cans (14-1/2 ounces each) chicken broth
1 can (14-1/2 ounces) DEL MONTE® Original Recipe Stewed Tomatoes
1/4 teaspoon dried thyme
1 cup half & half

1. Cut shrimp into small pieces; set aside. In large saucepan, cook onion, celery and carrot in butter until onion is tender.

2. Add shrimp; cook 1 minute. Add broth, tomatoes and thyme; simmer 10 minutes. Ladle 1/3 of soup into blender container or food processor.

3. Cover and process until smooth. Repeat for remaining soup. Add half & half to saucepan. Return soup to pan. Heat through. *Do not boil.*
Makes 6 servings (approximately 1 cup each)

Chunky Potato Soup

6 slices OSCAR MAYER® Bacon, chopped
1 large leek, chopped or 1/2 cup chopped green onions
1 can (14-1/2 ounces) chicken broth
1 cup milk
1 package (8 ounces) PHILADELPHIA® Cream Cheese, cubed
4 cups chopped peeled potatoes

COOK bacon in Dutch oven or large saucepan on medium heat until crisp, stirring frequently. Drain bacon, reserving 2 tablespoons drippings in Dutch oven. Set bacon aside.

ADD leek to reserved drippings; cook and stir 5 minutes or until tender. Add broth, milk and cream cheese; cook on low heat until cream cheese is melted, stirring frequently.

ADD potatoes; cook, uncovered, 20 to 25 minutes or until potatoes are tender, stirring occasionally.
Makes 6 (1-cup) servings

Country Vegetable Soup

3 cans (13-3/4 ounces each) chicken broth
1 cup water
1 package (4-1/2 ounces) creamy chicken, rice and sauce mix
1/2 teaspoon dried basil
1 bag (16 ounces) BIRDS EYE® frozen Farm Fresh Mixtures Broccoli, Green Beans, Pearl Onions and Red Peppers

• Bring broth, water, rice and sauce mix, and basil to boil in large saucepan over high heat.

• Reduce heat to medium. Cook, uncovered, 7 minutes.

• Add vegetables; cook 6 to 7 minutes or until rice and vegetables are tender. *Makes 4 servings*

Velveeta® Spicy Southwest Corn Cheese Soup

(Pictured at right)

1 package (10 ounces) frozen sweet corn, thawed, drained
1 clove garlic, minced
1 tablespoon butter or margarine
3/4 pound (12 ounces) VELVEETA® Pasteurized Prepared Cheese Product, cut up
3/4 cup chicken broth
3/4 cup milk
1 can (4 ounces) chopped green chilies
2 tablespoons chopped fresh cilantro

1. Cook and stir corn and garlic in butter in large saucepan on medium-high heat until tender. Reduce heat to medium.

2. Stir in remaining ingredients; cook until VELVEETA is melted and soup is thoroughly heated. Top each serving with crushed tortilla chips, if desired.   *Makes 4 (1-cup) servings*

Tip: A serving of Spicy Southwest Corn Cheese Soup is high in calcium. In addition, it is also an excellent source of vitamins A and C.

Quick and Zesty Vegetable Soup

1 pound lean ground beef
1/2 cup chopped onion
Salt and pepper
2 cans (14-1/2 ounces each) DEL MONTE® Italian Recipe Stewed Tomatoes
2 cans (14-1/2 ounces each) beef broth
1 can (14-1/2 ounces) DEL MONTE® Mixed Vegetables
1/2 cup uncooked medium egg noodles
1/2 teaspoon dried oregano

1. Brown meat with onion in large pot. Cook until onion is tender; drain. Season to taste with salt and pepper.

2. Stir in remaining ingredients. Bring to boil; reduce heat.

3. Cover and simmer 15 minutes or until noodles are tender.   *Makes 8 servings*

Chunky Chicken Noodle Soup with Vegetables

2 envelopes LIPTON® RECIPE SECRETS® Noodle Soup Mix with Real Chicken Broth
6 cups water
1/2 small head escarole, torn into pieces (about 2 cups)*
1 large stalk celery, sliced
1 small carrot, sliced
1/4 cup frozen peas (optional)
1 small clove garlic, finely chopped
1/2 teaspoon dried thyme leaves, crushed
2 whole cloves
1 bay leaf
2 cups cut-up cooked chicken
1 tablespoon finely chopped parsley

Or substitute 2 cups shredded cabbage.

In large saucepan or stockpot, combine noodle soup mix, water, escarole, celery, carrot, peas, garlic, thyme, cloves and bay leaf. Bring to a boil, then simmer, uncovered, stirring occasionally, 15 minutes or until vegetables are tender. Stir in chicken and parsley; heat through. Remove bay leaf and cloves.
                    Makes about 4 (1-3/4-cup) main-dish or 7 (1-cup) appetizer servings

Microwave Directions: In 3-quart microwave-safe casserole, combine as above. Microwave uncovered at HIGH (Full Power), stirring occasionally, 20 minutes or until vegetables are tender. Stir in chicken and parsley; microwave, uncovered, 1 minute or until heated through. Remove bay leaf. Let stand covered 5 minutes.

Helpful Hint

Escarole, well wrapped, will keep in the refrigerator about one week. All greens should be stored unwashed. To clean escarole, separate the leaves from the head and swish the leaves in a large bowl or sinkful of water. Repeat this process several times, if necessary, to remove embedded sand or soil. Drain and pat dry.

Velveeta® Spicy Southwest Corn Cheese Soup

Tomato Onion Soup

(Pictured below)

2 large onions, thinly sliced
1 clove garlic, minced
1/4 cup butter
1-3/4 cups tomato juice
3 cups beef broth
2/3 cup picante sauce
1 cup croutons
1 cup (4 ounces) shredded Monterey Jack cheese (optional)

1. Cook onions, garlic and butter in 3-quart saucepan over medium-low heat 20 minutes or until onions are tender and golden brown.

2. Stir in tomato juice, broth and picante sauce. Bring to a boil over medium-high heat. Reduce heat to low. Simmer, uncovered, 20 minutes.

3. Ladle soup into bowls and sprinkle with croutons and cheese, if desired. Serve with additional picante sauce. *Makes 6 servings*

Tomato Onion Soup

StarKist® Vegetable Gazpacho

1 large onion, quartered
1 medium zucchini, halved lengthwise
1 yellow or crookneck squash, halved lengthwise
1 red bell pepper
1 yellow bell pepper
3/4 cup bottled olive oil vinaigrette dressing
1 (3-ounce) pouch of STARKIST® Premium Albacore or Chunk Light Tuna
3 pounds firm ripe tomatoes, chopped
2 cucumbers, peeled, seeded and chopped
2 to 3 cloves fresh garlic, minced or pressed
1/2 cup fresh sourdough bread crumbs
1-1/2 to 2 cups tomato juice

Preheat broiler. Brush onion quarters, zucchini halves, squash halves and whole peppers with dressing; reserve remaining dressing. Broil 6 to 8 minutes, turning occasionally, until vegetables are roasted and pepper skins blister and turn black. Remove from broiler. Place peppers in bowl; cover and let stand 15 minutes before peeling. Cool remaining vegetables. Peel skin from peppers; seed and remove membranes.

Cut roasted vegetables into large pieces; place in food processor bowl. Process until coarsely chopped. Transfer to large bowl; add tuna, tomatoes, cucumbers, garlic, bread crumbs, 1-1/2 cups tomato juice and remaining dressing. Blend thoroughly. Add remaining 1/2 cup tomato juice to thin, if desired. *Makes 6 to 8 servings*

Ham and Cauliflower Chowder

1 bag (16 ounces) BIRDS EYE® frozen Cauliflower
2 cans (10-3/4 ounces each) cream of mushroom or cream of celery soup
2-1/2 cups milk or water
1/2 pound fully-cooked ham, cubed
1/3 cup shredded Colby cheese (optional)

• Cook cauliflower according to package directions; drain.

• Combine cauliflower, soup, milk and ham in saucepan; mix well.

• Cook over medium heat 4 to 6 minutes, stirring occasionally. Top individual servings with cheese. *Makes 4 to 6 servings*

Apple and Chicken Soup

Apple and Chicken Soup

(Pictured above)

1 sweet potato (8 ounces)
1 tablespoon olive oil
2 ribs celery, thinly sliced
1/2 medium onion, chopped
1 teaspoon dried thyme leaves
1/2 teaspoon dried rosemary, crushed
1/4 teaspoon dried sage leaves
1/4 teaspoon ground nutmeg
2 cans (14-1/2 ounces each) chicken broth
1 cup apple juice
1 large McIntosh apple, peeled and chopped
2/3 cup uncooked small pasta shells
3/4 pound boneless skinless chicken breasts

1. Pierce sweet potato in several places with fork. Microwave at HIGH 6 to 8 minutes or until crisp-tender; set aside (sweet potato will finish cooking and become tender as it stands).

2. Heat oil in 3-quart saucepan over medium-high heat until hot. Add celery, onion, thyme, rosemary, sage and nutmeg. Cook, covered, 3 to 4 minutes or until onion is tender. Add chicken broth, juice and apple. Bring to a boil over high heat; stir in pasta. Reduce heat to medium-high; boil, uncovered, 8 to 10 minutes.

3. Cut chicken into 1/4-inch-wide strips. Remove skin from sweet potato; cut sweet potato into 1-inch pieces. Add chicken and sweet potato to soup. Reduce heat to medium; simmer 3 to 5 minutes or until chicken is no longer pink in center and pasta is tender. *Makes 4 to 6 servings*

Serving Suggestion: Serve with wedges of warm herb-cheese bread.

Ground Beef, Spinach and Barley Soup

(Pictured at right)

12 ounces lean ground beef
4 cups water
1 can (14-1/2 ounces) stewed tomatoes, undrained
1-1/2 cups thinly sliced carrots
1 cup chopped onion
1/2 cup quick-cooking barley
1-1/2 teaspoons beef bouillon granules
1-1/2 teaspoons dried thyme leaves, crushed
1 teaspoon dried oregano leaves, crushed
1/2 teaspoon garlic powder
1/4 teaspoon black pepper
1/8 teaspoon salt
3 cups torn stemmed washed spinach leaves

Cook beef in large saucepan over medium heat until no longer pink, stirring to separate; drain fat from beef. Add water, stewed tomatoes with juice, carrots, onion, barley, bouillon granules, thyme, oregano, garlic powder, pepper and salt. Bring to a boil over high heat. Reduce heat to medium-low. Cover and simmer 12 to 15 minutes or until barley and vegetables are tender, stirring occasionally. Stir in spinach; cook until spinach starts to wilt. Garnish as desired. *Makes 4 servings*

Tomato Vegetable Soup

1 bag SUCCESS® Rice
1 can (6 ounces) tomato paste
1 teaspoon sugar
1 teaspoon salt
1 teaspoon pepper
1/2 teaspoon dried oregano leaves, crushed
1/4 teaspoon dried basil leaves, crushed
2 cans (14-1/2 ounces *each*) stewed tomatoes
1/2 cup chopped onion
1/2 cup sliced celery
1/2 cup sliced carrots

Prepare rice according to package directions.

Combine tomato paste, sugar and seasonings in large saucepan or Dutch oven. Add all remaining ingredients except rice. Bring to a boil over medium-high heat. Reduce heat to low; simmer, uncovered, 20 minutes. Stir in rice; heat thoroughly, stirring occasionally. *Makes 6 servings*

Corn and Onion Chowder

1/4 pound uncooked bacon, chopped
2 medium potatoes (3/4 pound), peeled and cut into 1/4-inch cubes
1-1/3 cups *French's®* French Fried Onions, divided
1/2 cup chopped celery
1 tablespoon fresh thyme *or* 3/4 teaspoon dried thyme leaves
1 bay leaf
1-1/2 cups water
2 cans (14-3/4 ounces each) cream-style corn, undrained
1-1/2 cups milk
1/2 teaspoon salt
1/4 teaspoon ground white or black pepper

Cook and stir bacon in large saucepan over medium-high heat until crisp and browned. Remove with slotted spoon to paper towels. Pour off all but 1 tablespoon drippings.

Add potatoes, *2/3 cup* French Fried Onions, celery, thyme and bay leaf to saucepan. Stir in water. Bring to a boil over medium-high heat. Reduce heat to low. Cover; simmer 10 to 12 minutes or until potatoes are fork-tender, stirring occasionally.

Stir in corn, milk, salt, pepper and reserved bacon. Cook until heated through. *Do not boil.* Discard bay leaf. Ladle into individual soup bowls. Sprinkle with remaining *2/3 cup* onions. *Makes 6 to 8 servings*

Helpful Hint

To freeze soup, first refrigerate the soup until the fat rises to the surface. Skim the fat and discard. Divide the soup into portions to serve two or four. To save freezer space, store the soup in self-sealing plastic bags, stacking them in the freezer. Be sure to label each bag with its contents and the date that the soup was made.

Ground Beef, Spinach and Barley Soup

Chickpea and Shrimp Soup

(Pictured at right)

1 tablespoon olive or vegetable oil
1 cup diced onion
2 cloves garlic, minced
4 cans (10.5 ounces each) condensed beef broth
1 can (14.5 ounces) CONTADINA® Recipe Ready Diced Tomatoes with Roasted Garlic, undrained
1 can (15 ounces) chickpeas or garbanzo beans, rinsed and drained
1 can (6 ounces) CONTADINA Italian Paste with Italian Seasonings
8 ounces small cooked shrimp
2 tablespoons chopped fresh Italian parsley *or* 2 teaspoons dried parsley flakes, crushed
1/2 teaspoon salt
1/4 teaspoon ground black pepper

1. Heat oil over medium-high heat in large saucepan. Add onion and garlic; sauté for 1 minute.

2. Stir in broth, undrained tomatoes, chickpeas and tomato paste. Bring to boil.

3. Reduce heat to low; simmer, uncovered, 10 minutes. Add shrimp, parsley, salt and pepper; simmer 3 minutes or until heated through. Stir before serving. Garnish with additional chopped fresh parsley, if desired. *Makes 8 to 10 servings*

Calico Wild Rice Soup

4 cups chicken broth
2 cups cooked wild rice
1 cup frozen corn
1/2 cup sliced green onions
2 tablespoons chopped red bell pepper
2 tablespoons chopped green bell pepper
1 tablespoon chopped fresh parsley
1 teaspoon dried tarragon leaves, crushed
2 tablespoons cornstarch
2 tablespoons water

Combine broth, rice, corn, green onions, red and green bell pepper, parsley and tarragon in large saucepan; mix well. Cook over medium heat until mixture boils; reduce heat and simmer 5 minutes or until corn is tender. Combine cornstarch and water in small bowl. Stir into broth mixture; cook 5 minutes or until soup thickens slightly, stirring occasionally. *Makes 4 to 6 servings*

Favorite recipe from **Minnesota Cultivated Wild Rice Council**

Dijon Roasted Vegetable Soup

2 plum tomatoes, halved
1 medium zucchini, split lengthwise and halved
1 large onion, quartered
1 red bell pepper, sliced
1 cup sliced carrots
2 to 3 cloves garlic
5 cups chicken broth
1/4 teaspoon ground cumin
1/4 teaspoon crushed red pepper flakes
2 cups diced cooked chicken (about 10 ounces)
1/2 cup GREY POUPON® Dijon Mustard
1/4 cup chopped parsley

Arrange tomatoes, zucchini, onion, bell pepper, carrots and garlic on large baking sheet. Bake at 325°F for 30 to 45 minutes or until golden and tender. Remove from oven and cool. Chop vegetables.

Heat chicken broth, chopped vegetables, cumin and red pepper flakes to a boil in 3-quart pot, over high heat; reduce heat. Simmer for 5 minutes. Stir in chicken and mustard; cook for 5 minutes more. Stir in parsley and serve warm. *Makes 8 servings*

Cream of Asparagus Soup

1 tablespoon margarine or butter
1 small onion, chopped
2 cans (14-1/2 ounces each) chicken broth
1 jar (16 ounces) RAGÚ® Cheese Creations!® Classic Alfredo Sauce
2 packages (10 ounces each) frozen asparagus spears, thawed

1. In 3-1/2-quart saucepan, melt margarine over medium heat and cook onion, stirring occasionally, 5 minutes or until tender. Stir in broth, Ragú Cheese Creations! Sauce and asparagus. Bring to a boil over medium heat, stirring frequently. Reduce heat to low and simmer 5 minutes or until asparagus is tender.

2. In blender or food processor, purée hot soup mixture in batches until smooth. Return soup to saucepan and heat through. Season, if desired, with salt and ground black pepper. *Makes 8 servings*

Chickpea and Shrimp Soup

Classic Meatball Soup

(Pictured at right)

2 pounds beef bones
3 ribs celery
2 carrots
1 medium onion, cut in half
1 bay leaf
6 cups cold water
1 egg
4 tablespoons chopped fresh parsley, divided
1 teaspoon salt, divided
1/2 teaspoon dried marjoram leaves, crushed
1/4 teaspoon black pepper, divided
1/2 cup soft fresh bread crumbs
1/4 cup grated Parmesan cheese
1 pound ground beef
1 can (14-1/2 ounces) diced tomatoes, undrained
1/2 cup uncooked rotini or small macaroni

1. To make stock, rinse bones and combine with celery, carrots, onion and bay leaf in 6-quart stockpot. Add water. Bring to a boil; reduce heat to low. Cover partially and simmer 1 hour, skimming foam occasionally.

2. Preheat oven to 400°F. Spray 13×9-inch baking pan with nonstick cooking spray. Combine egg, 3 tablespoons parsley, 1/2 teaspoon salt, marjoram and 1/8 teaspoon pepper in medium bowl; whisk lightly. Stir in bread crumbs and cheese. Add beef; mix well. Place meat mixture on cutting board; pat evenly into 1-inch-thick square. With sharp knife, cut meat into 1-inch squares; shape each square into a ball. Place meatballs in prepared pan; bake 20 to 25 minutes until meat is no longer pink, turning occasionally. Drain on paper towels.

3. Strain stock through sieve into medium bowl. Slice celery and carrots; reserve. Discard bones, onion and bay leaf. To degrease stock, let stand 5 minutes to allow fat to rise. Skim fat.

4. Return stock to stockpot. Add tomatoes with juice to stock. Bring to a boil; boil 5 minutes. Stir in rotini, remaining 1/2 teaspoon salt and 1/8 teaspoon pepper. Cook 6 minutes, stirring occasionally. Add reserved vegetables and meatballs. Reduce heat to medium; cook 10 minutes until hot. Stir in remaining 1 tablespoon parsley. Season to taste.

Makes 4 to 6 servings

Tortilla Soup

(Pictured on page 66)

1 tablespoon butter or margarine
1/2 cup chopped green bell pepper
1/2 cup chopped onion
1/2 teaspoon ground cumin
2 cans (14-1/2 ounces each) chicken broth
1-3/4 cups (16-ounce jar) ORTEGA® Salsa Prima-Thick & Chunky or Garden Style
1 cup whole-kernel corn
1 tablespoon vegetable oil
6 corn tortillas, cut into 1/2-inch strips
3/4 cup (3 ounces) shredded 4 cheese Mexican blend
Sour cream (optional)

MELT butter in medium saucepan over medium heat. Add bell pepper, onion and cumin; cook for 3 to 4 minutes or until tender. Stir in broth, salsa and corn. Bring to a boil. Reduce heat to low; cook for 5 minutes.

HEAT vegetable oil in medium skillet over medium-high heat. Add tortilla strips; cook for 3 to 4 minutes or until tender.

SERVE soup in bowls. Top with tortilla strips, cheese and a dollop of sour cream. Garnish as desired.

Makes 6 servings

Creamy Turkey Soup

2 tablespoons butter
1/2 cup chopped onion
1 cup sliced fresh mushrooms
2 packages (.88 ounce each) LAWRY'S® Gravy Mix for Chicken
4 cups milk
1 cup cooked, cubed turkey
1/8 teaspoon white pepper

In medium saucepan, heat butter. Add onion and mushrooms and cook over medium-high heat until tender. Add Gravy Mix for Chicken and milk, stirring constantly until blended. Add turkey and pepper. Bring to a boil over medium-high heat; reduce heat to low and simmer, uncovered, 3 to 5 minutes.

Makes 4 servings

Sandwiches

Maple Francheezies

(Pictured at left)

    Mustard Spread (recipe follows)
1/4 cup maple syrup
  2 teaspoons garlic powder
  1 teaspoon black pepper
1/2 teaspoon ground nutmeg
  4 slices bacon
  4 jumbo hot dogs
  4 hot dog buns, split
1/2 cup (2 ounces) shredded cheddar cheese

Prepare Mustard Spread; set aside.

Prepare grill for direct cooking.

Combine maple syrup, garlic powder, pepper and nutmeg in small bowl. Brush syrup mixture onto bacon slices. Wrap 1 slice bacon around each hot dog.

Brush hot dogs with remaining syrup mixture. Place hot dogs on grid. Grill, covered, over medium-high heat 8 minutes or until bacon is crisp and hot dogs are heated through, turning halfway through grilling time. Place hot dogs in buns, top with Mustard Spread and cheese. Serve with carrots and potato chips. *Makes 4 servings*

Mustard Spread

1/2 cup prepared yellow mustard
  1 tablespoon finely chopped onion
  1 tablespoon diced tomato
  1 tablespoon chopped fresh parsley
  1 teaspoon garlic powder
1/2 teaspoon black pepper

Combine all ingredients in small bowl; mix well.
Makes about 3/4 cup

Clockwise from top left: *Maple Francheezie, The Meatless Dagwood (p. 100), Broccoli Melts (p. 94) and Ranch Burger (p. 96)*

Mediterranean Chicken Salad Sandwiches

(Pictured at right)

    4 boneless skinless chicken breast halves
1/2 cup water
    1 teaspoon dried basil leaves
1/4 teaspoon salt
1/4 teaspoon black pepper
    1 cup chopped cucumber
1/2 cup mayonnaise
1/4 cup chopped roasted red pepper
1/4 cup sliced pitted black olives
1/4 cup yogurt
1/4 teaspoon garlic powder
    6 Kaiser rolls, split
       Additional mayonnaise and lettuce leaves

Place chicken, water, basil, salt and pepper in medium saucepan; bring to a boil. Reduce heat; simmer covered 10 to 12 minutes or until chicken is no longer pink in center. Remove chicken from saucepan; cool. Cut into 1/2-inch pieces. Combine chicken, cucumber, mayonnaise, red pepper, olives, yogurt and garlic powder in medium bowl; toss to coat well. Spread rolls with additional mayonnaise. Top with lettuce and chicken salad mixture. Garnish as desired.   *Makes 6 servings*

Cajun Chicken Sandwiches

    3 tablespoons *Frank's® RedHot®* Cayenne Pepper
       Sauce, divided
    2 tablespoons vegetable oil
    4 teaspoons Cajun seasoning blend, divided
    4 thin sliced boneless chicken breast cutlets
       (about 1 pound)
    1 cup mild chunky-style salsa
       Lettuce
    4 soft rolls, split

Combine 2 tablespoons *Frank's RedHot* Sauce, oil and 3 teaspoons Cajun seasoning in cup. Brush mixture onto both sides of chicken. Cover and marinate in refrigerator 30 minutes. Combine salsa, remaining 1 tablespoon *Frank's RedHot* Sauce and 1 teaspoon Cajun seasoning in small bowl; set aside. Place chicken on grid. Grill over medium-high coals 10 minutes or until chicken is no longer pink in center, turning once. To serve, layer lettuce, cooked chicken and salsa mixture on rolls, dividing evenly.
                Makes 4 servings

Caramelized Onion & Eggplant Sandwiches

       Grilled Garlic Aioli (recipe follows) or
          mayonnaise
1/2 cup packed brown sugar
1/2 cup water
1/2 cup soy sauce
    2 tablespoons molasses
    5 slices fresh gingerroot
1/4 teaspoon ground coriander
       Dash black pepper
    1 large yellow onion
    4 large eggplant slices, 1 inch thick
    4 round buns, split
    4 tomato slices
       Mixed salad greens
       Radishes
       Carrot curls

Prepare Grilled Garlic Aioli; set aside. Combine sugar, water, soy sauce, molasses, ginger, coriander and pepper in small saucepan. Bring to boil, stirring constantly. Reduce heat; simmer marinade 5 minutes, stirring occasionally. Cool. Cut onion into 1/2-inch-thick slices. Insert wooden picks into onion slices from edges to prevent separating into rings. (Soak wooden picks in hot water 15 minutes to prevent burning.) Marinate eggplant and onion in marinade 10 to 15 minutes. Remove vegetables from marinade; reserve marinade. Lightly oil grid to prevent sticking. Grill vegetables on covered grill around edge of medium-hot KINGSFORD® Briquets about 20 minutes or until tender, turning once or twice and brushing with reserved marinade. Place buns on grill, cut sides down, until toasted. Serve eggplant and onion on grilled buns with tomato, greens and Grilled Garlic Aioli. Garnish with radishes and carrot curls.   *Makes 4 sandwiches*

Grilled Garlic Aioli: Prepare Grilled Garlic (recipe follows). Mash 8 cloves Grilled Garlic in small bowl. Add 1/4 cup mayonnaise; mix until blended.

Grilled Garlic: Peel outermost papery skin from 1 or 2 garlic bulbs. Brush garlic with olive oil. Grill at edge of grid on covered grill over medium-hot Kingsford® Briquets 30 to 45 minutes or until cloves are soft and buttery. Remove from grill; cool slightly. Gently squeeze softened garlic bulb from root end so that cloves slip out of skins into small bowl. Use immediately or cover and refrigerate up to 1 week.

                Mediterranean Chicken Salad Sandwich

Hot Crab and Cheese on Muffins

(Pictured at right)

4 English muffins, split
1 tablespoon butter or margarine
3 green onions, chopped
1/3 cup chopped red bell pepper
2 cans (6 ounces each) fancy crabmeat, drained*
1 to 2 teaspoons hot pepper sauce
1 cup (4 ounces) shredded cheddar cheese
1 cup (4 ounces) shredded Monterey Jack cheese

*1/2 pound fresh crabmeat, drained and flaked can be substituted for canned crabmeat.

1. Preheat broiler. Place muffin halves on lightly greased baking sheet. Broil 4 inches from heat 2 minutes or until muffins are lightly toasted. Place on large microwavable plate.

2. Melt butter in medium skillet over medium heat. Add green onions and bell pepper; cook and stir 3 to 4 minutes or until tender. Remove from heat; stir in crabmeat, hot pepper sauce and cheeses. Spoon about 1/3 cup crab mixture onto muffin halves.

3. Microwave at HIGH 2 to 3 minutes, rotating platter once, or until crab mixture is heated through. Serve with fresh fruit, if desired.   *Makes 8 servings*

Broccoli Melts

(Pictured on page 90)

2 tablespoons vegetable oil
1 cup broccoli florets
1 cup sliced fresh mushrooms
1/4 cup chopped green onions
2 English muffins, split
8 teaspoons Dijon mustard
1/2 cup (2 ounces) shredded sharp cheddar cheese

1. Preheat broiler. Heat oil in large skillet over medium-high heat until hot. Add broccoli, mushrooms and onions. Cook and stir 3 minutes or until crisp-tender; set aside.

2. Place English muffin halves on baking sheet. Broil 1 to 2 minutes or until light golden brown. Remove from oven and spread each half with 2 teaspoons mustard. Top with vegetable mixture. Sprinkle each with about 2 tablespoons cheese. Broil 1 to 2 minutes more or until cheese is melted. Garnish as desired. Serve immediately.   *Makes 4 servings*

Italian Meatball Subs

Nonstick cooking spray
1/2 cup chopped onion
3 teaspoons finely chopped garlic, divided
1 can (14-1/2 ounces) Italian-style crushed tomatoes, undrained
2 bay leaves
2-1/2 teaspoons dried basil leaves, divided
2 teaspoons dried oregano leaves, divided
3/4 teaspoon black pepper, divided
1/4 teaspoon red pepper flakes
1/2 pound lean ground beef
1/3 cup chopped green onions
1/3 cup dry bread crumbs
1/4 cup chopped fresh parsley
1 egg white
2 tablespoons water
1/2 teaspoon dried marjoram leaves
1/2 teaspoon ground mustard
4 French bread rolls, warmed and cut in half lengthwise

1. Spray large nonstick saucepan with cooking spray. Heat over medium heat until hot. Add onion and 2 teaspoons garlic. Cook and stir 5 minutes or until onion is tender. Add tomatoes with juice, bay leaves, 2 teaspoons basil, 1 teaspoon oregano, 1/2 teaspoon black pepper and red pepper flakes; cover. Simmer 30 minutes, stirring occasionally. Remove and discard bay leaves.

2. Combine meat, green onions, bread crumbs, parsley, egg white, water, remaining 1 teaspoon garlic, 1/2 teaspoon basil, 1 teaspoon oregano, 1/4 teaspoon black pepper, marjoram and mustard in medium bowl until well blended. Shape into 16 small meatballs.

3. Spray large nonstick skillet with cooking spray. Heat over medium heat until hot. Add meatballs. Cook 5 minutes or until meatballs are no longer pink in centers, turning occasionally.

4. Add meatballs to tomato sauce. Cook 5 minutes, stirring occasionally.

5. Place 4 meatballs in each roll. Spoon additional sauce over meatballs. Serve immediately.
    Makes 4 servings

Hot Crab and Cheese on Muffin

Tasty Turkey Turnovers

Tasty Turkey Turnovers

(Pictured at left)

1 package (11.3 ounces) refrigerated dinner rolls
2 tablespoons prepared honey mustard
3 ounces thinly sliced deli turkey breast
3/4 cup packaged broccoli coleslaw
1 egg white, beaten
Prepared mustard (optional)

1. Preheat oven to 425°F. Spray baking sheet with nonstick cooking spray.

2. Separate dinner rolls; place on lightly floured surface. With lightly floured rolling pin, roll each dinner roll into 3-1/2-inch circle. Spread honey mustard lightly over dinner rolls; top with turkey and broccoli coleslaw. Brush edges of dinner rolls with beaten egg white. Fold dough over forming a half circle; squeeze edges together firmly with fingers. Press edges with tines of fork to finish sealing.

3. Place on prepared baking sheet; brush egg white over tops of turnovers. Bake about 15 minutes or until golden brown. Let stand 5 minutes before serving. Serve warm or at room temperature with additional mustard for dipping, if desired.

Makes 8 turnovers

Ranch Burgers

(Pictured on page 90)

1-1/4 pounds lean ground beef
3/4 cup prepared HIDDEN VALLEY® The Original Ranch® Dressing
3/4 cup dry bread crumbs
1/4 cup minced onions
1 teaspoon salt
1/4 teaspoon black pepper
Sesame seed buns
Lettuce, tomato slices and red onion slices (optional)
Additional HIDDEN VALLEY® The Original Ranch® Dressing

In large bowl, combine ground beef, salad dressing, bread crumbs, onions, salt and pepper. Shape mixture into 6 patties. Grill over medium-hot heat until no longer pink. Place on sesame seed buns with lettuce, tomato and red onion slices, if desired. Serve with a generous amount of additional salad dressing. Garnish as desired. *Makes 6 servings*

Hot Dogs with Dijon Kraut

1 (14-ounce) can sauerkraut, rinsed and drained
1/4 cup GREY POUPON® Dijon Mustard
1/4 cup prepared barbecue sauce
1/3 cup chopped onion
1 tablespoon sweet pickle relish
1 teaspoon caraway seeds
6 hot dogs, grilled
6 oblong sandwich buns or hot dog rolls, toasted
1-1/2 cups shredded cheddar cheese (6 ounces)

Heat sauerkraut, mustard, barbecue sauce, onion, pickle relish and caraway seeds to a boil in medium saucepan over medium heat; reduce heat. Cover; simmer for 2 minutes. Keep warm.

Place hot dogs in buns; top each with 1/4 cup cheese. Broil for 1 minute or until cheese melts. Top with sauerkraut mixture and serve immediately.

Makes 6 servings

Muffuletta

(Pictured below)

1 (12-ounce) loaf focaccia bread
3 tablespoons prepared Italian salad dressing
1/2 cup sliced Spanish olives
8 ounces thinly sliced salami or baked ham
4 ounces thinly sliced provolone or sharp
   cheddar cheese
Lettuce leaves

1. Cut bread crosswise into halves; brush cut sides of both halves generously with salad dressing. Pour any remaining salad dressing over olives.

2. Arrange meat and cheese on bottom half of bread; top with olives, lettuce leaves and top half of bread. Cut into wedges to serve.   *Makes 4 servings*

Helpful Hint

Leftover olives should be kept refrigerated in their brine in a tightly covered container. Stored properly they will keep for several weeks.

Cheeseburger Calzones

1 pound ground beef
1 medium onion, chopped
1/2 teaspoon salt
1 jar (26 to 28 ounces) RAGÚ® Robusto!™ Pasta
   Sauce
1 jar (8 ounces) marinated mushrooms, drained
   and chopped (optional)
1 cup shredded cheddar cheese (about 4 ounces)
1 package (2 pounds) frozen pizza dough,
   thawed

1. Preheat oven to 375°F. In 12-inch skillet, brown ground beef with onion and salt over medium-high heat; drain. Stir in 1 cup Ragú Pasta Sauce, mushrooms and cheese.

2. On floured surface, cut each pound of dough into 4 pieces; press to form 6-inch circles. Spread 1/2 cup beef mixture on each dough circle; fold over and pinch edges to close.

3. With large spatula, gently arrange on cookie sheets. Bake 25 minutes or until golden. Serve with remaining sauce, heated.   *Makes 8 servings*

Muffuletta

Southern Barbecue Sandwich

(Pictured at right and on back cover)

    1 pound boneless sirloin or flank steak
  3/4 cup *French's®* Worcestershire Sauce, divided
  1/2 cup ketchup
  1/2 cup light molasses
  1/4 cup *French's®* Classic Yellow® Mustard
    2 tablespoons *Frank's® RedHot®* Cayenne Pepper
      Sauce
  1/2 teaspoon hickory salt
    4 sandwich buns, split

Place steak in large resealable plastic food storage bag. Pour 1/2 cup Worcestershire over steak. Seal bag and marinate meat in refrigerator 20 minutes. To prepare barbecue sauce, combine ketchup, molasses, remaining 1/4 cup Worcestershire, mustard, **Frank's RedHot** Sauce and hickory salt in medium saucepan. Bring to a boil over high heat. Reduce heat to low. Cook 5 minutes until slightly thickened, stirring occasionally. Set aside. Place steak on grid, discarding marinade. Grill over hot coals 15 minutes, turning once. Remove steak from grid; let stand 5 minutes. Cut steak diagonally into thin slices. Stir meat into barbecue sauce. Cook until heated through, stirring often. Serve steak and sauce in sandwich buns. *Makes 4 servings*

Beef & Bean Burritos

    1 pound lean ground beef
  1/2 cup chopped onion
  1/2 cup enchilada sauce
  1/4 teaspoon salt
    1 can (about 16 ounces) refried beans
    1 cup (4 ounces) shredded Monterey Jack cheese
    2 cups shredded lettuce
    1 cup sour cream
    1 cup guacamole
    8 (10- or 12-inch) flour tortillas, warmed

Cook and stir beef and onion in skillet over medium heat until beef is browned and onion is tender; drain. Stir in enchilada sauce and salt. Cover and simmer 10 minutes; keep warm. Place beans in another skillet and heat through; keep warm. Serve meat mixture, beans, cheese, lettuce, sour cream and guacamole in separate bowls with warmed tortillas. To assemble burritos, place about 1/4 cup meat filling and 1/4 cup refried beans on each tortilla; top with condiments and guacamole as desired. Roll up burritos to eat. *Makes 8 burritos*

Italian Chicken Roll-Ups

  3/4 pound boneless, skinless chicken breasts
  1/4 cup plus 1 tablespoon Italian salad dressing,
      divided
  1/2 cup dairy sour cream
    1 tablespoon grated Parmesan cheese
    1 tablespoon CRISCO® Oil*
    4 (10-inch) flour tortillas, warmed
    1 large tomato, chopped (optional)
  1/3 cup chopped green onions
  3/4 cup (3 ounces) shredded cheddar cheese

Use your favorite Crisco Oil product.

Rinse chicken; pat dry. Cut widthwise into 1-inch slices. Place in bowl. Pour 1/4 cup Italian dressing over chicken. Toss to coat. Let stand 5 minutes or longer. Drain.

Combine sour cream, remaining 1 tablespoon Italian dressing and Parmesan cheese. Refrigerate.

Heat oil in medium skillet on medium-high heat. Add chicken. Cook for 5 to 10 minutes, stirring occasionally, or until no longer pink in center. Cool. Shred.

Combine chicken and sour cream mixture. Spoon onto warm tortillas. Top with chopped tomato, if desired, green onions and cheese. Fold or roll-up tortillas and serve. *Makes 4 servings*

Chicago Fire Italian Sausage Sandwiches

    1 package BUTTERBALL® Lean Fresh Turkey Hot
      Italian Sausage
    5 large hot dog buns
    5 teaspoons yellow mustard
    5 tablespoons chopped onion
    5 tablespoons pickle relish
   10 tomato wedges
   10 hot sport peppers

Grill sausage according to package directions. Place in buns. Add mustard, onion, relish, tomato wedges and peppers to each sandwich.

Makes 5 sandwiches

Southern Barbecue Sandwich

Amigo Pita Pocket Sandwiches

(Pictured at right)

1 pound ground turkey
1 can (7 ounces) whole kernel corn, drained
1 can (6 ounces) tomato paste
1/2 cup water
1/2 cup chopped green bell pepper
1 package (1.0 ounce) LAWRY'S® Taco Spices & Seasonings
8 pita breads
  Curly lettuce leaves
  Shredded cheddar cheese

In large skillet, brown ground turkey until no longer pink; drain fat. Add corn, tomato paste, water, green pepper and Taco Spices & Seasonings; mix well. Bring to a boil over medium-high heat; reduce heat to low and cook, uncovered, 15 minutes. Cut off top quarter of pita breads and open to form pockets. Line each with lettuce leaves. Spoon about 1/2 cup filling into each pita bread and top with cheese.

Makes 8 servings

Serving Suggestion: Serve with vegetable sticks and fresh fruit.

The Meatless Dagwood

(Pictured on page 90)

1-1/4 cups deli egg salad
1/4 cup coarsely chopped pitted ripe olives
4 thin slices (2 ounces) deli brick or provolone cheese
6 slices marble rye or pumpernickel bread
2 large dill pickles, thinly sliced
2 romaine or red leaf lettuce leaves
  Cherry tomato for garnish

1. Combine egg salad and olives in small bowl.

2. To assemble each sandwich, layer 1 cheese slice on 1 bread slice. Place 1/4 of egg salad mixture and 1/4 of pickle slices on cheese.

3. Top pickles with 1 bread slice and 1 cheese slice. Place 1/4 of egg salad mixture and 1/4 of pickle slices on cheese; top with lettuce leaf and 1 bread slice. Garnish with cherry tomato, if desired.

Makes 2 servings

Serving Suggestion: Serve with carrot sticks, celery sticks and potato chips.

Grilled Chicken Croissant Monterey

1/2 cup A.1.® Steak Sauce, divided
1 tablespoon olive oil
1 tablespoon finely chopped parsley
1 teaspoon dried minced onion
1/4 cup mayonnaise
4 boneless chicken breasts, gently pounded (about 1 pound)
4 slices Muenster cheese (about 3 ounces)
4 croissants (6×3 inches each), split
4 lettuce leaves
1 small avocado, peeled, pitted and sliced
4 slices tomato

Blend 1/4 cup steak sauce, oil, parsley and onion; set aside for basting.

Blend remaining 1/4 cup steak sauce and mayonnaise; reserve.

Grill chicken over medium heat for 6 minutes or until juices run clear, turning and brushing often with basting sauce. Top each chicken breast with cheese slice; grill until cheese melts.

Spread 1 tablespoon reserved steak sauce mixture on bottom of each croissant; top with lettuce leaf, avocado slices, tomato slice and chicken breast. Spread 1 tablespoon steak sauce mixture on each chicken breast; top with croissant top. Serve immediately.

Makes 4 servings

Cheesy Spinach Burgers

1 envelope LIPTON® RECIPE SECRETS® Onion Soup Mix
2 pounds ground beef
1 package (10 ounces) frozen chopped spinach, thawed and squeezed dry
1 cup shredded mozzarella or cheddar cheese (about 4 ounces)

1. In large bowl, combine all ingredients; shape into 8 patties.

2. Grill or broil until done. Serve, if desired, on hamburger buns.

Makes 8 servings

Amigo Pita Pocket Sandwiches

Open-Faced Reuben with Mustard-Caraway Hollandaise

(Pictured at right)

1/4 cup butter or margarine
1 teaspoon caraway seeds
1 package (1-1/4 ounces) hollandaise sauce mix
2 tablespoons Dijon mustard
 Dash cayenne pepper
4 slices pumpernickel or rye bread
8 ounces sliced pastrami
1-1/3 to 2 cups sauerkraut, rinsed and drained
1 green bell pepper, thinly sliced in rings
3 ounces thinly sliced or shredded Swiss cheese
 Dash paprika (optional)

1. Heat butter and caraway in 1- to 2-quart saucepan over medium heat until butter is melted. Mix in sauce mix with wire whisk. While whisking, slowly add water according to package directions. Add mustard and cayenne pepper; whisk until bubbly. Simmer and stir 1 minute or until thickened; set aside.

2. Preheat broiler. Place bread on baking sheet. Broil 4 inches from heat 1-1/2 to 2 minutes per side or until crisp; set aside. Place pastrami on plate; cover with plastic wrap. Microwave at HIGH 1 minute or until heated through; set aside. Place sauerkraut in small bowl. Cover with plastic wrap and microwave at HIGH 1 minute or until heated through; set aside.

3. Spread 2 to 3 teaspoons sauce on each slice of toast. Place pastrami on toast; top with sauerkraut. Drizzle each serving with about 1 tablespoon sauce. Lay 2 pepper rings on sauerkraut; top with cheese. Sprinkle with paprika, if desired. Broil 2 to 3 minutes or until cheese bubbles. Serve with remaining sauce. *Makes 4 servings*

Serving Suggestion: Serve with pickle spears and fresh vegetables.

Helpful Hint

Sauerkraut is chopped cabbage that has been salted and fermented. It is German in origin and literally means "sour cabbage." However, this does not mean you can ignore the expiration date on the package. Sauerkraut that has gone sour is not the same thing as cabbage that has been fermented and salt-pickled.

Mississippi Barbecue Burgers

1 cup FRANK'S® or SNOWFLOSS® Kraut, drained
1/3 cup jellied cranberry sauce
1/4 cup MISSISSIPPI® Barbecue Sauce
2 tablespoons brown sugar
1 egg, lightly beaten
1 envelope dried onion soup mix
1/4 cup water
1 pound ground beef
4 onion or sesame seed hamburger rolls, split, lightly toasted

1. Mix kraut, cranberry sauce, barbecue sauce and brown sugar in small saucepan; bring to a boil. Reduce heat and simmer about 15 minutes, stirring occasionally.

2. Meanwhile, in medium bowl combine egg, soup mix and water. Let stand 5 minutes. Add ground beef; mix thoroughly. Form into 4 patties.

3. Grill patties over mesquite or charcoal until no longer pink. Serve on toasted rolls topped with kraut mixture. *Makes 4 servings*

Hot Sausage on a Bun

1 package BOB EVANS® Italian Grillin' Sausage (approximately 5 links)
1 medium green bell pepper, chopped
1 medium onion, chopped
4 medium mushrooms, sliced
1 clove garlic, minced
1 (16-ounce) jar pepperoni-flavored pizza sauce
1 tomato, chopped
5 Italian sandwich rolls, split
1 cup (4 ounces) shredded mozzarella cheese
1/4 cup grated Parmesan cheese

Place sausage in saucepan; cover with water. Bring to a boil; cover and simmer 30 to 40 minutes. Drain all but 5 tablespoons liquid. Cook bell pepper, onion, mushrooms and garlic with sausage in reserved liquid until vegetables are soft. Stir in pizza sauce and tomato; simmer 15 to 20 minutes over low heat. Place 1 sausage in each roll; cover with sauce and sprinkle with cheeses. Place open sandwiches under broiler just until cheese melts. *Makes 5 sandwiches*

Open-Faced Reuben with Mustard-Caraway Hollandaise

Easy Salmon Burger with Honey Barbecue Sauce

Easy Salmon Burgers with Honey Barbecue Sauce

(Pictured above)

1/3 cup honey
1/3 cup ketchup
1-1/2 teaspoons cider vinegar
1 teaspoon prepared horseradish
1/4 teaspoon minced garlic
1/8 teaspoon crushed red pepper flakes (optional)
1 can (7-1/2 ounces) salmon, drained, bones and skin removed
1/2 cup dry bread crumbs
1/4 cup chopped onion
3 tablespoons chopped green bell pepper
1 egg white
2 hamburger buns, toasted

In small bowl, combine honey, ketchup, vinegar, horseradish, garlic and red pepper flakes until well blended. Set aside half of sauce. In separate bowl, mix together salmon, bread crumbs, onion, green pepper and egg white. Blend in 2 tablespoons remaining sauce. Divide salmon mixture into 2 patties, 1/2 to 3/4 inch thick. Place patties on well-oiled grill, 4 to 6 inches from hot coals. Grill, turning 2 to 3 times and basting with sauce, until burgers are browned and meat thermometer reads 160°F. Or place patties on lightly greased baking sheet. Broil 4 to 6 inches from heat source, turning 2 to 3 times and basting with remaining sauce, until meat thermometer reads 160°F. Place on hamburger buns and serve with reserved sauce. Garnish with tomato and lemon slices, if desired.   *Makes 2 servings*

Favorite recipe from **National Honey Board**

Ham and Cheese Strudels with Mustard Sauce

2 cups (12 ounces) diced CURE 81® ham
1 cup shredded Swiss cheese
1 cup sliced fresh mushrooms
1 egg, beaten
1/4 cup chopped green onions
8 sheets frozen phyllo dough, thawed
1/2 cup butter or margarine, melted
Mustard Sauce (recipe follows)

Heat oven to 350°F. In bowl, combine ham, cheese, mushrooms, egg and green onions; mix well. Brush 1 sheet phyllo dough with butter. Keep remaining phyllo sheets covered with a dampened towel to prevent drying. To assemble, fold phyllo sheet in half crosswise; brush with butter. Fold in half crosswise again; brush with butter. Place 1/3 cup ham mixture in center of phyllo sheet. Fold long sides up and over filling, overlapping slightly. Fold into thirds from narrow edge. Place strudel, seam side down, on baking sheet. Cover with dampened towel to prevent drying. Repeat with remaining phyllo sheets, ham mixture and butter. Bake 20 minutes or until golden brown. Serve with Mustard Sauce.   *Makes 8 servings*

Mustard Sauce: In saucepan, combine 1/2 cup sour cream, 1/2 cup mayonnaise or salad dressing, 2 tablespoons ground mustard and 1/2 teaspoon sugar. Heat over low heat, stirring occasionally, until warm.

Grilled Club Sandwiches

(Pictured below)

- 1 long thin loaf (18 inches) French bread
- 1/2 cup mayonnaise
- 1/4 cup *French's®* Zesty Deli Mustard
- 2 tablespoons finely chopped red onion
- 2 tablespoons prepared horseradish
- 1/2 pound sliced smoked boiled ham
- 1/2 pound sliced honey-baked deli turkey
- 1 large ripe tomato, sliced
- 8 ounces Brie cheese, thinly sliced
- 1 bunch watercress, washed and drained

Cut bread in half lengthwise. Combine mayonnaise, mustard, onion and horseradish in small bowl; mix well. Spread mixture on both halves of bread. Layer ham, turkey, tomato, cheese and watercress on bottom half of bread. Cover with top half; press down firmly. Cut loaf crosswise into 1-1/2-inch pieces. Thread two mini sandwiches through crusts onto metal skewer. Repeat with remaining sandwiches.

Place sandwiches on well-oiled grid. Grill over medium-low coals about 5 minutes or until cheese is melted and bread is toasted, turning once. Serve warm with fruit, if desired. *Makes 6 servings*

Chicken, Feta and Pepper Subs

- 1 pound boneless, skinless chicken breasts
- 3 tablespoons olive oil, divided
- 2 teaspoons TABASCO® brand Pepper Sauce
- 1/2 teaspoon salt
- 1/2 teaspoon ground cumin
- 1 red bell pepper, cut into strips
- 1 yellow or green bell pepper, cut into strips
- 1/2 cup crumbled feta cheese
- 4 (6-inch) French rolls

Cut chicken breasts into thin strips. Heat 1 tablespoon oil in 12-inch skillet over medium-high heat. Add chicken; cook until well browned on all sides, stirring frequently. Stir in TABASCO® Sauce, salt and cumin. Remove mixture to medium bowl. Add remaining 2 tablespoons oil to same skillet over medium heat. Add bell peppers; cook about 5 minutes or until tender-crisp, stirring occasionally. Toss with chicken and feta cheese.

To serve, cut rolls in half widthwise. Cover bottom halves with chicken mixture and top with remaining roll halves. *Makes 4 servings*

Grilled Club Sandwiches

Barbecued Pork Tenderloin Sandwiches

(Pictured at right)

1/2 cup ketchup
1/3 cup packed brown sugar
1 tablespoon Worcestershire sauce
1/2 teaspoon ground mustard
1/4 teaspoon cayenne pepper
1 clove garlic, minced
2 whole pork tenderloins (about 3/4 pound each), well trimmed
1 large red onion, cut into 6 (1/4-inch-thick) slices
6 hoagie rolls or Kaiser rolls, split

1. Prepare barbecue grill for direct cooking.

2. Combine ketchup, sugar, Worcestershire sauce, mustard, cayenne pepper and garlic in small, heavy saucepan with ovenproof handle; mix well.

3. Set saucepan on one side of grid.* Place tenderloins on center of grid. Grill tenderloins, on uncovered grill, over medium-hot coals 8 minutes. Simmer sauce, uncovered, 5 minutes or until thickened, stirring occasionally.

4. Turn tenderloins with tongs; continue to grill, uncovered, 5 minutes. Add onion slices to grid. Reserve half of sauce. Brush tenderloins and onion with some remaining sauce.

5. Continue to grill, uncovered, 7 to 10 minutes or until internal temperature reaches 160°F when tested with meat thermometer inserted into the thickest part of meat.**

6. Transfer roast to cutting board; cover with foil. Let stand 5 to 10 minutes before carving. Internal temperature will continue to rise 5°F to 10°F during stand time. Carve tenderloins crosswise into thin slices; separate onion slices into rings. Divide meat and onion rings among rolls; drizzle with reserved sauce. Serve with mixed green salad, if desired.

Makes 6 servings

*If desired, sauce may be prepared on range-top. Combine ketchup, sugar, Worcestershire sauce, mustard, cayenne pepper and garlic in small saucepan. Bring to a boil over medium-high heat. Reduce heat to low and simmer, uncovered, 5 minutes or until thickened, stirring occasionally.

**If using an instant read thermometer, do not leave thermometer in tenderloins during grilling since the thermometer is not heatproof.

Monte Cristo Sandwiches

2 tablespoons honey mustard, divided
12 thin slices white or egg bread, divided
4 ounces sliced deli turkey breast
8 thin slices (4 ounces) Swiss cheese, divided
4 ounces smoked sliced deli ham, divided
2 eggs, beaten
1/4 cup milk
1/16 teaspoon ground nutmeg
2 to 3 tablespoons butter or margarine
Powdered sugar and raspberry preserves

1. Preheat oven to 450°F.

2. To assemble 3-decker sandwich, spread 1/2 teaspoon mustard over 1 side of each of 3 bread slices. Place 1/4 of turkey and 1 cheese slice over mustard on 1 bread slice. Top with second bread slice, mustard side up.

3. Place 1/4 of ham and 1 cheese slice on top of bread. Top with remaining bread slice, mustard side down, pressing gently together. Repeat with remaining mustard, bread, turkey, cheese and ham to make 4 sandwiches.

4. Combine eggs, milk and nutmeg in shallow dish or pie plate.

5. Melt 1 tablespoon butter in large nonstick skillet over medium heat. Dip both sides of each sandwich in egg mixture, letting excess drip back into dish.

6. Fry 1 sandwich at a time in skillet 4 minutes or until browned, turning halfway through cooking. Transfer sandwiches to greased or foil-lined baking sheet. Repeat with remaining sandwiches, adding butter to skillet as needed.

7. Bake sandwiches 5 to 7 minutes or until heated through and cheese is melted. Cut each sandwich in half; sprinkle lightly with powdered sugar. Serve immediately with preserves.

Makes 4 servings

Helpful Hint

If you don't have honey mustard on hand, make your own! Start with 2 tablespoons of your favorite mustard, preferably Dijon, and stir in honey, 1 teaspoon at a time, until the mustard has reached the desired sweetness.

Barbecued Pork Tenderloin Sandwich

Breads

Raspberry Tea Cake

(Pictured at left)

    1/3 cup whole almonds, toasted
      2 cups all-purpose flour
    3/4 cup sugar
    1/2 teaspoon salt
    1/2 cup cold butter
    3/4 teaspoon baking powder
    1/2 cup milk
    1/2 teaspoon vanilla extract
      1 egg
    3/4 cup seedless raspberry jam

1. Preheat oven to 350°F. Grease 9-inch round cake pan; set aside.

2. Place almonds in food processor. Process using on/off pulsing action until almonds are ground, but not pasty.

3. Combine flour, sugar and salt in large bowl. Cut in butter with pastry blender or 2 knives until mixture resembles coarse crumbs. Place 1/2 cup mixture in small bowl; set aside. Stir almonds and baking powder into remaining flour mixture.

4. Combine milk, vanilla and egg in medium bowl with wire whisk until well blended. Make well in center of flour mixture. Add milk mixture; stir until mixture forms soft dough. Spread half of dough evenly on bottom of prepared pan. Bake 10 minutes.

5. Remove crust from oven. Spread evenly with jam. Drop remaining dough by teaspoonfuls over jam. Sprinkle with reserved flour mixture. Bake 20 to 25 minutes or until golden brown and toothpick inserted in center comes out clean. Cool cake in pan on wire rack 20 minutes. To serve, cut into wedges and garnish as desired. Store covered at room temperature.

Makes 10 servings

Clockwise from top left: *Chocolate Chunk Cinnamon Coffee Cake (p. 118), Savory Summertime Oat Bread (p. 114), Peach Gingerbread Muffins (p. 116) and Raspberry Tea Cake*

Dinner Rolls

(Pictured at right)

1-1/4 cups milk
1/2 cup vegetable shortening
3-3/4 to 4-1/4 cups all-purpose flour, divided
1/4 cup sugar
2 packages active dry yeast
1 teaspoon salt
2 eggs

Heat milk and shortening in saucepan over low heat until mixture is 120° to 130°F. (Shortening does not need to melt completely.) Mix 1-1/2 cups flour, sugar, yeast and salt in bowl; set aside. Gradually beat milk mixture into flour mixture with electric mixer at low speed. Increase speed to medium; scrape down side of bowl once. Reduce speed to low. Beat in eggs and 1 cup flour. Increase speed to medium and beat 2 minutes; scrape down side of bowl once. Stir in additional flour, about 1-1/4 cups to make soft dough.

Turn out dough onto lightly floured surface; flatten slightly. Knead 5 minutes or until smooth and elastic, gradually adding remaining flour to prevent sticking, if necessary. Shape dough into ball; place in large, lightly greased bowl. Turn dough over so top is greased. Cover with towel; let rise in warm place 1 hour or until doubled in bulk.

Punch down dough. Knead on lightly floured surface 1 minute. Cover with towel; let rest 10 minutes. Grease two 8-inch square pans. Cut dough in half. Cut one half into 12 pieces, keeping remaining half covered with towel. Shape pieces into balls; place in rows in 1 prepared pan. Repeat with remaining dough. Cover pans with towels; let rise in warm place 30 minutes or until doubled in bulk.

Preheat oven to 375°F. Bake 15 to 20 minutes or until golden brown. Remove immediately from pans. Cool on wire racks. Serve warm.   *Makes 24 rolls*

Serving Suggestion: Serve these rolls for breakfast with butter and your favorite jelly or jam.

Honey Cloverleafs

1 package (16 ounces) hot roll mix
6 tablespoons honey, divided
1/4 cup butter or margarine
1 teaspoon grated lemon peel
1 cup sliced almonds

Prepare hot roll mix in large bowl according to package directions, adding 2 tablespoons honey to liquid. Cover kneaded dough with bowl and let rest 5 minutes.

Melt butter in saucepan over medium heat. Add remaining 4 tablespoons honey; stir in lemon peel.

Roll dough into 36 balls (about 1- to 1-1/2-inch diameter each). Form clusters of three balls; dip each in honey mixture then in almonds. Place each cluster in well-greased muffin cup. Cover and set in warm place to rise about 30 minutes or until doubled in bulk.

Bake in preheated 350°F oven 15 to 20 minutes or until lightly browned. Brush with honey mixture, if desired. Remove from pan and cool slightly on wire rack. Serve warm or cool.   *Makes 1 dozen rolls*

Variation: Dough may be dipped in honey mixture then in chopped parsley, rosemary or other fresh herbs.

Favorite recipe from **National Honey Board**

Tomato Cheese Bread

1 can (14.5 ounces) CONTADINA® Recipe Ready Diced Tomatoes
2 cups buttermilk biscuit/baking mix
2 teaspoons dried oregano leaves, crushed, divided
3/4 cup (3 ounces) shredded cheddar cheese
3/4 cup (3 ounces) shredded Monterey Jack cheese

1. Drain tomatoes, reserving 2/3 cup juice.

2. Combine baking mix, 1 teaspoon oregano, and reserved tomato juice in medium bowl.

3. Press dough evenly to edge of 11×7×2-inch greased baking dish. Sprinkle cheddar cheese and remaining oregano over batter. Distribute tomato pieces evenly over cheese; sprinkle with Monterey Jack cheese.

4. Bake in preheated 375°F oven 25 minutes, or until edges are golden brown and cheese is bubbly. Cool 5 minutes before cutting into squares to serve.
        Makes 12 servings

Easier Chocolate-Filled Braid

(Pictured below)

Chocolate Nut Filling (recipe follows)
2-1/2 to 2-3/4 cups all-purpose flour, divided
2 tablespoons sugar
1/2 teaspoon salt
1 package rapid-rise yeast
1/2 cup milk
1/4 cup water
1/2 cup (1 stick) butter or margarine
1 egg
Vegetable oil
Powdered Sugar Glaze (recipe follows, optional)

1. Heat oven to 375°F. Lightly grease large baking sheet; set aside. Prepare Chocolate Nut Filling and set aside.

2. Stir together 1-1/2 cups all-purpose flour, sugar, salt and yeast in large bowl. Combine milk, water and butter in small saucepan over low heat. Heat milk mixture just until very warm, 120° to 130°F.

(Butter might not be melted.) Gradually add milk mixture to dry ingredients; beat on medium speed of mixer 2 minutes. Add egg and 1 cup flour; beat 2 minutes. Stir in enough remaining flour to form stiff dough. Cover and let rest 10 minutes.

3. Turn out dough onto well-floured work surface; roll dough into 18×10-inch rectangle. Carefully transfer dough rectangle to prepared baking sheet. Spread Chocolate Nut Filling lengthwise down center third of dough rectangle. Cut 1-inch-wide strips diagonally on both sides of dough rectangle to within 3/4 inch of filling. Alternately fold opposite strips of dough at angle across Chocolate Nut Filling. Shape braid into ring; pinch ends together to seal. Brush braid lightly with vegetable oil; let braid stand 10 minutes.

4. Bake braid 20 to 25 minutes or until lightly browned. Remove from baking sheet to wire rack. Cool completely. Prepare Powdered Sugar Glaze, if desired; drizzle over braid.

Makes 10 to 12 servings

Chocolate Nut Filling

3/4 cup HERSHEY'S Semi-Sweet Chocolate Chips
2 tablespoons sugar
1/3 cup evaporated milk
1/2 cup chopped nuts
1 teaspoon vanilla extract
1/4 teaspoon ground cinnamon

1. Stir together chocolate chips, sugar and evaporated milk in small saucepan over low heat. Cook chocolate mixture, stirring constantly, until chips are melted and mixture is smooth. Remove from heat.

2. Stir in chopped nuts, vanilla extract and ground cinnamon. Cool Chocolate Nut Filling completely.

Powdered Sugar Glaze

1 cup powdered sugar
1 tablespoon milk
1 teaspoon butter or margarine, softened
1/2 teaspoon vanilla extract

1. Stir together powdered sugar, milk, butter and vanilla extract in small bowl. Beat glaze until smooth and of desired consistency.

2. Stir in additional milk, 1 teaspoon at a time, if needed to thin glaze.

Easier Chocolate-Filled Braid

Bacon-Cheese Muffins

Bacon-Cheese Muffins

(Pictured above)

1/2 pound bacon (10 to 12 slices)
    Vegetable oil
  1 egg, beaten
3/4 cup milk
1-3/4 cups all-purpose flour
  1/4 cup sugar
  1 tablespoon baking powder
  1 cup (4 ounces) shredded Wisconsin Cheddar
    cheese
1/2 cup crunchy nutlike cereal nuggets

Preheat oven to 400°F. In large skillet, cook bacon over medium-high heat until crisp. Drain, reserving drippings. If necessary, add oil to drippings to measure 1/3 cup. In small bowl, combine dripping mixture, egg and milk; set aside. Crumble bacon; set aside.

In large bowl, combine flour, sugar and baking powder. Make well in center. Add egg mixture all at once to flour mixture, stirring just until moistened. Batter should be lumpy. Fold in bacon, cheese and cereal. Spoon into greased or paper-lined 2-1/2-inch muffin cups, filling about 3/4 full. Bake 15 to 20 minutes or until golden. Remove from pan. Cool on wire rack.   *Makes 12 muffins*

Favorite recipe from **Wisconsin Milk Marketing Board**

Helpful Hint

Separating cold bacon can be a chore. Warming the whole package first makes the slices separate more easily. To warm, place the package of bacon in the microwave. Heat at HIGH 10 to 15 seconds; let stand 3 minutes.

Baked Doughnuts with Cinnamon Glaze

(Pictured at right)

5 to 5-1/2 cups all-purpose flour, divided
2/3 cup granulated sugar
2 packages active dry yeast
1 teaspoon salt
1 teaspoon grated lemon peel
1/2 teaspoon ground nutmeg
2 cups milk, divided
1/2 cup butter
2 eggs
2 cups sifted powdered sugar
1/2 teaspoon ground cinnamon

1. Combine 2 cups flour, granulated sugar, yeast, salt, lemon peel and nutmeg in large bowl. Combine 1-3/4 cups milk and butter in 1-quart saucepan. Heat over low heat until mixture is 120° to 130°F. (Butter does not need to melt completely.) Gradually beat milk mixture into flour mixture with electric mixer at low speed. Beat 2 minutes at medium speed.

2. Beat in eggs and 1 cup flour at low speed. Beat 2 minutes at medium speed. Stir in enough additional flour, about 2 cups, to make soft dough. Cover with greased plastic wrap; refrigerate at least 2 hours or up to 24 hours.

3. Punch down dough. Turn out dough onto lightly floured surface. Knead dough about 1 minute or until dough is no longer sticky, adding remaining 1/2 cup flour to prevent sticking if necessary.

4. Grease 2 large baking sheets. Roll out dough to 1/2-inch thickness with lightly floured rolling pin. Cut dough with floured 2-3/4-inch doughnut cutter. Reroll scraps, reserving doughnut holes. Place doughnuts and holes 2 inches apart on prepared baking sheets. Cover with towels; let rise in warm place about 30 minutes or until doubled in bulk.

5. To prepare glaze, combine powdered sugar and cinnamon in small bowl. Stir in enough remaining milk, about 1/4 cup, to make glaze of desired consistency. Cover; set aside.

6. Preheat oven to 400°F. Place pieces of waxed paper under wire racks to keep counter clean. Bake doughnuts and holes 8 to 10 minutes or until golden brown. Remove from pan; cool on wire racks 5 minutes. Dip warm doughnuts into glaze. Place right side up on racks. Serve warm.

Makes 2 dozen doughnuts and holes

Savory Summertime Oat Bread

(Pictured on page 108)

1/2 cup finely chopped onion
2 cups whole wheat flour
4-1/4 to 4-1/2 cups all-purpose flour, divided
2 cups uncooked old-fashioned oats
1/4 cup sugar
2 packages quick-rising yeast
1-1/2 teaspoons salt
1-1/2 cups water
1-1/4 cups milk
1/4 cup butter
1 cup finely shredded carrots
3 tablespoons dried parsley flakes
1 tablespoon butter, melted

1. Spray small nonstick skillet with nonstick cooking spray; heat over medium heat until hot. Cook onion, stirring frequently, 3 minutes or until tender. Set aside.

2. Stir together whole wheat flour, 1 cup all-purpose flour, oats, sugar, yeast and salt in large bowl. Heat water, milk and 1/4 cup butter in medium saucepan over low heat until mixture reaches 120° to 130°F. Gradually add milk mixture to flour mixture. Blend at low speed of electric mixer just until dry ingredients are moistened; beat 3 minutes at medium speed. Stir in carrots, onion, parsley and remaining 3-1/4 to 3-1/2 cups all-purpose flour until dough is no longer sticky.

3. Knead dough on lightly floured surface 5 to 8 minutes or until smooth and elastic. Place in large bowl lightly sprayed with nonstick cooking spray; turn dough over. Cover with towel and let rise in warm place about 30 minutes or until doubled in bulk.

4. Spray two 8×4-inch loaf pans with nonstick cooking spray. Punch dough down. Cover with towel and let rest 10 minutes. Shape into 2 loaves; place in pans. Brush with melted butter. Cover with towel; let rise in warm place 30 minutes or until doubled in bulk. Meanwhile, preheat oven to 350°F.

5. Bake 40 to 45 minutes or until bread sounds hollow when tapped and top is golden brown. Remove from pans; cool on wire racks.

Makes 2 loaves (24 slices)

Baked Doughnuts with Cinnamon Glaze

Golden Apple Buttermilk Bread

(Pictured at right)

1-1/2 cups unsifted all-purpose flour
1 cup whole wheat flour
1/2 cup natural bran cereal
1 teaspoon baking soda
1/2 teaspoon baking powder
1/4 teaspoon ground ginger
1-1/3 cups buttermilk
3/4 cup sugar
1/4 cup vegetable oil
1 large egg
1 teaspoon grated orange peel
1 cup chopped Washington Golden Delicious
    apples

1. Heat oven to 350°F. Grease 9×5-inch loaf pan. In medium bowl, combine flours, bran, baking soda, baking powder and ginger. In large bowl, beat together buttermilk, sugar, oil, egg and orange peel.

2. Add flour mixture to buttermilk mixture, stirring just until combined. Fold in apples. Spread batter in prepared pan and bake 45 to 50 minutes or until wooden toothpick inserted in center comes out clean. Cool bread in pan 10 minutes. Remove from pan and cool on wire rack.

Makes 1 loaf (8 servings)

Favorite recipe from **Washington Apple Commission**

Peach Gingerbread Muffins

(Pictured on page 108)

2 cups all-purpose flour
2 teaspoons baking powder
1 teaspoon ground ginger
1/2 teaspoon salt
1/2 teaspoon ground cinnamon
1/4 teaspoon ground cloves
1/2 cup sugar
1/2 cup MOTT'S® Chunky Apple Sauce
1/4 cup MOTT'S® Apple Juice
1/4 cup GRANDMA'S® Molasses
1 egg
2 tablespoons vegetable oil
1 (16-ounce) can peaches in juice, drained and
    chopped

1. Preheat oven to 400°F. Line 12 (2-1/2-inch) muffin cups with paper liners or spray with nonstick cooking spray.

2. In large bowl, combine flour, baking powder, ginger, salt and spices.

3. In small bowl, combine sugar, apple sauce, apple juice, molasses, egg and oil.

4. Stir apple sauce mixture into flour mixture just until moistened. Fold in peaches.

5. Spoon batter evenly into prepared muffin cups.

6. Bake 20 minutes or until toothpick inserted in centers comes out clean. Immediately remove from pan; cool on wire rack 10 minutes. Serve warm or cool completely.
Makes 12 servings

Dilly of a Batter Bread

3-1/4 cups all-purpose flour, divided
2 packages RED STAR® Active Dry Yeast or
    QUICK•RISE™ Yeast
2 tablespoons sugar
1 tablespoon dried minced onion
2 teaspoons dill seed
1 teaspoon salt
1 carton (8 ounces) plain yogurt
1/2 cup water
2 tablespoons shortening
1 egg

In large mixer bowl, combine 1-1/2 cups flour, yeast, sugar, onion, dill seed and salt; mix well. Heat yogurt, water and shortening until very warm (120° to 130°F; shortening does not need to melt). Add to flour mixture. Add egg. Blend at low speed until moistened; beat 3 minutes at medium speed. By hand, gradually stir in remaining flour to make a stiff batter.

Spoon into greased 1-1/2- or 2-quart casserole. Cover; let rise in warm place until light and double, about 1 hour (40 minutes for Quick•Rise™ Yeast). Bake at 375°F for 35 to 40 minutes or until golden brown. Remove from casserole; serve warm or cold.
Makes 1 round loaf

Cranberry-Cheese Batter Bread

Cranberry-Cheese Batter Bread

(Pictured above)

    3 cups all-purpose flour
1/2 cup sugar
    1 package active dry yeast
    1 teaspoon salt
1/2 cup (1 stick) butter, chilled
1/2 cup (4 ounces) cream cheese, chilled
    1 cup dried cranberries
1-1/4 cups milk, warmed to 120° to 130°F

Grease 8-inch square baking pan; set aside. Combine flour, sugar, yeast and salt in large bowl.

Cut butter and cream cheese into 1-inch chunks; add to flour mixture. Cut in butter and cream cheese with pastry blender until mixture resembles coarse crumbs. Add cranberries; toss. Add warm milk; beat 1 minute or until dough looks stringy. Place batter in prepared pan. Cover with towel; let rise in warm place about 1 hour.

Preheat oven to 375°F. Bake 35 minutes or until golden brown. *Makes 1 loaf*

Chocolate Chunk Cinnamon Coffee Cake

(Pictured on page 108)

    1 package (12 ounces) BAKER'S® Semi-Sweet
      Chocolate Chunks
3/4 cup chopped nuts
    2 cups sugar, divided
1-1/2 teaspoons ground cinnamon
2-2/3 cups flour
1-1/2 teaspoons baking soda
3/4 teaspoon CALUMET® Baking Powder
1/2 teaspoon salt
3/4 cup (1-1/2 sticks) butter, softened
    1 teaspoon vanilla extract
    3 eggs
1-1/2 cups BREAKSTONE'S® *or* KNUDSEN® Sour
      Cream

HEAT oven to 350°F. Grease 13×9-inch baking pan.

MIX chocolate, nuts, 2/3 cup of the sugar and cinnamon; set aside. Mix flour, baking soda, baking powder and salt; set aside.

BEAT butter, remaining 1-1/3 cups sugar and vanilla in large bowl with electric mixer on medium speed until light and fluffy. Add eggs, 1 at a time, beating well after each addition. Add flour mixture alternately with sour cream, beating after each addition until smooth. Spoon 1/2 of the batter into prepared pan. Top with 1/2 of the chocolate-nut mixture. Repeat layers.

BAKE 40 to 45 minutes or until toothpick inserted in center comes out clean. Cool in pan on wire rack. *Makes 16 servings*

Barbecued French Bread

    2 tablespoons butter
1/3 cup chopped onion
1/2 clove garlic, minced
1/3 cup chili sauce
    2 tablespoons cider vinegar
    1 tablespoon brown sugar
    1 tablespoon prepared mustard
1-1/2 teaspoons TABASCO® brand Pepper Sauce
    1 large loaf French bread
      Grated Parmesan cheese

Preheat oven to 400°F. Melt butter in medium saucepan over medium heat. Add onion and garlic; cook and stir about 3 minutes. Stir in chili sauce, vinegar, brown sugar, mustard and TABASCO® Sauce; simmer about 5 minutes or until mixture thickens.

Cut French bread diagonally into 3/4-inch slices, almost but not through to bottom of loaf. Spread sauce between slices; sprinkle with Parmesan cheese. Wrap in aluminum foil and heat in oven 15 minutes. *Makes 1 loaf*

Onion-Zucchini Bread

(Pictured below)

    1 large zucchini (3/4 pound), shredded
2-1/2 cups all-purpose flour
1-1/3 cups *French's*® French Fried Onions
    1/3 cup grated Parmesan cheese
      1 tablespoon baking powder
      1 tablespoon chopped fresh basil
    1/2 teaspoon salt
    3/4 cup milk
    1/2 cup (1 stick) butter or margarine, melted
    1/4 cup packed light brown sugar
      2 eggs

Preheat oven to 350°F. Lightly grease 9×5×3-inch loaf pan; set aside.

Place shredded zucchini in colander to drain.

Combine flour, French Fried Onions, Parmesan cheese, baking powder, basil and salt in large bowl.

Combine milk, melted butter or margarine, light brown sugar and eggs in medium bowl. Whisk mixture until well blended. Place zucchini on kitchen towel; gently squeeze out any excess liquid. Stir zucchini into milk mixture.

Gradually stir milk mixture into flour mixture, stirring just until dry ingredients are moistened. Do not overmix. (Batter will be very stiff and dry.) Pour batter into prepared pan. Run knife down center of batter.

Bake for 50 to 65 minutes or until toothpick inserted in center of bread comes out clean. Cool bread in pan on wire rack about 10 minutes. Carefully remove bread from pan to wire rack; let cool completely. To serve, cut bread into slices and garnish as desired.* *Makes 10 to 12 servings*

For optimum flavor, wrap bread overnight and serve the next day. Great when toasted!

Onion-Zucchini Bread

Orange Streusel Coffeecake

(Pictured at right)

> Cocoa Streusel (recipe follows)
> 3/4 cup (1-1/2 sticks) butter, softened
> 1 cup sugar
> 3 eggs
> 1 teaspoon vanilla extract
> 1/2 cup dairy sour cream
> 3 cups all-purpose flour
> 2 teaspoons baking powder
> 1 teaspoon baking soda
> 1 cup orange juice
> 2 teaspoons freshly grated orange peel
> 1/2 cup orange marmalade or apple jelly

1. Prepare Cocoa Streusel. Heat oven to 350°F. Generously grease 12-cup fluted tube pan.

2. Beat butter and sugar in large bowl until well blended. Add eggs and vanilla; beat well. Add sour cream; beat until blended. Stir together flour, baking powder and baking soda; add alternately with orange juice to butter mixture, beating until well blended. Stir in orange peel.

3. Spread marmalade in bottom of prepared pan; sprinkle half of streusel over marmalade. Pour half of batter into pan, spreading evenly. Sprinkle remaining streusel over batter; spread remaining batter evenly over streusel.

4. Bake about 1 hour or until toothpick inserted in center of cake comes out clean. Loosen cake from side of pan with spatula; immediately invert onto serving plate. Garnish with fresh orange pieces and orange peel curls, if desired.   *Makes 12 servings*

Cocoa Streusel: Stir together 2/3 cup packed light brown sugar, 1/2 cup chopped walnuts, 1/4 cup HERSHEY'S Cocoa and 1/2 cup MOUNDS® Sweetened Coconut Flakes, if desired.

Cinnamon Chip Danish

> 6 ounces cream cheese, softened
> 3 tablespoons sugar
> 1 egg yolk
> 1-2/3 cups (10-ounce package) HERSHEY'S
>   Cinnamon Chips, divided*
> 10 frozen yeast rolls, thawed and risen
> Vanilla Glaze (recipe follows)

*REESE'S® Peanut Butter Chips or HERSHEY'S Semi-Sweet Chocolate Chips can be substituted for the cinnamon chips.

1. For filling, beat cream cheese, sugar and egg yolk until well blended. Set aside 3 tablespoons cinnamon chips for garnish. Stir remaining chips into cream cheese mixture.

2. Spray work surface with nonstick cooking spray. Combine rolls and roll to an 18×12-inch rectangle. Spread filling over center-third (lengthwise portion) of rectangle. Cut 1-inch-wide strips from edge of filling to edge of dough along 18-inch sides. Begin braid by folding top row toward filling. Alternately fold strips at an angle from each side across filling toward opposite side. Fold bottom row toward filling and finish by stretching last strip and tucking under.

3. Spray baking sheet with nonstick cooking spray. Support braid with both hands and place diagonally on baking sheet. Cover with sprayed plastic wrap; let rise 25 to 30 minutes. Heat oven to 350°F. Bake 30 minutes or until golden brown. Cool; drizzle with Vanilla Glaze. Garnish with reserved chips.
Makes about 12 servings

Vanilla Glaze: Stir together 1/2 cup powdered sugar, 1-1/2 teaspoons softened butter and enough milk until of desired consistency.

Nutty Cinnamon Sticky Buns

> 1/3 cup margarine or butter
> 1/2 cup packed brown sugar
> 1/2 cup PLANTERS® Pecans, chopped
> 1 teaspoon ground cinnamon
> 1 (17.3-ounce) package refrigerated biscuits
>   (8 large biscuits)

1. Melt margarine or butter in 9-inch round baking pan in 350°F oven.

2. Mix brown sugar, pecans and cinnamon in small bowl; sprinkle over melted margarine or butter in pan. Arrange biscuits in pan with sides touching (biscuits will fit tightly in pan).

3. Bake at 350°F for 25 to 30 minutes or until biscuits are golden brown and center biscuit is fully cooked. Invert pan immediately onto serving plate. Spread any remaining topping from pan on buns. Serve warm.   *Makes 8 buns*

Orange Streusel Coffeecake

Parmesan Garlic Twists

(Pictured at right)

1/3 Butter Flavor CRISCO® Stick or 1/3 cup Butter
    Flavor CRISCO® all-vegetable shortening
    plus additional for greasing
1 cup all-purpose flour
1/2 teaspoon baking powder
1/2 teaspoon salt
1/2 teaspoon Italian seasoning*
3/4 cup grated Parmesan cheese, divided
3 egg yolks
4 cloves garlic, minced or crushed, or
    1/2 teaspoon garlic powder
2 teaspoons water
1 egg white
Paprika

**Or, substitute 1/2 teaspoon of dried oregano, basil, rosemary or
marjoram or some combination of these herbs.*

Heat oven to 400°F. Grease baking sheets with
shortening. Place sheets of foil on countertop for
cooling garlic twists.

Combine flour, baking powder, salt and Italian
seasoning in large bowl. Reserve 1 tablespoon
Parmesan cheese. Add remaining cheese. Cut in
1/3 cup shortening with pastry blender (or two
knives) until mixture resembles coarse crumbs.
Beat egg yolks, garlic and water lightly. Sprinkle
over flour mixture. Toss lightly with fork until dough
forms ball. Flour lightly.

Roll dough out on floured surface or between
two sheets of waxed paper to form 13×9-inch
rectangle. Trim edges to straighten.

Cut in half widthwise. Cut strips 1/4 inch wide (they
will be 6-1/2 inches long). Twist two strips together,
overlapping each strip over the other. Place about
2 inches apart on prepared baking sheets. Repeat
until all strips are twists. Brush with egg white.
Sprinkle with reserved Parmesan cheese.

Bake at 400°F. for 8 to 10 minutes or until lightly
browned. *Do not overbake.* Cool one minute.
Remove to foil to cool completely. Sprinkle with
paprika.   *Makes 3 dozen twists*

Serving Suggestion: Serve these twists as an
appetizer with warmed chunky tomato sauce for
dipping.

Orange Fruit Bread

2 cups all-purpose flour
1/4 cup sugar
1-1/2 teaspoons baking powder
1/2 teaspoon baking soda
1/2 teaspoon salt
1/4 cup Dried Plum Purée (recipe follows) or
    prepared dried plum butter
3/4 cup orange juice
1/2 cup orange marmalade
    Grated peel of 1 orange
1 package (6 ounces) mixed dried fruit bits
1/4 cup chopped pecans, toasted

Preheat oven to 350°F. Coat 8×4×2-inch loaf
pan with vegetable cooking spray. In mixer bowl,
combine flour, sugar, baking powder, baking soda
and salt. Add Dried Plum Purée; beat at low speed
until blended. Add juice, marmalade and orange
peel. Beat at low speed just until blended. Stir in
fruit bits and pecans. Spoon batter into prepared
pan. Bake in center of oven about 1 hour until
toothpick inserted into center comes out clean.
Cool in pan 5 minutes; remove from pan to wire
rack. Cool completely. For best flavor, wrap securely
and store overnight before slicing. Serve with
orange marmalade, if desired.

Makes 1 loaf (12 slices)

Dried Plum Purée: Combine 1-1/3 cups (8 ounces)
pitted dried plums and 6 tablespoons hot water in
container of food processor or blender. Pulse on
and off until dried plums are finely chopped and
smooth. Store leftovers in a covered container in
the refrigerator for up to two months. Makes 1 cup.

Favorite recipe from **California Dried Plum Board**

Helpful Hint

*Store quick breads in plastic bags
or wrapped in plastic at room
temperature for up to three days.
Freeze them in plastic bags or
tightly wrapped in heavy-duty foil
for up to three months. Reheat
frozen breads wrapped in foil in a
300°F oven for 15 to 18 minutes.*

Apple Sauce Cinnamon Rolls

(Pictured at right)

ROLLS

4 cups all-purpose flour, divided
1 package active dry yeast
1 cup MOTT'S® Natural Apple Sauce, divided
1/2 cup skim milk
2 tablespoons plus 1/3 cup granulated sugar, divided
2 tablespoons margarine
1/2 teaspoon salt
1 egg, beaten lightly
2 teaspoons ground cinnamon

ICING

1 cup sifted powdered sugar
1 tablespoon skim milk
1/2 teaspoon vanilla extract

1. To prepare rolls, in large bowl, mix 1-1/2 cups flour and yeast. In small saucepan, combine 3/4 cup apple sauce, 1/2 cup milk, 2 tablespoons granulated sugar, margarine and salt. Cook over medium heat, stirring often, until mixture reaches 120° to 130°F and margarine is almost melted (milk will appear curdled). Add to flour mixture along with egg. Beat with electric mixer on low speed 30 seconds, scraping bowl often. Beat on high speed 3 minutes. Stir in 2-1/4 cups flour until soft dough forms.

2. Turn out dough onto lightly floured surface; flatten slightly. Knead 3 to 5 minutes or until smooth and elastic, adding remaining 1/4 cup flour to prevent sticking if necessary. Shape dough into ball; place in large bowl sprayed with nonstick cooking spray. Turn dough over so that top is greased. Cover with towel; let rise in warm place about 1 hour or until doubled in bulk.

3. Spray two 8- or 9-inch round baking pans with nonstick cooking spray.

4. Punch down dough; turn out onto lightly floured surface. Cover with towel; let rest 10 minutes. Roll out dough into 12-inch square. Spread remaining 1/4 cup apple sauce over dough, to within 1/2 inch of edges. In small bowl, combine remaining 1/3 cup granulated sugar and cinnamon; sprinkle over apple sauce. Roll up dough jelly-roll style. Moisten edge with water; pinch to seal seam. Cut roll into 12 (1-inch) slices with sharp floured knife. Arrange 6 rolls 1/2 inch apart in each prepared pan. Cover with towel; let rise in warm place about 30 minutes or until nearly doubled in bulk.

5. Preheat oven to 375°F. Bake 20 to 25 minutes or until lightly browned. Cool on wire rack 5 minutes. Invert each pan onto serving plate.

6. To prepare icing, in bowl, mix powdered sugar, 1 tablespoon milk and vanilla until smooth. Drizzle over rolls. Serve warm.   *Makes 12 servings*

Cheese and Beef Snacking Bread

1 cup milk
1/4 cup water
3 tablespoons vegetable oil
1 egg, yolk
2 tablespoons sugar
1 teaspoon salt
1 tablespoon dried minced onion
1 teaspoon caraway seeds
3 cups all-purpose flour
2-1/4 teaspoons RED STAR® Active Dry Yeast

TOPPING

1 egg white
1-1/2 cups shredded cheddar cheese
1 package (2.5 ounces) smoked sliced beef or corned beef, snipped

BREAD MACHINE METHOD

Place room temperature ingredients, except egg white, cheese and beef, in pan in order listed. Select dough cycle. Because this is a batter bread you will need to help the mixing using a rubber spatula. At end of kneading cycle, remove batter and follow shaping and baking instructions. Do not allow dough to rise in the machine.

TRADITIONAL METHOD

Combine 1 cup flour, yeast, caraway seeds, onion, salt and sugar. Heat milk, water and oil to 120° to 130°F; add to flour mixture. Beat 3 minutes on medium speed. Add egg yolk; beat 1 minute. Add remaining flour to make stiff batter.

SHAPING AND BAKING

Spread batter evenly in greased 15×10-inch baking pan. Brush with lightly beaten egg white. Sprinkle with beef and cheese. Bake in preheated 375°F oven 25 to 30 minutes or until golden brown. Cut into squares and serve warm.   *Makes 1 loaf*

Apple Sauce Cinnamon Rolls

Main Dishes

Chicken Enchiladas

(Pictured at left)

2 cups chopped cooked chicken or turkey
1 cup chopped green pepper
1 package (8 ounces) PHILADELPHIA® Cream Cheese, cubed
1 cup TACO BELL® HOME ORIGINALS®* Thick 'N Chunky Salsa, divided
8 (6-inch) flour tortillas
3/4 pound (12 ounces) VELVEETA® Pasteurized Prepared Cheese Product, cut up
1/4 cup milk

TACO BELL and HOME ORIGINALS are registered trademarks owned and licensed by Taco Bell Corp.

MIX chicken, green pepper, cream cheese and 1/2 cup of the salsa in saucepan, stirring occasionally; cook over low heat until cream cheese is melted.

SPOON 1/3 cup chicken mixture down center of each tortilla; roll up. Place, seam-side down, in lightly greased 11×7-inch baking dish.

MIX VELVEETA and milk in saucepan; cook over low heat until VELVEETA is completely melted, stirring frequently. Pour over enchiladas; cover with foil.

BAKE, uncovered, at 350°F for 20 minutes or until thoroughly heated. Top with remaining salsa. Garnish as desired.

Makes 4 to 6 servings

Clockwise from top left: *Swanson® Savory Pot Roast with Harvest Vegetables (p. 178), Campbell's® Baked Macaroni & Cheese (p. 138), Cajun-Style Rubbed Steak (p. 128) and Chicken Enchiladas*

Pepperidge Farm® Turkey & Stuffing Bake

(Pictured at right)

1 can (14 ounces) SWANSON® Chicken Broth
    (1-3/4 cups)
    Generous dash pepper
1 stalk celery, chopped (about 1/2 cup)
1 small onion, coarsely chopped (about 1/4 cup)
4 cups PEPPERIDGE FARM® Herb Seasoned
    Stuffing
4 servings sliced roasted *or* deli turkey (about
    12 ounces)
1 jar (12 ounces) FRANCO-AMERICAN® Slow
    Roast™ Turkey Gravy

1. In medium saucepan mix broth, pepper, celery and onion. Over high heat, heat to a boil. Reduce heat to low. Cover and cook 5 minutes or until vegetables are tender. Add stuffing. Mix lightly.

2. Spoon into 2-quart shallow baking dish. Arrange turkey over stuffing. Pour gravy over turkey.

3. Bake at 350°F. for 30 minutes or until hot.

Makes 4 servings

Cajun-Style Rubbed Steaks

(Pictured on page 126)

1/3 cup A.1.® Original or A.1.® BOLD & SPICY
    Steak Sauce
1/4 cup margarine or butter, melted
3/4 teaspoon each garlic powder, onion powder
    and ground black pepper
1/2 teaspoon ground white pepper
1/4 teaspoon cayenne pepper
4 (4- to 6-ounce) beef shell top loin or strip
    steaks, about 1/2 inch thick

In small bowl, blend steak sauce and margarine; set aside.

In another small bowl, combine garlic powder, onion powder and peppers. Brush both sides of steaks with reserved steak sauce mixture, then sprinkle with seasoning mixture. Grill steaks over medium-high heat or broil 4 inches from heat source 5 minutes on each side or to desired doneness. Garnish as desired. Serve with mashed potatoes and peas, if desired.

Makes 4 servings

Grilled Fish Steaks with Tomato Basil Butter Sauce

Tomato Basil Butter Sauce (recipe follows)
4 fish steaks, such as halibut, swordfish, tuna or
    salmon (at least 3/4 inch thick)
    Olive oil
    Salt and black pepper
    Fresh basil leaves and summer squash slices for
    garnish
    Hot cooked seasoned noodles (optional)

Prepare Tomato Basil Butter Sauce; set aside. Rinse fish; pat dry with paper towels. Brush one side of fish lightly with oil; season with salt and pepper.

Coat grill rack with oil before starting grill. Grill fish, oil side down, on a covered grill, over medium KINGSFORD® Briquets, 6 to 10 minutes. Halfway through cooking time, brush top with oil and season with salt and pepper, then turn and continue grilling until fish flakes easily with fork. (Grilling time depends on the thickness of fish; allow 3 to 5 minutes for each 1/2 inch of thickness.) Serve with Tomato Basil Butter Sauce. Garnish with basil leaves and squash slices. Serve with noodles, if desired.

Makes 4 servings

Tomato Basil Butter Sauce

4 tablespoons butter or margarine, softened,
    divided
1-1/2 cups chopped seeded peeled tomatoes (about
    1 pound)
1/2 teaspoon sugar
1 clove garlic, minced
    Salt and black pepper
4-1/2 teaspoons very finely chopped fresh basil

Melt 1 tablespoon butter in small skillet. Add tomatoes, sugar and garlic. Cook over medium-low heat, stirring frequently, until liquid evaporates and mixture thickens. Remove pan from heat; stir in remaining butter until mixture has a saucelike consistency. Season to taste with salt and pepper, then stir in basil.

Makes about 1 cup

*Pepperidge Farm® Turkey
& Stuffing Bake*

Zesty Italian Stuffed Peppers

(Pictured at right)

3 bell peppers (green, red or yellow)
1 pound ground beef
1 jar (14 ounces) spaghetti sauce
1-1/3 cups *French's* French Fried Onions, divided
2 tablespoons *Frank's* *RedHot* Cayenne Pepper Sauce
1/2 cup uncooked instant rice
1/4 cup sliced ripe olives
1 cup (4 ounces) shredded mozzarella cheese

Preheat oven to 400°F. Cut bell peppers in half lengthwise through stems; discard seeds. Place pepper halves, cut side up, in shallow 2-quart baking dish; set aside.

Place beef in large microwavable bowl. Microwave on HIGH 5 minutes or until meat is no longer pink, stirring once. Drain. Stir in spaghetti sauce, *2/3 cup* French Fried Onions, **Frank's RedHot** Sauce, rice and olives. Spoon evenly into bell pepper halves.

Cover; bake 35 minutes or until bell peppers are tender. Uncover; sprinkle with cheese and remaining *2/3 cup* onions. Bake 1 minute or until onions are golden. *Makes 6 servings*

Serving Suggestion: Serve with tossed salad.

Campbell's® Asian Chicken Stir-Fry

1 tablespoon vegetable oil
1 pound skinless, boneless chicken breasts, cut into strips
1 can (10-3/4 ounces) CAMPBELL'S® Condensed Golden Mushroom Soup
3 tablespoons soy sauce
1 teaspoon garlic powder
1 bag (16 ounces) any frozen vegetable combination, thawed
4 cups hot cooked rice

1. In medium skillet over medium-high heat, heat oil. Add chicken and stir-fry until browned and juices evaporate.

2. Add soup, soy sauce and garlic powder. Heat to a boil. Reduce heat to medium. Add vegetables and cook until vegetables are tender-crisp, stirring often. Serve over rice. *Makes 4 servings*

Southwest White Chili

SPICE BLEND
1 teaspoon McCORMICK® California Style Garlic Powder
1 teaspoon McCORMICK® Ground Cumin
1/2 teaspoon McCORMICK® Oregano Leaves
1/2 teaspoon McCORMICK® Cilantro Leaves
1/8 to 1/4 teaspoon McCORMICK® Ground Red Pepper

CHILI
1 tablespoon olive oil
1-1/2 pounds boneless, skinless chicken breasts, cut into 1/2-inch cubes
1/4 cup chopped onion
1 cup chicken broth
1 can (4 ounces) chopped green chilies, undrained
1 can (15 ounces) white kidney beans (cannellini), undrained
Shredded Monterey Jack cheese
Sliced green onions, for garnish

1. Place all ingredients for spice blend in small dish and stir until well blended. Set aside.

2. Heat oil in 2- to 3-quart saucepan over medium-high heat. Add chicken; cook and stir 4 to 5 minutes. Remove chicken with slotted spoon; cover and keep warm.

3. Add chopped onion to saucepan; cook and stir 2 minutes. Stir in chicken broth, chilies and reserved spice blend. Simmer, covered, over low heat 20 minutes.

4. Stir in beans and reserved chicken; simmer, uncovered, 10 minutes.

5. Spoon into serving dish and sprinkle with cheese and green onions. *Makes 4 servings*

Serving Suggestion: For a quick accompaniment, whip up a batch of cornbread or corn muffins from a mix. For extra flavor in the muffins, simply stir grated cheese, chopped green onions, chopped jalapeño peppers, or crumbled crisply cooked bacon into the batter.

Zesty Italian Stuffed Pepper

Ensenada Fish Tacos

(Pictured at right)

10 ounces halibut or orange roughy fillets, cut
     into 1-inch cubes
1 tablespoon vegetable oil
1 tablespoon lime juice
1 package (1.27 ounces) LAWRY'S® Spices
     & Seasonings for Fajitas
6 corn or flour tortillas (about 8 inches)
2-1/2 cups shredded lettuce
1/2 cup diced fresh tomatoes
3/4 cup (3 ounces) shredded Monterey Jack or
     cheddar cheese
2 tablespoons thinly sliced green onion
     Dairy sour cream (optional)
     Guacamole (optional)
     Salsa (optional)
     Chopped fresh cilantro (optional)

In shallow glass baking dish, place fish. Pour oil
and lime juice over fish. Sprinkle with Spices &
Seasonings for Fajitas; toss lightly to coat. Cover.
Refrigerate 2 hours to marinate, occasionally
spooning marinade over fish. In same dish, bake fish
in 450°F oven 10 minutes or until fish flakes easily
with fork; drain. To serve, evenly divide fish; place
in center of each tortilla. Top with lettuce,
tomatoes, cheese and green onion.

Makes 6 servings

Serving Suggestion: Garnish with sour cream,
guacamole, salsa and cilantro to taste.

Helpful Hint

*When storing fresh fish, wrap it
tightly in plastic wrap. If possible,
place the package on ice and store
it in the coldest part of the
refrigerator. Be sure that melting
ice drains away from the fish. If
the flesh comes in contact with
moisture, it may become discolored.
Fresh fish should be used within
one day of purchase.*

Swedish Meatballs

1-1/2 cups soft bread crumbs
1 cup (1/2 pint) heavy cream
2 tablespoons butter or margarine, divided
1 small onion, chopped
1 pound ground beef
1/2 pound ground pork
3 tablespoons chopped fresh parsley, divided
1-1/2 teaspoons salt
1/4 teaspoon black pepper
1/4 teaspoon ground allspice
1 cup beef broth
1 tablespoon all-purpose flour
1 cup sour cream

Combine bread crumbs and cream in small bowl;
mix well. Let stand 10 minutes. Melt 1 tablespoon
butter in large skillet over medium heat. Add onion.
Cook and stir 5 minutes or until onion is tender.
Combine beef, pork, bread crumb mixture, onion,
2 tablespoons parsley, salt, pepper and allspice in
large bowl; mix well. Cover; refrigerate 1 hour.

Pat meat mixture into 1-inch-thick square on cutting
board. Cut into 36 squares. Shape each square into
a ball. Melt remaining 1 tablespoon butter in large
skillet over medium heat. Add meatballs. Cook
10 minutes or until browned on all sides and no
longer pink in centers. Remove meatballs from
skillet; drain on paper towels.

Drain drippings from skillet; discard. Pour broth
into skillet. Heat over medium-high heat, stirring
frequently and scraping up any browned bits.
Reduce heat to low.

Combine flour and sour cream in small bowl until
smooth; mix well. Stir sour cream mixture into
skillet. Cook 5 minutes, stirring constantly. Do not
boil. Add meatballs. Cook 5 minutes more. Sprinkle
with remaining 1 tablespoon parsley. Garnish as
desired. *Makes 5 to 6 servings*

Note: Mashed potatoes, boiled red potatoes or
broad egg noodles are wonderful accompaniments.

Skillet Pork Chop with Maple Apples

Skillet Pork Chops with Maple Apples

(Pictured above)

    1 package (12 ounces) uncooked egg noodles
    1 teaspoon dried oregano leaves
    1 teaspoon dried thyme leaves
    1/2 teaspoon salt
    1/2 teaspoon ground nutmeg
    1/4 teaspoon black pepper
    4 well-trimmed center-cut bone-in pork chops,
        cut 1/2 inch thick
    2 tablespoons margarine or butter, divided
    1 red apple
    1/4 cup maple syrup
    2 tablespoons lemon juice
    1/2 teaspoon ground ginger

1. Prepare noodles according to package directions; drain.

2. While noodles are cooking, combine oregano, thyme, salt, nutmeg and pepper in small bowl; sprinkle over pork chops.

3. Heat 1 tablespoon margarine in large skillet until hot. Add pork chops and cook over medium heat 5 to 7 minutes per side or until pork is no longer pink. Remove from skillet and cover to keep warm.

4. Cut apple in half; core and cut into slices. Add remaining 1 tablespoon margarine and apple to skillet. Cook, stirring occasionally, about 3 minutes or until tender. Stir in syrup, lemon juice, ginger and additional salt and pepper to taste. Cook about 2 minutes or until slightly thickened.

5. Serve pork chops and apple mixture over noodles. Garnish with fresh oregano leaves, if desired.   *Makes 4 servings*

Zesty Seafood Lasagna

    2 packages (1.8 ounces each) white sauce mix
4-1/2 cups milk
    1 teaspoon dried basil leaves
    1/2 teaspoon dried thyme leaves
    1/2 teaspoon garlic powder
    3/4 cup grated Parmesan cheese, divided
    3 tablespoons *Frank's® RedHot®* Cayenne Pepper
        Sauce
    9 oven-ready lasagna pasta sheets
    2 packages (10 ounces each) frozen chopped
        spinach, thawed and squeezed
    1/2 pound cooked shrimp
    1/2 pound raw bay scallops or flaked imitation
        crabmeat
    2 cups (8 ounces) shredded mozzarella cheese,
        divided

1. Preheat oven to 400°F. Prepare white sauce according to package directions using milk and adding basil, thyme and garlic powder in large saucepan. Stir in 1/2 cup Parmesan cheese and *Frank's RedHot* Sauce.

2. Spread 1 cup sauce in bottom of greased 13×9×2-inch casserole. Layer 3 pasta sheets widthwise over sauce. (Do not let edges touch.) Layer half of the spinach and seafood over pasta. Spoon 1 cup sauce over seafood; sprinkle with 3/4 cup mozzarella cheese. Repeat layers a second time. Top with final layer of pasta sheets, remaining sauce and cheeses.

3. Cover pan with greased foil. Bake 40 minutes. Remove foil; bake 10 minutes or until top is browned and pasta is tender. Let stand 15 minutes before serving.   *Makes 8 servings*

Swanson® Rosemary Chicken & Vegetables

(Pictured below)

3- to 4-pound whole broiler-fryer chicken
1 tablespoon butter *or* margarine, melted
4 medium red potatoes, quartered
2 cups fresh *or* frozen baby carrots
2 stalks celery, cut into chunks
12 small white onions, peeled
1-1/2 teaspoons chopped fresh rosemary *or*
      1/2 teaspoon dried rosemary leaves, crushed
1 cup SWANSON® Chicken Broth
1/2 cup orange juice

BRUSH chicken with butter. Place chicken and vegetables in roasting pan. Sprinkle with rosemary. Mix broth and orange juice and pour **half** of broth mixture over all.

ROAST at 375°F. for 1 hour.

STIR vegetables. Add remaining broth mixture to pan. Roast 30 minutes or until done.

Makes 4 servings

Tip: To quickly peel onions, pour boiling water over onions and let stand 5 minutes. Then slip off skins.

Campbell's® 15-Minute Chicken & Rice Dinner

1 tablespoon vegetable oil
4 skinless, boneless chicken breast halves (about 1 pound)
1 can (10-3/4 ounces) CAMPBELL'S® Condensed Cream of Chicken Soup *or* 98% Fat Free Cream of Chicken Soup
1-1/2 cups water*
1/4 teaspoon paprika
1/4 teaspoon pepper
1-1/2 cups *uncooked* Minute® Original Rice
2 cups fresh *or* thawed frozen broccoli flowerets

For creamier rice, increase water to 1-2/3 cups.

1. In medium skillet over medium-high heat, heat oil. Add chicken and cook 8 minutes or until browned. Set chicken aside. Pour off fat.

2. Add soup, water, paprika and pepper. Heat to boil.

3. Stir in rice and broccoli. Place chicken on rice mixture. Season chicken with additional paprika and pepper. Reduce heat to low. Cover and cook 5 minutes or until chicken is no longer pink.

Makes 4 servings

Swanson® Rosemary Chicken & Vegetables

Shrimp & Ham Jambalaya

(Pictured at right)

1 onion, cut into wedges
1 large green bell pepper, chopped
2 cloves garlic, minced
1/4 teaspoon cayenne pepper
2 tablespoons FLEISCHMANN'S® Original
    Margarine
3 cups cooked rice
2 cups large shrimp, cleaned and cooked (about
    1 pound)
2 cups cubed cooked ham (about 1-1/4 pounds)
1 (16-ounce) can whole tomatoes, chopped
    (undrained)
1 teaspoon natural hickory seasoning

1. Cook and stir onion, bell pepper, garlic and cayenne pepper in margarine in large skillet over medium heat until vegetables are tender.

2. Stir in remaining ingredients. Cook for 10 to 15 minutes or until heated through, stirring often. Serve immediately. Garnish as desired.

Makes 8 servings

Chicken and Broccoli Crepes

10 prepared Basic Crepes (recipe follows)
1/2 cup all-purpose flour
1/2 cup half-and-half cream
1/2 teaspoon garlic salt
1-1/4 cups chicken broth
    2 cups (8 ounces) shredded Wisconsin Cheddar
        cheese, divided
1/2 cup (2 ounces) shredded Wisconsin Monterey
        Jack cheese
1-1/2 cups dairy sour cream, divided
    2 tablespoons diced pimientos
    1 tablespoon dried parsley flakes
    1 teaspoon paprika
    2 tablespoons butter
    1 can (4 ounces) sliced mushrooms, drained
    2 packages (10 ounces each) frozen broccoli
        spears, cooked and drained
    2 cups cubed cooked chicken

Prepare Basic Crepes; set aside. Combine flour, half-and-half and garlic salt in medium saucepan; beat with wire whisk until smooth. Blend in chicken broth. Stir in 1 cup Cheddar cheese, Monterey Jack cheese, 1/2 cup sour cream, pimientos, parsley and paprika. Cook sauce over medium-low heat until

mixture thickens, stirring constantly. Remove from heat; set aside. Melt butter in small skillet over medium-high heat. Cook and stir mushrooms in butter.

On half of each crepe, place equally divided portions of cooked broccoli, chicken and mushrooms. Spoon 1 to 2 tablespoons cheese sauce over each.

Fold crepes. Place in large, shallow baking dish. Pour remaining cheese sauce over crepes. Top with remaining 1 cup sour cream and 1 cup Cheddar cheese. Bake, uncovered, in preheated 350°F oven 5 to 10 minutes or until cheese melts. Garnish with chopped fresh parsley, if desired.

Makes 10 crepes

Basic Crepes

3 eggs
1/2 teaspoon salt
2 cups plus 2 tablespoons all-purpose flour
2 cups milk
1/4 cup melted butter

Beat eggs and salt together in medium bowl with electric mixer or wire whisk. Add flour alternately with milk, beating until smooth. Stir in melted butter.

Allow crepe batter to stand 1 hour or more in refrigerator before cooking. The flour may expand and bubbles will collapse. The batter should be the consistency of heavy cream. If the batter is too thick, add 1 to 2 tablespoons additional milk and stir well.

Cook crepes in heated, nonstick pan over medium-high heat. With one hand, pour 3 tablespoons batter into pan; with other hand, lift pan off heat. Quickly rotate pan until batter covers bottom; return pan to heat. Cook until light brown; turn and brown other side for a few seconds.   *Makes about 30 crepes*

Note: To store crepes, separate with pieces of waxed paper and wrap airtight. They may be frozen for up to 3 months.

Favorite recipe from **Wisconsin Milk Marketing Board**

Shrimp & Ham Jambalaya

Bacon & Cheese Stuffed Chicken

(Pictured at right)

4 boneless, skinless chicken breast halves (about 1-1/4 pounds), pounded 1/4 inch thick
1 cup shredded mozzarella cheese (about 4 ounces)
4 slices bacon, crisp-cooked and crumbled
1 egg, lightly beaten
1/2 cup Italian seasoned dry bread crumbs
2 tablespoons olive or vegetable oil
1 jar (26 to 28 ounces) RAGÚ® Robusto!™ Pasta Sauce
1 cup chicken broth
8 ounces linguine or spaghetti, cooked and drained

1. Evenly top each chicken breast half with cheese and bacon. Roll up and secure with wooden toothpicks. Dip chicken in egg, then bread crumbs.

2. In 12-inch nonstick skillet, heat oil over medium heat and brown chicken, turning occasionally. Stir in Ragú Pasta Sauce and broth. Bring to a boil over high heat. Reduce heat to low and simmer, covered, 10 minutes or until chicken is no longer pink.

3. To serve, arrange chicken and sauce over hot linguine. Garnish, if desired, with fresh basil or parsley.   *Makes 4 servings*

Italian Porketta

2 to 4 pounds boneless whole pork loin roast
3 tablespoons dill seed
1 tablespoon fennel seed
1 teaspoon lemon-pepper seasoning
1/4 teaspoon onion powder
1/4 teaspoon garlic powder
1/4 teaspoon dried oregano

Combine seasonings together and coat roast with mixture. Roast in a shallow pan at 325°F for 45 minutes to 1 hour, until meat thermometer registers 155° to 160°F. Let roast rest 5 to 10 minutes before carving.   *Makes 8 to 12 servings*

Favorite recipe from **National Pork Board**

Kielbasa Kabobs

1/2 cup A.1.® Steak Sauce
1/4 cup GREY POUPON® Dijon Mustard
3 tablespoons light molasses
2 tablespoons cider vinegar
1 tablespoon vegetable oil
1 clove garlic, minced
1 teaspoon cornstarch
1 pound kielbasa, sliced into 1-inch pieces
6 small red skin potatoes, parboiled and cut into wedges (about 12 ounces)
1 medium onion, cut into wedges
1 medium apple, cut into wedges
   Steamed shredded red and green cabbage

Soak 6 (10-inch) wooden skewers in water for at least 30 minutes. Blend steak sauce, mustard, molasses, vinegar, oil, garlic and cornstarch in small saucepan. Cook and stir over medium heat until sauce thickens and begins to boil; cool.

Alternately thread kielbasa, vegetables and apple onto skewers. Grill kabobs over medium heat for 12 to 15 minutes or until done, turning and brushing often with prepared sauce. Serve hot with prepared cabbage.   *Makes 6 servings*

Campbell's® Baked Macaroni & Cheese

(Pictured on page 126)

1 can (10-3/4 ounces) CAMPBELL'S® Condensed Cheddar Cheese Soup
1/2 soup can milk
1/8 teaspoon pepper
2 cups hot cooked corkscrew *or* medium shell macaroni (about 1-1/2 cups uncooked)
1 tablespoon dry bread crumbs
2 teaspoons margarine *or* butter, melted

1. In 1-quart casserole mix soup, milk, pepper and macaroni.

2. Mix bread crumbs with margarine and sprinkle over macaroni mixture.

3. Bake at 400°F. for 20 minutes or until hot.   *Makes 4 servings*

Biscuit-Topped Hearty Steak Pie

(Pictured at right)

1-1/2 pounds top beef round steak, cooked and cut into 1-inch cubes
1 package (9 ounces) frozen baby carrots
1 package (9 ounces) frozen peas and pearl onions
1 large baking potato, cooked and cut into 1/2-inch pieces
1 jar (18 ounces) home-style brown gravy
1/2 teaspoon dried thyme leaves
1/2 teaspoon black pepper
1 can (12 ounces) flaky buttermilk biscuits

Preheat oven to 375°F. Spray 2-quart casserole with nonstick cooking spray.

Combine steak, frozen vegetables and potato in prepared dish. Stir in gravy, thyme and pepper.

Bake, uncovered, 40 minutes. Remove from oven. *Increase oven temperature to 400°F.* Top with biscuits and bake 8 to 10 minutes or until biscuits are golden brown.   *Makes 6 servings*

Note: This casserole can be prepared with leftovers of almost any kind. Other steaks, roast beef, stew meat, pork, lamb or chicken can be substituted for round steak; adjust gravy flavor to complement meat. Red potatoes can be used in place of baking potato. Choose your favorite vegetable combination, such as broccoli, cauliflower and carrots or broccoli, corn and red peppers, as a substitute for the peas and carrots.

Honey Nut Stir-Fry

1 pound pork steak, pork loin or boneless chicken breast
1 tablespoon cornstarch
3/4 cup orange juice
1/3 cup honey
3 tablespoons soy sauce
1/4 teaspoon ground ginger
2 tablespoons vegetable oil, divided
2 large carrots, sliced diagonally
2 stalks celery, sliced diagonally
1/2 cup cashews or peanuts
Hot cooked rice

Cut pork into thin strips; set aside. Combine cornstarch, orange juice, honey, soy sauce and ginger in small bowl; mix well. Heat 1 tablespoon oil in large skillet over medium-high heat. Add carrots and celery; stir-fry about 3 minutes. Remove vegetables; set aside. Pour remaining 1 tablespoon oil into skillet. Add pork; stir-fry about 3 minutes. Return vegetables to skillet; add honey mixture and nuts. Cook and stir over medium-high heat until sauce comes to a boil and thickens. Serve over rice.

Makes 4 to 6 servings

Favorite recipe from **National Honey Board**

Spicy Lasagna Roll-Ups

1 pound ground turkey breast or ground beef
1/2 cup chopped onion
2 cloves garlic, minced
1 teaspoon dried Italian seasoning
1/4 teaspoon crushed red pepper flakes
1 can (10-3/4 ounces) condensed tomato soup
1 cup chopped zucchini
3/4 cup water
1 container (15 ounces) ricotta cheese
1/2 cup shredded mozzarella cheese
1 egg
4 cooked lasagna noodles

1. Preheat oven to 350°F. Spray large nonstick skillet with nonstick cooking spray; heat over medium heat until hot. Add turkey, onion, garlic, Italian seasoning and red pepper flakes; cook and stir until turkey is no longer pink and onion is tender. Add soup, zucchini and water; simmer 5 minutes. Pour soup mixture into shallow 2-quart baking dish.

2. Combine ricotta and mozzarella cheeses and egg in medium bowl; mix well. Lay lasagna noodles on work surface; spread 1/2 cup cheese mixture on each noodle. Roll up noodles, enclosing filling; place rolls seam sides down over soup mixture.

3. Cover and bake 30 minutes; uncover and continue baking an additional 10 minutes or until sauce is bubbly. Place lasagna rolls on serving dish; spoon remaining sauce over rolls.   *Makes 4 servings*

Quick 'n' Tangy Beef Stir-Fry

Barbecued Ribs with Oriental Plum Sauce

(Pictured on front cover)

3 pounds pork spareribs
1/2 cup water
Oriental Plum Sauce (recipe follows)

Arrange ribs in single layer in 13×9-inch microwave-safe dish. Pour water over ribs. Cover loosely with plastic wrap. Microwave on MEDIUM-HIGH (70% power) 20 minutes, rearranging ribs once.

Place ribs on grid. Grill over medium coals 20 minutes or until barely pink near bone, basting with Oriental Plum Sauce during last 10 minutes of cooking. Serve with remaining sauce.

Makes 4 servings

Oriental Plum Sauce

1 jar (10 ounces) plum jam
2 tablespoons *Frank's*® *RedHot*® Cayenne Pepper Sauce
2 tablespoons prepared seafood cocktail sauce or chili sauce
1 teaspoon grated peeled fresh ginger

Combine ingredients in small saucepan. Cook over medium heat 3 minutes or until hot and bubbly, stirring occasionally. Cool completely.

Makes about 1-1/2 cups

Beef Sonoma & Rice

1 pound ground beef
1 clove garlic, minced
1 package (6.8 ounces) RICE-A-RONI® Beef Flavor
1/2 cup chopped green bell pepper *or* 1 can (4 ounces) chopped green chiles, undrained
1/4 cup sliced green onions
1 medium tomato, chopped
2 tablespoons chopped parsley or cilantro

1. In large skillet, brown ground beef and garlic; drain. Remove from skillet; set aside.

2. In same skillet, prepare Rice-A-Roni Mix as package directs, stirring in beef mixture, green pepper and onions during last 5 minutes of cooking.

3. Sprinkle with tomato and parsley.

Makes 4 servings

Quick 'n' Tangy Beef Stir-Fry

(Pictured above)

SAUCE
1/2 cup *French's*® Worcestershire Sauce
1/2 cup water
2 tablespoons sugar
2 teaspoons cornstarch
1/2 teaspoon ground ginger
1/2 teaspoon garlic powder

STIR-FRY
1 pound thinly sliced beef steak
3 cups sliced bell peppers

1. Combine ingredients for sauce. Marinate beef in *1/4 cup* sauce 5 minutes. Heat *1 tablespoon oil* in large skillet or wok over high heat. Stir-fry beef in batches 5 minutes or until browned.

2. Add peppers; cook 2 minutes. Add remaining sauce; stir-fry until sauce thickens. Serve over hot cooked ramen noodles or rice, if desired. Garnish as desired.

Makes 4 servings

Ham-Broccoli Quiche

(Pictured below)

1 cup sliced fresh mushrooms
1 clove garlic, minced
2 teaspoons butter or margarine
1/2 cup shredded Swiss cheese
1 (9-inch) pastry shell
1-1/2 cups (8 ounces) chopped CURE 81® ham
1 cup cooked, chopped broccoli
1 cup milk
3 eggs
2 teaspoons all-purpose flour
1/4 teaspoon ground white pepper
Dash ground nutmeg
2 tablespoons grated Romano or Parmesan cheese

Heat oven to 350°F. In skillet over medium-high heat, sauté mushrooms and garlic in butter until tender. Sprinkle Swiss cheese in pastry shell. Top with mushroom mixture, ham and broccoli. In bowl, beat together milk, eggs, flour, white pepper and nutmeg; pour into pastry shell. Sprinkle with Romano or Parmesan cheese. Bake 35 to 40 minutes or until knife inserted near center comes out clean. Stand 10 minutes before serving. Garnish as desired.

Makes 6 servings

Meatless Ravioli Bake

4 cups finely chopped eggplant
1/2 cup chopped onion
1/4 cup chopped carrots
1/4 cup chopped celery
3 tablespoons olive oil
2 cans (8 ounces each) HUNT'S® No Salt Added Tomato Sauce
1 can (14.5 ounces) HUNT'S® Crushed Tomatoes
1/2 teaspoon sugar
1/8 teaspoon pepper
1 package (25 ounces) frozen large ravioli, prepared according to package directions

1. Preheat oven to 375°F.

2. In saucepan, sauté eggplant, onion, carrots and celery in hot oil; cook until tender.

3. Stir in Hunt's Tomato Sauce, Hunt's Tomatoes, sugar and pepper. Simmer, uncovered, 10 minutes; stirring occasionally.

4. Spoon *1-1/2 cups* of tomato mixture into 13×9×2-inch baking dish; top with half the ravioli and *half* of the *remaining* sauce. Repeat layers.

5. Bake, uncovered, 30 minutes or until bubbly.

Makes 6 servings

Ham-Broccoli Quiche

German-Style Bratwurst & Sauerkraut

(Pictured at right)

6 slices bacon
1 small onion, chopped
1 clove garlic, minced
1 (32-ounce) jar or can sauerkraut, rinsed and well drained
2 medium potatoes, peeled and sliced
1-1/2 to 2 cups water, divided
1/2 cup apple juice or dry white wine
2 tablespoons brown sugar
1 teaspoon instant chicken bouillon granules
1 teaspoon caraway seeds
1 dried bay leaf
1 pound BOB EVANS® Bratwurst (5 links)
2 medium apples, cored and sliced
Fresh bay leaves (optional)

Cook bacon in large skillet over medium-high heat until crisp. Remove bacon; drain and crumble on paper towel. Set aside. Drain off all but 2 tablespoons drippings in skillet. Add onion and garlic to drippings; cook over medium heat until tender, stirring occasionally. Stir in sauerkraut, potatoes, 1-1/2 cups water, apple juice, brown sugar, bouillon, caraway and dried bay leaf. Add remaining 1/2 cup water, if necessary, to cover potatoes. Bring to a boil over high heat.

Meanwhile, make 3 or 4 diagonal 1/4-inch-deep cuts into one side of each bratwurst. Cook bratwurst in large skillet over medium heat until browned, turning occasionally. Add bratwurst to sauerkraut mixture. Reduce heat to low; simmer, covered, 20 to 30 minutes or until potatoes are just tender, stirring occasionally. Add apples; cook, covered, 5 to 10 minutes or until apples are just tender. Stir in reserved bacon. Remove and discard dried bay leaf. Garnish with fresh bay leaves, if desired. Serve hot. Refrigerate leftovers. *Makes 5 servings*

Cheesy Crispy Chicken

12 chicken drumsticks
Vegetable cooking spray
1 bottle (8 ounces) blue cheese salad dressing
2 cups dry bread crumbs
1/2 teaspoon celery salt
1/2 teaspoon dried dill weed
1/4 teaspoon black pepper

Preheat oven to 350°F. Spray baking sheet with cooking spray; set aside. Pour dressing in medium bowl. Combine bread crumbs, celery salt, dill and pepper in shallow dish. Dip chicken into dressing; roll in bread crumb mixture. Place chicken in single layer on prepared baking sheet. Bake, uncovered, 50 minutes or until juices run clear, turning once. Serve hot or cold. *Makes 6 servings*

Favorite recipe from **National Chicken Council**

Carolina Barbecue

1 (5-pound) Boston butt roast
2 teaspoons vegetable oil
1-1/2 cups water
1 can (8 ounces) tomato sauce
1/4 cup packed brown sugar
1/4 cup cider vinegar
1/4 cup Worcestershire sauce
1 teaspoon celery seeds
1 teaspoon chili powder
Salt and black pepper to taste
Dash hot pepper sauce

Randomly pierce roast with sharp knife. In Dutch oven, brown roast on all sides in hot oil. In mixing bowl, combine remaining ingredients; mix well. Pour sauce over roast and bring to a boil. Reduce heat; cover and simmer 2 hours or until roast is fork-tender. Baste roast with sauce during cooking time. Slice or chop to serve. *Makes 20 servings*

Favorite recipe from **National Pork Board**

Helpful Hint

When simmering or braising a roast, it is important not to let the liquid boil once the heat has been reduced. Cooking the meat at a low, even temperature helps to prevent it from becoming tough.

German-Style Bratwurst & Sauerkraut

Fish with Hidden Valley Ranch® Tartar Sauce

(Pictured at right)

1 cup (1/2 pint) sour cream
1/4 cup chopped sweet pickles
1 packet (1 ounce) HIDDEN VALLEY® The
    Original Ranch® Salad Dressing & Seasoning
    Mix
3/4 cup dry bread crumbs
1-1/2 pounds whitefish fillets (sole, flounder,
    snapper or turbot)
1 egg, beaten
    Vegetable oil
    French fried shoestring potatoes (optional)
    Lemon wedges (optional)

To make sauce, in small bowl, combine sour cream, pickles and 2 tablespoons of the salad dressing & seasoning mix; cover and refrigerate. On large plate, combine bread crumbs and remaining salad dressing mix. Dip fillets in egg, then coat with bread crumb mixture. Fry fillets in 3 tablespoons oil until golden and fish flakes easily with fork. (Add more oil to pan if necessary to prevent sticking.) Serve with chilled sauce. Serve with French fries and lemon wedges, if desired.
Makes 4 servings

Chili Cornbread Casserole

1 pound ground beef
1 medium onion, chopped
1 jar (16 ounces) RAGÚ® Cheese Creations!®
    Double Cheddar Sauce
1 can (16 ounces) red kidney beans, rinsed and
    drained
1 can (8-3/4 ounces) whole kernel corn, drained
2 to 3 teaspoons chili powder
1 package (8-1/2 ounces) cornbread mix

1. Preheat oven to 400°F. In 12-inch skillet, brown ground beef and onion over medium-high heat; drain. Stir in Ragú Cheese Creations! Sauce, beans, corn and chili powder.

2. Meanwhile, prepare cornbread mix according to package directions. Do not bake.

3. In ungreased 2-quart baking dish, spread ground beef mixture. Top with cornbread mixture. Bake, uncovered, 20 minutes or until toothpick inserted in center of cornbread comes out clean and top is golden.
Makes 6 servings

Roast Turkey Breast with Apple-Cornbread Stuffing

    Nonstick cooking spray
1 medium onion, chopped
1-1/4 cups chicken broth
1 package (8 ounces) cornbread stuffing mix
1 Granny Smith apple, diced
3/4 teaspoon dried sage, divided
3/4 teaspoon dried thyme leaves, divided
1 boneless turkey breast (1-1/2 pounds)
1 teaspoon paprika
1/4 teaspoon black pepper
1 cup whole-berry cranberry sauce (optional)

1. Preheat oven to 450°F. Spray 1-1/2-quart casserole with cooking spray; set aside.

2. Spray large saucepan with cooking spray; heat over medium heat. Add chopped onion; cook and stir 5 minutes. Add chicken broth; bring to a simmer. Stir in cornbread stuffing mix, diced apple, 1/4 teaspoon dried sage and 1/4 teaspoon dried thyme. Transfer mixture to prepared casserole; set aside.

3. Spray shallow roasting pan with cooking spray. Place turkey breast in pan, skin side up; coat with cooking spray. Combine paprika, remaining 1/2 teaspoon dried sage, 1/2 teaspoon dried thyme and black pepper in small bowl; sprinkle over turkey. Spray lightly with cooking spray.

4. Place turkey in preheated oven; roast 15 minutes. *Reduce oven temperature to 350°F.* Place stuffing in oven alongside turkey; continue to roast 35 minutes or until internal temperature of turkey reaches 170°F when tested with meat thermometer inserted into thickest part of breast.

5. Transfer turkey to cutting board; cover with foil and let stand 10 to 15 minutes before carving. (Internal temperature will rise 5°F to 10°F during stand time.)

6. Remove stuffing from oven; cover to keep warm. Carve turkey into thin slices; serve immediately with stuffing and cranberry sauce, if desired.
Makes 6 servings

Fish with Hidden Valley Ranch®
Tartar Sauce

Old-Fashioned Beef Stew

(Pictured at right)

1 tablespoon CRISCO® Oil*
1-1/4 pounds boneless beef round steak, trimmed and cut into 1-inch cubes
2-3/4 cups water, divided
1 teaspoon Worcestershire sauce
2 bay leaves
1 clove garlic, minced
1/2 teaspoon paprika
1/4 teaspoon pepper
8 medium carrots, quartered
8 small potatoes, peeled and quartered
4 small onions, quartered
1 package (9 ounces) frozen cut green beans
1 tablespoon cornstarch
Salt (optional)

Use your favorite Crisco Oil product.

1. Heat oil in Dutch oven on medium-high heat. Add beef. Cook and stir until browned. Add 1-1/2 cups water, Worcestershire sauce, bay leaves, garlic, paprika and pepper. Bring to a boil. Reduce heat to low. Cover. Simmer 1 hour 15 minutes, stirring occasionally. Remove and discard bay leaves.

2. Add carrots, potatoes and onions. Cover. Simmer 30 to 45 minutes or until vegetables are almost tender. Add beans. Simmer 5 minutes or until tender. Remove from heat. Add 1 cup water to Dutch oven.

3. Combine cornstarch and remaining 1/4 cup water in small bowl. Stir well. Stir into ingredients in Dutch oven. Return to low heat. Cook and stir until thickened. Season with salt, if desired.

Makes 8 servings

Apricot Glazed Chicken

1 roasting chicken (4 to 5 pounds)
1 cup seedless red or green grapes
4 tablespoons honey, divided
1 can (15 ounces) apricot halves, divided
1/4 cup butter or margarine, melted
2 teaspoons seasoned salt
1/4 teaspoon pepper
1/2 cup dry white wine or chicken broth
Grape clusters and fresh herbs for garnish (optional)

Pat chicken dry with paper towels. Toss 1 cup grapes with 2 tablespoons honey in small bowl. Place grapes in body cavity. Tie legs close to body and fold wing tips back or secure with skewers or cotton string. Place chicken, breast side up, on rack in roasting pan.

Drain apricot halves, reserving syrup. Set aside 6 halves for garnish. Purée remaining apricots in blender or food processor with melted butter, seasoned salt, pepper and remaining 2 tablespoons honey. Brush over chicken. Pour wine and 1/4 cup apricot syrup in bottom of pan. Cover chicken loosely with tented foil.

Roast at 350°F 1-3/4 to 2 hours or until chicken is tender and thermometer inserted in thigh registers 180°F. Baste occasionally with pan drippings to glaze. Remove foil during last 30 minutes of roasting. Bring apricot mixture to a boil in small saucepan over medium heat. Boil 1 to 2 minutes. Serve chicken on platter with apricot sauce, garnished with clusters of grapes, apricot halves and fresh herbs, if desired.

Makes 6 to 8 servings

Favorite recipe from **National Honey Board**

Italian Pasta Bake

1 pound ground beef *or* Italian sausage
4 cups cooked mostaccioli *or* penne pasta
1 jar (28 to 30 ounces) spaghetti sauce (about 2-3/4 cups)
3/4 cup KRAFT® 100% Grated Parmesan Cheese, divided
2 cups KRAFT® Shredded Low-Moisture Part-Skim Mozzarella Cheese

BROWN meat in large skillet; drain.

STIR in mostaccioli, spaghetti sauce and 1/2 cup of the Parmesan cheese. Spoon into 13×9-inch baking dish. Top with mozzarella cheese and remaining 1/4 cup Parmesan cheese.

BAKE, uncovered, at 375°F for 20 minutes.

Makes 6 servings

Campbell's® Turkey Stuffing Divan

(Pictured at right)

1-1/4 cups boiling water
    4 tablespoons margarine or butter, melted
    4 cups PEPPERIDGE FARM® Herb Seasoned
       Stuffing
    2 cups cooked broccoli cuts
    2 cups cubed cooked turkey
    1 can (10-3/4 ounces) CAMPBELL'S® Condensed
       Cream of Celery Soup *or* 98% Fat Free
       Cream of Celery Soup
1/2 cup milk
    1 cup shredded Cheddar cheese (4 ounces)

1. Mix water and margarine. Add stuffing. Mix lightly.

2. Spoon into 2-quart shallow baking dish. Arrange broccoli and turkey over stuffing. In small bowl mix soup, milk and *1/2 cup* cheese. Pour over broccoli and turkey. Sprinkle remaining cheese over soup mixture.

3. Bake at 350°F. for 30 minutes or until hot.

Makes 6 servings

Variation: Substitute 1 can (10-3/4 ounces) CAMPBELL'S® Condensed Cream of Chicken Soup *or* 98% Fat Free Cream of Chicken Soup for Cream of Celery Soup. Substitute 2 cups cubed cooked chicken for turkey.

Tip: For 2 cups cooked broccoli cuts use about 1 pound fresh broccoli, trimmed, cut into 1-inch pieces (about 2 cups) *or* 1 package (10 ounces) frozen broccoli cuts (2 cups).

Mediterranean Cod

    1 bag (16 ounces) BIRDS EYE® frozen Farm Fresh
       Mixtures Broccoli, Green Beans, Pearl
       Onions and Red Peppers
    1 can (14-1/2 ounces) stewed tomatoes
1/2 teaspoon dried basil leaves
    1 pound cod fillets, cut into serving pieces
1/2 cup orange juice, divided
    2 tablespoons all-purpose flour
1/4 cup sliced black olives (optional)

• Combine vegetables, tomatoes and basil in large skillet. Bring to boil over medium-high heat.

• Place cod on vegetables. Pour 1/4 cup orange juice over fish. Cover and cook 5 to 7 minutes or until fish is tender and flakes with fork.

• Remove cod and keep warm. Combine flour with remaining 1/4 cup orange juice until smooth; stir into skillet. Cook until liquid is thickened and vegetables are coated.

• Serve fish with vegetables; sprinkle with olives.

Makes about 4 servings

Serving Suggestion: Serve with rice or couscous.

Pork Chops Dijon

    4 boneless pork chops (1-1/4 inches thick)
1/2 teaspoon salt
1/2 teaspoon freshly ground pepper
    2 tablespoons CRISCO® Oil*
1/2 cup finely chopped onion
    2 teaspoons jarred minced garlic *or* 1 large clove
       garlic, peeled and minced
1/2 cup dry white wine, beef stock or beef broth
    1 cup brown gravy
    3 tablespoons sweet pickle relish
    2 tablespoons Dijon mustard
    2 teaspoons cornstarch
    2 tablespoons cold water

Use your favorite Crisco Oil product.

1. Trim fat from pork chops. Sprinkle with salt and pepper. Heat oil in 10- or 12-inch skillet on medium heat. Add chops. Brown well on both sides. Remove chops from pan.

2. Add onion and garlic to pan. Cook on medium heat 3 minutes, or until onion is translucent. Add wine, gravy, relish and mustard to skillet. Stir well. Return chops to pan. Bring to boil. Reduce heat to low. Cook chops, covered, 20 to 30 minutes, or until tender.

3. Mix cornstarch with water. Add mixture to gravy. Simmer 2 minutes, or until lightly thickened. Serve immediately. *Makes 4 servings*

Note: This dish can be prepared up to two days in advance and refrigerated, tightly covered. Reheat on low heat until hot. The same sauce works well with chicken breast halves, thighs or drumsticks.

Campbell's® Turkey Stuffing Divan

Cheese-Stuffed Meat Loaf

(Pictured below)

1-1/2 pounds ground beef
1 jar (26 to 28 ounces) RAGÚ® Chunky
   Gardenstyle Pasta Sauce
1 large egg, lightly beaten
1/4 cup plain dry bread crumbs
   Salt and pepper to taste
2 cups shredded mozzarella cheese (about
   8 ounces)
1 tablespoon finely chopped fresh parsley

1. Preheat oven to 350°F. In large bowl, combine ground beef, 1/3 cup Ragú Pasta Sauce, egg and bread crumbs. Season, if desired, with salt and ground black pepper. In 13×9-inch baking or roasting pan, shape into 12×8-inch rectangle.

2. Sprinkle 1-1/2 cups cheese and parsley down center leaving 3/4-inch border. Roll, starting at long end, jelly-roll style. Press ends together to seal.

3. Bake, uncovered, 45 minutes. Pour remaining sauce over meat loaf and sprinkle with remaining 1/2 cup cheese. Bake an additional 15 minutes or

Cheese-Stuffed Meat Loaf

until sauce is heated through and cheese is melted. Let stand 5 minutes before serving. Garnish as desired. *Makes 6 servings*

Tip: Molding the meat mixture onto waxed paper helps make rolling easier. Just lift waxed paper to curl the meat over cheese filling, then carefully remove meat from paper. Continue rolling in this manner until filling is enclosed in roll and meat is off paper.

Turkey Picadillo

1 tablespoon vegetable oil
1 large onion, chopped
2 cloves garlic, minced
1 pound ground turkey
1 can (14-1/2 ounces) diced tomatoes,
   undrained
1/3 cup golden raisins
3 to 4 tablespoons *Frank's*® *RedHot*® Cayenne
   Pepper Sauce
1 tablespoon balsamic vinegar
1/2 teaspoon dried oregano leaves
1/8 teaspoon ground cinnamon
1/3 cup blanched slivered almonds, chopped
1/4 cup chopped fresh parsley
   Shredded lettuce (optional)

1. Heat oil in large nonstick skillet over medium-high heat. Add onion and garlic; cook and stir until tender. Add turkey; cook and stir until no longer pink.

2. Add tomatoes with liquid, raisins, **Frank's RedHot** Sauce, vinegar, oregano and cinnamon to turkey mixture. Bring to a boil. Reduce heat to low; cook, uncovered, 15 minutes or until thickened and most of liquid is absorbed, stirring occasionally. Stir in almonds and parsley.

3. Spoon turkey mixture over bed of shredded lettuce, if desired. Serve with sour cream, cheddar cheese, chopped green onions and red bell peppers, if desired. *Makes 4 main-dish servings*

Tip: Serve this delicious turkey dish with rice, red beans and tortilla chips. It also makes a wonderful filling for tacos.

Swanson® Teriyaki Pork Kabobs

Swanson® Teriyaki Pork Kabobs

(Pictured above)

- 2 tablespoons cornstarch
- 1 can (14 ounces) SWANSON® Beef Broth
- 2 tablespoons soy sauce
- 1 tablespoon packed brown sugar
- 1/4 teaspoon garlic powder *or* 2 cloves garlic, minced
- 1/4 teaspoon ground ginger
- 1 pound boneless pork loin, cut into 1-inch cubes
- 12 medium mushrooms
- 1 large red onion, cut into 12 wedges
- 4 cherry tomatoes
- 4 cups hot cooked rice

MIX cornstarch, broth, soy, brown sugar, garlic and ginger in saucepan. Cook and stir until mixture boils and thickens.

THREAD alternately pork, mushrooms and onion on 4 long skewers.

GRILL or broil kabobs 20 minutes or until done, turning and brushing often with broth mixture. Place a tomato on each skewer.

HEAT remaining broth mixture to a boil. Serve with kabobs and rice.   *Makes 4 servings*

Helpful Hint

Cornstarch has about twice the thickening ability of flour. In order to avoid lumps when using cornstarch as a thickener, it should be mixed with a cold liquid until smooth before cooking or adding it to a hot liquid.

Campbell's® Chicken & Broccoli Alfredo

(Pictured at right)

1/2 package *uncooked* linguine (8 ounces)
1 cup fresh or frozen broccoli flowerets
2 tablespoons butter or margarine
1 pound skinless, boneless chicken breasts, cubed
1 can (10-3/4 ounces) CAMPBELL'S® Condensed Cream of Mushroom Soup *or* 98% Fat Free Cream of Mushroom Soup
1/2 cup milk
1/2 cup grated Parmesan cheese
1/4 teaspoon freshly ground pepper

1. Prepare linguine according to package directions. Add broccoli for last 4 minutes of cooking time.

2. In medium skillet over medium-high heat, heat butter. Add chicken and cook until browned, stirring often. Drain.

3. Add soup, milk, cheese, pepper and linguine mixture and cook through, stirring occasionally. Serve with additional Parmesan cheese.

Makes 4 servings

Turkey Tenderloin with Mushroom Sauce

1 package BUTTERBALL® Fresh Boneless Turkey Breast Tenderloins, use 1 tenderloin, cut into 1/2-inch-thick slices
1 tablespoon butter or margarine
4 ounces fresh mushrooms, sliced
1/2 small onion, minced
1 cup chicken broth, divided
1 tablespoon cornstarch
1-1/2 teaspoons tomato paste
1 tablespoon chopped parsley
Salt and black pepper

Melt butter in large nonstick skillet over medium heat. Brown tenderloin slices in skillet about 5 minutes, turning frequently. Add mushrooms and onion; cook 3 minutes. Add 1/2 cup chicken broth; cover and simmer about 5 minutes. Combine cornstarch, remaining 1/2 cup chicken broth and tomato paste; pour into skillet; stir to blend. Cook and stir until thickened. Stir in parsley. Add salt and pepper to taste.

Makes 2 servings

Wild Rice Shrimp Paella

1-1/2 cups canned chicken broth
2 tablespoons butter or margarine
1/16 teaspoon saffron or 1/8 teaspoon turmeric
2 boxes UNCLE BEN'S® Butter & Herb Fast Cook Recipe Long Grain & Wild Rice
1 pound uncooked medium shrimp, peeled and deveined
1 can (14-1/2 ounces) diced tomatoes, undrained
1 cup frozen green peas, thawed
2 jars (6 ounces each) marinated artichoke hearts, drained

1. Combine broth, butter, saffron and contents of seasoning packets, reserving rice, in large saucepan. Bring to a boil.

2. Add shrimp; cook over medium-high heat 2 minutes or until shrimp turn pink. Remove shrimp with slotted spoon and set aside.

3. Add tomatoes and reserved rice. Bring to a boil. Cover; reduce heat and simmer 15 minutes.

4. Stir in peas; cover and cook 5 minutes. Add artichoke hearts and reserved shrimp; cover and cook 5 minutes or until hot and rice is tender. Stand 3 minutes before serving.

Makes 6 servings

Confetti Pineapple Baked Ham Steak

1 pound ready-to-serve ham steak
1 can (8 ounces) crushed pineapple, drained
1 cup diced red or green bell peppers
3 tablespoons *French's®* Sweet & Tangy Honey Mustard
2 tablespoons lightly packed brown sugar
1/16 teaspoon ground cloves
Hot cooked rice

1. Preheat oven to 425°F. Score edge of ham steak. Place in 2-quart baking dish. Combine remaining ingredients in small bowl. Spoon pineapple mixture on top of ham steak.

2. Bake, uncovered, 20 minutes or until hot and bubbly. Serve with hot cooked rice, if desired.

Makes 4 servings

Campbell's® Chicken & Broccoli Alfredo

Shepherd's Pie

(Pictured at right)

1-1/3 cups instant mashed potato buds
1-2/3 cups milk
   2 tablespoons margarine or butter
   1 teaspoon salt, divided
   1 pound ground beef
1/4 teaspoon black pepper
   1 jar (12 ounces) beef gravy
   1 package (10 ounces) frozen mixed vegetables, thawed and drained
3/4 cup grated Parmesan cheese

1. Preheat broiler. Prepare 4 servings of mashed potatoes according to package directions using milk, margarine and 1/2 teaspoon salt.

2. While mashed potatoes are cooking, brown meat in medium broilerproof skillet over medium-high heat, stirring to separate meat. Drain drippings. Sprinkle meat with pepper and remaining 1/2 teaspoon salt. Add gravy and vegetables; mix well. Cook over medium-low heat 5 minutes or until hot.

3. Spoon prepared potatoes around outside edge of skillet, leaving 3-inch circle in center. Sprinkle cheese evenly over potatoes. Broil 4 to 5 inches from heat source 3 minutes or until cheese is golden brown and meat mixture is bubbly.

Makes 4 servings

Chicken Fajitas

1/4 cup orange juice
   2 tablespoons lime juice
   2 tablespoons lemon juice
   1 clove garlic, minced
   4 boneless skinless chicken breast halves (about 1-1/2 pounds)
   1 teaspoon chili powder
1/2 teaspoon salt
   1 tablespoon vegetable oil
   1 medium-size red bell pepper, cut into strips
   1 medium-size green bell pepper, cut into strips
   1 medium-size yellow bell pepper, cut into strips
   1 medium onion, sliced
 10 flour tortillas, warmed
   1 cup sour cream
   1 cup salsa
   1 can (2-1/4 ounces) sliced black olives, drained

Combine orange juice, lime juice, lemon juice and garlic in large bowl. Season chicken with chili powder and salt. Place chicken in juice mixture, turning to coat. Cover; marinate in refrigerator 30 minutes. Remove chicken. Place marinade in small saucepan. Bring to a rolling boil over medium-high heat; keep warm. Place chicken on broiler rack or grill about 6 inches from heat. Broil or grill, turning and basting with marinade, 10 minutes or until no longer pink in center. Heat oil in large skillet over medium-high heat until hot. Add peppers and onion; cook and stir about 5 minutes or until onion is tender. Slice chicken into strips; add to pepper-onion mixture. Divide chicken-pepper mixture evenly in centers of tortillas. Roll up tortillas; top each with dollop of sour cream, salsa and olives.

Makes 5 servings (2 fajitas each)

Favorite recipe from **National Chicken Council**

Bistro Steak with Mushrooms

1-1/2 to 2 pounds boneless beef sirloin steak (1-1/2 inches thick)
   2 cups sliced mushrooms
   1 can (10-3/4 ounces) condensed golden mushroom soup
1/2 cup dry red wine or beef broth
   3 tablespoons *French's*® Worcestershire Sauce

1. Rub sides of steak with *1/4 teaspoon pepper*. Heat *1 tablespoon oil* over medium-high heat in nonstick skillet. Cook steak about 5 minutes per side for medium-rare or to desired doneness. Transfer steak to platter.

2. Stir-fry mushrooms in same skillet in *1 tablespoon oil* until browned. Stir in soup, wine, Worcestershire and *1/4 cup water*. Bring to a boil. Simmer, stirring, 3 minutes. Return steak and juices to skillet. Cook until heated through. Serve with mashed potatoes, if desired.
Makes 6 servings

Shepherd's Pie

Tex-Mex Stir-Fry

(Pictured at right)

1 package (1.27 ounces) LAWRY'S® Spices
     & Seasonings for Fajitas
1/3 cup water
2 tablespoons vegetable oil, divided
1-1/2 cups broccoli florets
2 carrots, thinly sliced diagonally
1 red or green bell pepper, thinly sliced
1/2 cup thinly sliced celery
1 pound medium shrimp, peeled and deveined
4-1/2 teaspoons brown sugar
1 teaspoon ground ginger
1 teaspoon dry mustard

In small bowl, combine Spices & Seasonings for
Fajitas and water; set aside. In large skillet or wok,
heat 1 tablespoon oil. Add broccoli, carrots, bell
pepper and celery and stir-fry over medium-high
heat 3 minutes. Remove; set aside. Add remaining
1 tablespoon oil and shrimp to same hot skillet;
stir-fry over medium-high heat 3 minutes. Add
vegetables back to skillet. Pour in Spices &
Seasonings for Fajitas mixture, brown sugar, ginger
and mustard. Cook additional 2 minutes longer,
tossing gently to blend.   *Makes 6 servings*

Serving Suggestion: Serve over hot cooked rice and
garnish with sliced almonds, if desired.

Beef Tenderloin with Dijon-Cream Sauce

2 tablespoons olive oil
3 tablespoons balsamic vinegar*
1 beef tenderloin roast (about 1-1/2 to
     2 pounds)
Salt
4-1/2 teaspoons white peppercorns
4-1/2 teaspoons black peppercorns
3 tablespoons mustard seeds
Dijon-Cream Sauce (recipe follows)

*Substitute 2 tablespoons red wine vinegar plus 1-1/2 teaspoons
sugar for the balsamic vinegar.*

Combine oil and vinegar in a cup; rub onto beef.
Season generously with salt. Let stand 15 minutes.
Meanwhile, coarsely crush peppercorns and
mustard seeds in a blender or food processor or by
hand with a mortar and pestle. Roll beef in crushed
mixture, pressing it into the surface to coat.

Coat grill rack with nonstick cooking spray before
starting the grill. Grill beef, on a covered grill, over
medium KINGSFORD® Briquets, 16 to 24 minutes
(depending on size and thickness) until a meat
thermometer inserted in the center almost registers
150°F for medium-rare. (Cook until 160°F for
medium or 170°F well-done; add another 5 minutes
for every 10°F.) Turn halfway through cooking. Let
stand 5 to 10 minutes before slicing. Slice and serve
with a few spoonfuls of sauce.   *Makes 6 servings*

Dijon-Cream Sauce

1 can (14-1/2 ounces) beef broth
1 cup whipping cream
2 tablespoons butter, softened
4-1/2 to 6 teaspoons Dijon mustard
3 to 4-1/2 teaspoons balsamic vinegar*
     Coarsely crushed black peppercorns and
     mustard seeds for garnish

*Substitute 2 teaspoons red wine vinegar plus 1 teaspoon sugar for
the balsamic vinegar.*

Bring beef broth and whipping cream to a boil in a
saucepan. Boil gently until reduced to about 1 cup;
sauce will be thick enough to coat a spoon. Remove
from heat; stir in the butter, a little at a time, until
completely melted. Stir in the mustard and vinegar,
adjusting amounts to taste. Sprinkle with the
peppercorns and mustard seeds.

Makes about 1 cup

Creamy Pasta Primavera

1 bag (16 ounces) BIRDS EYE® frozen Pasta
     Secrets Primavera
1/2 cup milk
2 packages (3 ounces each) cream cheese, cubed
1 cup cubed cooked ham
1/4 cup grated Parmesan cheese

• In large skillet, heat Pasta Secrets in milk over
medium heat to a simmer; cover and simmer 7 to
9 minutes or until vegetables are tender.

• Add cream cheese; reduce heat to low and cook
until cream cheese is melted, stirring often.

• Stir in ham and Parmesan cheese; cover and cook
5 minutes more.   *Makes 4 servings*

Tex-Mex Stir-Fry

Pork Chop with Orange-Radish Relish

Pork Chops with Orange-Radish Relish

(Pictured above)

    2 cups orange juice
1/3 cup lime juice
1/3 cup packed brown sugar
    3 medium oranges, peeled, seeded and cut into
        1/4-inch pieces
1/4 cup chopped red onion
1/4 cup diced radishes
    2 tablespoons finely chopped fresh cilantro
    6 bone-in pork chops (about 3/4 inch thick)
        Salt and black pepper
        Orange curls and radishes for garnish

Combine both juices and brown sugar in saucepan. Cook mixture at a low boil, stirring often, about 20 minutes until reduced to about 1/2 cup and it has a syrup consistency. Set aside 1/4 cup sauce for basting.

Meanwhile, prepare Orange-Radish Relish by combining oranges, onion and diced radishes in colander or strainer and drain well; transfer to bowl.

Add cilantro and gently stir in remaining orange syrup. Season pork with salt and pepper.

Oil hot grid to help prevent sticking. Grill pork, on covered grill, over medium KINGSFORD® Briquets, 7 to 10 minutes. (Pork is done at 160°F.) Halfway through cooking, turn chops and brush with reserved 1/4 cup orange syrup. Serve with Orange-Radish Relish. Garnish with orange curls and radishes.   *Makes 6 servings*

Sautéed Turkey with Spring Vegetables

    1 pound turkey cutlets or 1/4-inch-thick turkey
        breast slices, cut into 1-inch-wide strips
1/2 teaspoon dried tarragon leaves, divided
1/2 teaspoon dried thyme leaves
1/2 teaspoon salt
1/4 teaspoon freshly ground black pepper
    2 tablespoons CRISCO® Oil*
    2 bunches green onions, trimmed and sliced into
        1/2-inch pieces
    2 large carrots, peeled and cut into 1/2-inch
        slices
    2 tablespoons all-purpose flour
    1 can (14 ounces) chicken stock or broth
        (1-3/4 cups)
1/4 cup dry white wine or additional chicken stock
    1 cup fresh or frozen peas

Use your favorite Crisco Oil product.

1. Pat turkey dry. Sprinkle with 1/4 teaspoon tarragon, thyme, salt and pepper.

2. Heat oil in large skillet on medium-high heat. Add turkey. Sauté 2 minutes, or until outside is no longer pink. Remove from skillet with slotted spoon. Set aside. Add green onions and carrots to skillet. Sauté 3 minutes. Reduce heat to low. Stir in flour and remaining tarragon. Stir 1 minute.

3. Add stock and wine to skillet. Stir well. Increase heat to medium-high. Boil 10 minutes, or until carrots are tender and sauce has thickened. Add turkey and peas. Simmer 5 minutes, or until turkey is no longer pink in center. Serve immediately.
                      Makes 4 servings

Note: Boneless, skinless chicken breast pounded to even 1/4-inch thickness can be substituted for turkey.

Hearty Lasagna Rolls

(Pictured below)

1-1/2 pounds ground beef
   1 cup chopped fresh mushrooms
   1 medium onion, finely chopped
   1 small carrot, finely chopped
   1 clove garlic, finely chopped
  1/4 cup dry red wine or beef broth
  1/8 teaspoon cayenne pepper (optional)
   2 cups shredded mozzarella cheese
   1 egg, lightly beaten
   5 tablespoons grated Parmesan cheese, divided
   1 jar (1 pound 10 ounces) RAGÚ® Robusto! Pasta Sauce
  12 ounces lasagna noodles, cooked and drained

Preheat oven to 350°F. In 12-inch skillet, brown ground beef over medium-high heat; drain. Stir in mushrooms, onion, carrot and garlic; cook and stir over medium heat until vegetables are tender. Stir in wine and cayenne pepper; cook over high heat 3 minutes. Remove from heat; stand 10 minutes.

In medium bowl, thoroughly combine ground beef mixture, mozzarella cheese, egg and 2 tablespoons Parmesan cheese. In 13×9-inch baking dish, evenly pour 2 cups Ragú® Robusto! Pasta Sauce. Evenly spread 1/3 cup ground beef filling over each lasagna noodle. Carefully roll up noodles. Place seam-side-down in baking dish. Evenly spread remaining sauce over lasagna rolls. Bake, covered, 40 minutes. Sprinkle with remaining 3 tablespoons Parmesan cheese and bake, uncovered, 5 minutes or until bubbling.

Makes 6 servings

Campbell's® Cheeseburger Pasta

   1 pound ground beef
   1 can CAMPBELL'S® Cheddar Cheese Soup
   1 can (10-3/4 ounces) CAMPBELL'S® Tomato Soup
1-1/2 cups water
   2 cups *uncooked* medium shell pasta

COOK beef in skillet until browned. Pour off fat.

ADD soups, water and pasta. Heat to a boil. Cook over medium heat 10 minutes or until done, stirring often.

Makes 4 servings

Hearty Lasagna Rolls

Veggie Calzones

(Pictured at right)

1-1/2 cups BIRDS EYE® frozen Farm Fresh Mixtures Broccoli, Red Peppers, Onions & Mushrooms
1/2 cup ricotta cheese
1/2 cup shredded mozzarella cheese
1/4 cup grated Parmesan cheese
1 teaspoon dried Italian seasoning
1/4 teaspoon pepper
1 pound fresh pizza dough or thawed frozen bread dough
1 egg, beaten

• Preheat oven to 425°F.

• Rinse vegetables under warm water to thaw; drain well and pat gently with paper towel.

• In medium bowl, combine vegetables, cheeses, Italian seasoning and pepper.

• Divide dough into 4 pieces. Roll out each piece into 6-inch circle.* Spoon 1/4 of vegetable mixture over 1/2 of each circle, leaving 1/2-inch border. Moisten edge of dough with water; fold dough over filling to form half circle. Pinch edges well to seal. Cut several slits in top of dough; brush with egg.

• Place on greased baking sheet and bake 12 to 14 minutes or until golden brown. Serve with chunky tomato sauce and fresh fruit, if desired.

Makes 4 servings

*Dough is easier to work with on nonfloured surface.

Tuna and Broccoli Bake

1 (16-ounce) package frozen broccoli cuts, thawed and well drained
2 slices bread, cut in 1/2-inch cubes
1 (7-ounce) pouch of STARKIST® Premium Albacore or Chunk Light Tuna
3 eggs
2 cups cottage cheese
1 cup shredded cheddar cheese
1/4 teaspoon ground black pepper

Place broccoli on bottom of 2-quart baking dish. Top with bread cubes and tuna. In medium bowl, combine eggs, cottage cheese, cheddar cheese and pepper. Spread evenly over tuna mixture. Bake in 400°F oven 30 minutes or until golden brown and puffed.

Makes 4 servings

Peach-Glazed Virginia Ham

GLAZED HAM
1 (8-pound) smoked Virginia ham (shank end)
1/2 cup peach preserves
1 tablespoon coarse-grained mustard
3/4 teaspoon TABASCO® brand Pepper Sauce
1/8 teaspoon ground cloves

PEACH-CORN PICCALILLI
3 large ripe peaches
1 tablespoon vegetable oil
1 medium red bell pepper, seeded and diced
1/4 cup sliced green onions
1 (15-1/4-ounce) can whole kernel corn, drained
2 tablespoons brown sugar
2 tablespoons cider vinegar
1 teaspoon TABASCO® brand Pepper Sauce
1/4 teaspoon salt

Heat oven to 325°F. Remove skin from ham; trim off any excess fat. Score fat 1/4 inch deep in 1-inch diamonds. Place ham, fat side up, in roasting pan. Insert ovenproof meat thermometer into thickest part of ham, not touching the bone. Bake 1-1/2 hours until thermometer reaches 135°F.

Meanwhile, prepare glaze. Mix peach preserves, mustard, TABASCO® Sauce and cloves in small bowl. Remove ham from oven, maintaining oven temperature; brush with peach glaze. Bake 20 minutes longer or until the temperature reaches 160°F.

Meanwhile, prepare Peach-Corn Piccalilli. Cut peaches in half and remove pits. Chop two of the peach halves; set aside. Heat oil in 2-quart saucepan over medium heat. Add red pepper and green onions. Cook 3 minutes, stirring frequently. Add corn, brown sugar, vinegar, TABASCO® Sauce and salt. Heat to boiling; stir in chopped peaches. Reduce heat to low; cover and simmer 5 minutes or until peaches are just tender.

To serve, arrange ham on a large platter. Fill remaining peach halves with Peach-Corn Piccalilli and arrange around ham on platter.

Makes 8 to 12 servings

Veggie Calzone

Stir-Fried Scallops with Vegetables

(Pictured at right)

1 pound sea scallops
1/4 teaspoon salt
1/8 teaspoon black pepper
1 tablespoon cornstarch
1/2 cup vegetable broth
3 tablespoons butter or margarine, divided
1 package (6 ounces) red radishes, quartered
1/4 cup dry white wine or additional vegetable broth
1 package (6 ounces) frozen snow peas, partially thawed
1/2 cup sliced bamboo shoots
Hot cooked couscous

1. Rinse scallops and pat dry with paper towels. Sprinkle with salt and black pepper.

2. Combine cornstarch and broth in cup until smooth; set aside.

3. Heat wok over high heat about 1 minute or until hot. Add 1-1/2 tablespoons butter; swirl to coat bottom and heat 30 seconds. Arrange half the scallops in single layer in wok, leaving 1/2 inch between. (Scallops should not touch.) Cook scallops until browned on both sides. Remove scallops to large bowl. Repeat with remaining 1-1/2 tablespoons butter and scallops. Reduce heat to medium-high.

4. Add radishes to wok; stir-fry about 1 minute or until crisp-tender. Remove radishes to bowl with scallops.

5. Add wine or additional broth to wok. Stir cornstarch mixture; add to wok. Add snow peas and bamboo shoots; cook and stir until heated through.

6. Return scallops and radishes to wok; cook until scallops are firm and opaque. Serve over couscous. Garnish as desired. *Makes 4 servings*

Pizza Hot Dish

1-1/2 to 2 pounds ground beef
1/4 cup chopped onion
1 package (12 ounces) egg noodles
2 jars (15 ounces each) pizza sauce
1 can (10-3/4 ounces) condensed cheddar cheese soup
2 cups (8 ounces) shredded mozzarella cheese

1. In large skillet, brown ground beef with onion. Drain.

2. Prepare noodles according to package directions.

3. Add sauce, soup and cooked egg noodles to ground beef; mix well. Spoon into 13×9-inch baking pan or large casserole. Bake, covered, at 350°F for 30 minutes. Sprinkle with mozzarella cheese and bake, uncovered, an additional 15 minutes.
Makes 8 to 12 servings

Favorite recipe from **North Dakota Beef Commission**

Pork Schnitzel

4 boneless pork chops, 1/4 inch thick (3 ounces each)
1/2 cup cornflake crumbs or cracker crumbs
1 egg, lightly beaten
Pepper to taste
2 to 4 teaspoons olive oil, divided
1/3 cup lemon juice
1/4 cup chicken broth

1. Preheat oven to 200°F. Place baking sheet in oven. Trim fat from pork chops; discard. Place pork chops between layers of waxed paper; pound with smooth side of mallet to 1/8- to 1/4-inch thickness. Place crumbs in medium bowl. Dip 1 pork chop at a time in egg; gently shake off excess. Dip in crumbs to coat both sides. Place breaded pork chops in single layer on plate. Sprinkle with pepper.

2. Heat 2 teaspoons oil in large skillet over medium-high heat until hot. Add pork chops in single layer. Cook 1 minute or until golden brown on bottom. Turn and cook 1/2 to 1 minute or until golden brown and pork is no longer pink in center. Transfer to baking sheet in oven. Repeat to cook remaining pork chops, adding oil as needed to prevent meat from sticking to pan. Transfer to baking sheet in oven.

3. Remove skillet from heat. Add lemon juice and broth. Stir to scrape cooked bits from skillet bottom. Return to heat; bring to a boil, stirring constantly, until liquid is reduced to 3 to 4 tablespoons. Remove baking sheet from oven. Pour sauce over meat. *Makes 4 servings*

Stir-Fried Scallops with Vegetables

Roman Holiday

8 ounces BARILLA® Penne
1 tablespoon olive oil
8 ounces fresh mushrooms (such as portobello), trimmed and coarsely chopped
1 jar (26 ounces) BARILLA® Mushroom and Garlic Pasta Sauce
8 ounces Italian sausage, cooked and crumbled
2 tablespoons chopped flat leaf parsley
2 tablespoons grated Romano cheese

1. Cook penne according to package directions; drain.

2. Meanwhile, add olive oil to large skillet. Add mushrooms; cook over high heat until browned.

3. Reduce heat; stir in pasta sauce and cooked sausage. Cook 5 minutes.

4. Pour sauce over hot drained penne; sprinkle with parsley and cheese.   *Makes 6 to 8 servings*

30-Minute Chili Mac

30-Minute Chili Mac

(Pictured below left)

1 (1-pound) beef top round steak, cut into 1/4-inch-thick strips
1/2 cup chopped onion
1 tablespoon vegetable oil
1 (16-ounce) can whole tomatoes, undrained, coarsely chopped
1/2 cup A.1.® Original or A.1.® BOLD & SPICY Steak Sauce
2 tablespoons chili powder
1 cup uncooked elbow macaroni, cooked, drained
1 cup drained canned kidney beans, optional
1/3 cup shredded cheddar cheese (about 1-1/2 ounces)
1/4 cup chopped fresh cilantro

In large skillet, over medium heat, cook steak and onion in oil 8 to 10 minutes, stirring occasionally. Stir in tomatoes with liquid, steak sauce and chili powder. Heat to a boil; reduce heat. Cover; simmer 10 minutes or until steak is tender. Stir in macaroni and beans, if desired. Sprinkle with cheese and cilantro. Serve immediately.   *Makes 4 servings*

Fresh Herb Baked Drumsticks

8 TYSON® Individually Fresh Frozen® Chicken Drumsticks
1/4 cup chicken broth
1/4 cup wine vinegar
2 tablespoons corn oil
2 tablespoons chopped fresh parsley
2 tablespoons chopped fresh chives
1/2 teaspoon chopped fresh thyme
1/2 teaspoon chopped fresh marjoram
1/2 teaspoon salt
1/4 teaspoon coarsely ground black pepper
1/4 teaspoon ground cumin

PREP: Preheat oven to 400°F. Line 13×9-inch baking pan with foil; spray with nonstick cooking spray. CLEAN: Wash hands. Remove protective ice glaze from frozen chicken by holding under cool running water 1 to 2 minutes. Arrange chicken in single layer in prepared pan. CLEAN: Wash hands.

COOK: Bake 20 minutes; drain and discard juices. Combine remaining ingredients. Pour mixture over chicken. Bake 20 minutes. Turn chicken over and baste with juices. Bake 15 to 20 minutes or until

Peachy Pecan Ham

internal juices of chicken run clear. (Or insert instant-read meat thermometer in thickest part of chicken. Temperature should read 180°F.)

SERVE: Serve with mashed potatoes and green beans, if desired.

CHILL: Refrigerate leftovers immediately.

Makes 4 servings

Helpful Hint

Fresh herbs are used to enhance the flavor of food. The flavor in herbs comes from aromatic essential oils that are released by chopping or heating. When herbs are dried these oils become concentrated, so when substituting dried herbs for fresh use about one third as much.

Peachy Pecan Ham

(Pictured above)

    1 CURE 81® half ham
    1 cup peach preserves, divided
    1 tablespoon cornstarch
    2 cans (5-1/4 ounces each) peach nectar
    1 teaspoon dry mustard
1/2 cup packed brown sugar
1/2 cup chopped pecans, toasted
    2 large fresh peaches, peeled and sliced

Heat oven to 325°F. Place ham in shallow baking pan; score ham in diamond design. Cover. Bake according to package directions. Thirty minutes before ham is done, uncover and brush with 1/2 cup peach preserves. Bake 30 minutes longer, basting occasionally. In saucepan, combine cornstarch, peach nectar and dry mustard; stir until smooth. Add remaining 1/2 cup preserves and brown sugar. Cook and stir over medium heat until thickened. Stir in pecans and peaches; cook 1 minute. Slice ham; serve with peach sauce. *Makes 8 to 10 servings*

Crispy Italian Herb Chicken with Tri-Color Rotini Pasta

(Pictured at right)

2 BUTTERBALL® Chicken Requests™ Italian Style
    Herb Crispy Baked Breasts
1 cup uncooked tri-color rotini pasta
3 tablespoons water
1 tablespoon olive oil
2 cups broccoli florets
3 plum tomatoes, quartered
1 clove garlic, minced
    Grated Parmesan cheese

Prepare chicken according to package directions. Cook and drain pasta. Add water, oil and broccoli to skillet; cover. Cook 2 to 4 minutes. Stir in pasta, tomatoes and garlic; continue cooking 2 minutes longer. Serve chicken with pasta. Sprinkle with Parmesan cheese. *Makes 2 servings*

Zesty Cheddar Casserole

2 packages (1-1/2 ounces each) 4-cheese pasta
    sauce mix
2 cups milk
1 cup finely chopped celery
1/2 cup chopped onion
3 to 4 tablespoons *Frank's*® *RedHot*® Cayenne
    Pepper Sauce
1 bag (16 ounces) frozen vegetable combination
    such as broccoli, corn and red bell pepper
3 cups cooked diced chicken
6 slices crisply cooked bacon, crumbled
1-1/2 cups (6 ounces) shredded cheddar cheese,
    divided
1 package (7-1/2 ounces) refrigerated buttermilk
    biscuits

1. Preheat oven to 375°F. Prepare sauce mix according to package directions using milk, 1 cup water and omitting butter in 3-quart saucepan. Add celery, onion and *Frank's RedHot* Sauce. Cook and stir 1 minute.

2. Stir in vegetable combination, chicken, bacon and 1 cup cheese. Spoon into greased 3-quart casserole; cover. Bake 30 minutes; stir. Cut biscuits in half; arrange around edge of casserole. Sprinkle remaining 1/2 cup cheese over biscuits.

3. Bake, uncovered, 15 minutes or until biscuits are golden brown. *Makes 8 servings*

Herbed Tomato Pork Chops and Stuffing

1 tablespoon vegetable oil
4 boneless pork chops, 1/2 inch thick
1 can (8 ounces) stewed tomatoes
1 can (8 ounces) tomato sauce
1 medium green bell pepper, chopped
1/2 teaspoon dried oregano leaves
1/4 teaspoon ground pepper
2 cups STOVE TOP® Stuffing Mix for Chicken in
    the Canister
1 cup (4 ounces) shredded mozzarella cheese,
    divided

HEAT oil in large skillet on medium-high heat. Add chops; brown on both sides.

STIR in tomatoes, tomato sauce, green pepper, oregano and ground pepper. Bring to boil. Reduce heat to low; cover and simmer 15 minutes or until chops are cooked through. Remove chops from skillet.

STIR Stuffing Mix Pouch and 1/2 cup of the cheese into skillet. Return chops to skillet. Sprinkle with remaining 1/2 cup cheese; cover. Remove from heat. Let stand 5 minutes. *Makes 4 servings*

Turkey with Mustard Sauce

1 tablespoon butter or margarine
1 pound turkey cutlets
1 cup BIRDS EYE® frozen Mixed Vegetables
1 box (9 ounces) BIRDS EYE® frozen Pearl
    Onions in Cream Sauce
1 teaspoon spicy brown mustard

• In large nonstick skillet, melt butter over medium-high heat. Add turkey; cook until browned on both sides.

• Add mixed vegetables, onions with cream sauce and mustard; bring to boil. Reduce heat to medium-low; cover and simmer 6 to 8 minutes or until vegetables are tender and turkey is no longer pink in center. *Makes 4 servings*

Serving Suggestion: Serve with a fresh garden salad.

Crispy Italian Herb Chicken with Tri-Color Rotini Pasta

Pilaf-Stuffed Pork Loin Roast

(Pictured at right)

5 tablespoons butter or margarine, divided
1/4 cup chopped onion
1/4 cup chopped celery
1 clove garlic, minced
2 cups chicken broth
1 cup uncooked long grain and wild rice blend
1/2 cup finely chopped pecans, toasted*
3 tablespoons orange marmalade
4 teaspoons dried thyme leaves, divided
3/4 teaspoon salt
1/2 teaspoon black pepper
1 boneless, rolled and tied pork loin roast (5 to 6 pounds)**
1 onion, sliced and separated into rings
1/2 cup water
1 tablespoon vegetable oil
2 tablespoons soy sauce
   Orange juice
2 tablespoons all-purpose flour
   Plum slices and fresh chervil for garnish

To toast pecans, spread in single layer on baking sheet. Bake in preheated 350°F oven 6 to 8 minutes or until lightly browned, stirring often.

**Ask your meat retailer to try to keep the roast in 1 piece when boning.*

1. Preheat oven to 325°F. Melt 2 tablespoons butter in medium saucepan over medium heat; stir in chopped onion, celery and garlic. Cook until onion is tender, stirring frequently. Add broth; bring to a boil. Stir in rice blend. Reduce heat to low; cover and simmer 20 minutes. Remove from heat; let stand 5 minutes or until all liquid is absorbed.

2. Add pecans, marmalade, 1 teaspoon thyme, salt and pepper to rice blend; toss gently until blended. Cover; set aside.

3. Cut and remove strings from roast; discard. To butterfly roast, split roast in half where the 2 pieces fall apart. (If possible, keep roast in 1 piece.)

4. To butterfly each roast half, make horizontal cut starting from center crease of roast to within 1 inch of opposite edge. (If roast is in 2 pieces, butterfly 1 piece through center.) Open roast half and press uncut edge to flatten as much as possible.

5. Butterfly remaining roast half, starting from center crease and cutting to but not through outside edge. Open both sides of roast to obtain 1 piece with four sections of uniform thickness. (If roast is in 2 pieces, secure with wooden picks.)

6. Spoon rice mixture over roast, leaving 1-inch border. Cut enough heavy cotton string to tie roast at 1-inch intervals, making sure strings are long enough to tie securely. Place strings under roast. Beginning with 1 long side, roll roast jelly-roll fashion and tie with strings, being careful to keep 2 pieces together if necessary. Tie entire roast lengthwise with additional string.

7. Arrange onion rings in single layer in greased shallow roasting pan. Pour water over onion rings. Place meat rack in roasting pan. Place roast on rack; brush with oil and sprinkle with remaining 3 teaspoons thyme.

8. Cover with foil; roast in oven 2-1/2 hours or until internal temperature reaches 160°F when tested with meat thermometer inserted into the thickest part of roast but not in rice stuffing.

9. Transfer roast to cutting board; cover with foil. Let stand 10 to 15 minutes before carving. Internal temperature will rise 5°F to 10°F during stand time. Remove onion rings from roasting pan; discard. Meanwhile, to deglaze pan, pour soy sauce into pan drippings. Cook over medium-high heat, scraping up any browned bits and stirring frequently. Transfer mixture to deglazing measuring cup; let stand until fat rises to surface. Pour mixture into 2- or 4-cup measuring cup, stopping short of risen fat. (If deglazing measuring cup is unavailable, spoon fat from surface.) Add orange juice to measuring cup to equal 1-1/4 cups; set aside.

10. Melt remaining 3 tablespoons butter in small saucepan over medium heat; add flour, stirring until blended with wire whisk. Add orange juice mixture; cook until thickened and bubbly, whisking frequently. Season with additional salt and black pepper, if desired.

11. Remove strings from roast; discard. Carve roast and serve with orange sauce. Garnish, if desired.

Makes 12 servings

Helpful Hint

When cooking pork, such as this roast, never salt the meat before cooking it. The salt causes the juices in the meat to go to the surface and cook off, leaving the meat dry and tough.

Pilaf-Stuffed Pork Loin Roast

Campbell's® Beef Taco Bake

(Pictured at right)

    1 pound ground beef
    1 can (10-3/4 ounces) CAMPBELL'S® Condensed
        Tomato Soup
    1 cup PACE® Thick & Chunky Salsa *or* Picante
        Sauce
1/2 cup milk
    6 flour tortillas (8-inch) *or* 8 corn tortillas
        (6-inch), cut into 1-inch pieces
    1 cup shredded Cheddar cheese (4 ounces)

1. In medium skillet over medium-high heat, cook beef until browned, stirring to separate meat. Pour off fat.

2. Add soup, salsa, milk, tortillas and **half** the cheese. Spoon into 2-quart shallow baking dish. **Cover.**

3. Bake at 400°F. for 30 minutes or until hot. Sprinkle with remaining cheese.   *Makes 4 servings*

Normandy Pork and Cabbage

    1 pound boneless pork loin or tenderloin
    2 medium red baking apples, halved and cored
    1 tablespoon vegetable oil
    2 tablespoons butter or margarine, divided
    1 package (8 ounces) shredded green cabbage
        for coleslaw *or* 2 cups shredded red cabbage
    1 tablespoon all-purpose flour
    1 teaspoon ground sage
1/2 teaspoon salt
1/4 teaspoon black pepper
1/2 cup beef broth
1/2 cup apple juice or sweet apple cider
1/4 cup heavy cream
        Hot cooked egg noodles
        Green onion curls for garnish

Trim fat from pork; discard. Cut pork widthwise into 1/4-inch-thick slices. Cut each apple half into 6 wedges. Set aside.

Heat wok over high heat about 1 minute or until hot. Drizzle oil into wok and heat 30 seconds. Add 1 tablespoon butter and swirl to coat bottom. Add half the pork; stir-fry until no longer pink. Remove pork to large bowl. Repeat with remaining pork. Reduce heat to medium.

Add remaining 1 tablespoon butter to wok and swirl to coat bottom. Add apples; stir-fry about 2 minutes or just until apples soften. Remove apples to bowl with pork.

Add cabbage to wok; stir-fry just until wilted. Sprinkle with flour, sage, salt and black pepper; stir-fry until well mixed. Add broth and juice; cook and stir until sauce boils and thickens. Stir in cream; cook until heated through. Return pork and apples to wok. Stir in additional water if needed. Serve with noodles. Garnish, if desired.   *Makes 4 servings*

Note: For best results in this recipe, use Cortland, Rome Beauty, Winesap or Arkansas Black apples. They will remain flavorful and firm during cooking.

Spicy Tuna Empanadas

    1 (3-ounce) pouch of STARKIST® Premium
        Albacore or Chunk Light Tuna
    1 (4-ounce) can diced green chilies, drained
    1 (2-1/4-ounce) can sliced ripe olives, drained
1/2 cup shredded sharp cheddar cheese
    1 hard-cooked egg, chopped
        Salt and pepper to taste
1/4 teaspoon hot pepper sauce
1/4 cup medium thick and chunky salsa
    2 (15-ounce) packages refrigerated pie crusts
        Additional salsa

In medium bowl, place tuna, chilies, olives, cheese, egg, salt, pepper and hot pepper sauce; toss lightly with fork. Add 1/4 cup salsa and toss again; set aside. Following directions on package, unfold pie crusts (roll out slightly with rolling pin if you prefer thinner crust); cut 4 circles, 4 inches each, out of each crust. Place 8 circles on foil-covered baking sheets; wet edge of each circle with water. Top each circle with 1/4 cup lightly packed tuna mixture. Top with remaining circles, stretching pastry slightly to fit; press edges together and crimp with fork. Cut slits in top crust to vent. Bake in 425°F oven 15 to 18 minutes or until golden brown. Cool slightly. Serve with additional salsa.   *Makes 8 servings*

Asian Chicken and Noodles

(Pictured at right)

1 package (3 ounces) chicken flavor instant
    ramen noodles
1 bag (16 ounces) BIRDS EYE® frozen Farm Fresh
    Mixtures Broccoli, Carrots and Water
    Chestnuts*
1 tablespoon vegetable oil
1 pound boneless skinless chicken breasts, cut
    into thin strips
1/4 cup stir-fry sauce

Or, substitute 1 bag (16 ounces) Birds Eye® frozen Broccoli Cuts.

• Reserve seasoning packet from noodles.

• Bring 2 cups water to boil in large saucepan. Add
noodles and vegetables. Cook 3 minutes, stirring
occasionally; drain.

• Meanwhile, heat oil in large nonstick skillet over
medium-high heat. Add chicken; cook and stir until
no longer pink, about 8 minutes.

• Stir in noodles, vegetables, stir-fry sauce and
contents of reserved seasoning packet; heat
through. Garnish as desired.

Makes about 4 servings

Spicy Pot Roast

2 tablespoons vegetable oil, divided
4 pounds beef chuck or rump roast
2 tablespoons all-purpose flour
1 tablespoon chili powder
2 jars (8 ounces each) ORTEGA® Thick & Smooth
    Taco Sauce
1/2 cup beef broth

HEAT 1 tablespoon oil in large Dutch oven
over medium-high heat. Add roast; cook for 4 to
5 minutes or until brown on all sides. Remove from
pan; set aside.

HEAT remaining 1 tablespoon oil in saucepan. Add
flour and chili powder; cook for 30 seconds. Add
taco sauce and broth. Bring to a boil; reduce heat
to low. Add roast to sauce. Cover; cook, stirring
occasionally, for 1-1/2 to 2 hours or until roast is of
desired doneness. Serve with sauce.

Makes 6 to 8 servings

Tip: Shred cooked roast with a fork and use as a
meat filling for tacos, burritos or tamales.

Wild Rice Country Casserole

1 cup chopped onion
1/4 cup butter or margarine
1-1/4 pounds ground turkey
1/4 teaspoon black pepper
4 cups frozen potatoes O'Brien with onions and
    peppers, thawed
3 cups cooked wild rice
2 cups shredded mild cheddar cheese, divided
1 can (10-3/4 ounces) condensed cream of
    chicken soup
1 cup sour cream
1/3 cup bread crumbs

Preheat oven to 350°F. In large skillet, sauté onion in
butter; remove from skillet. In same skillet, brown
turkey. Sprinkle with pepper. Spread potatoes in
greased 13×9-inch baking pan. Combine onion,
turkey, wild rice, 1-1/2 cups cheese, soup and sour
cream in large bowl. Spread turkey mixture over
potatoes. Sprinkle remaining 1/2 cup cheese and
bread crumbs on top. Bake, uncovered, 40 minutes
or until heated through. *Makes 8 servings*

Favorite recipe from **Minnesota Cultivated Wild
Rice Council**

Manicotti alla Perdue

2 cups finely chopped cooked PERDUE® Chicken
    or Turkey
1 container (15 ounces) ricotta cheese
1 egg, slightly beaten
1 package (10 ounces) frozen chopped spinach,
    thawed and well drained
1/4 cup grated Parmesan cheese
1/2 teaspoon ground nutmeg
3 cups marinara or spaghetti sauce, divided
1 package (8 ounces) manicotti shells, cooked
1/2 to 3/4 cup shredded mozzarella cheese

Preheat oven to 350°F. In medium bowl, combine
first 6 ingredients. Into 13×9-inch baking pan, spoon
a thin layer of marinara sauce. Fill manicotti shells
with chicken or turkey mixture and arrange over
sauce. Pour remaining sauce on top; sprinkle with
mozzarella. Bake, covered, 25 to 30 minutes until
hot and bubbly. *Makes 4 to 6 servings*

Asian Chicken and Noodles

Mandarin Pork Stir-Fry

Mandarin Pork Stir-Fry

(Pictured above)

1-1/2 cups DOLE® Pineapple Orange or Pineapple
    Juice, divided
    Vegetable cooking spray
12 ounces lean pork tenderloin, chicken breast or
    turkey tenderloin, cut into thin strips
1 tablespoon finely chopped fresh ginger *or*
    1/2 teaspoon ground ginger
2 cups DOLE® Shredded Carrots
1/2 cup chopped DOLE® Pitted Prunes or Chopped
    Dates
4 green onions, cut into 1-inch pieces
2 tablespoons low-sodium soy sauce
1 teaspoon cornstarch

• Heat 2 tablespoons juice over medium-high heat
in large nonstick skillet sprayed with vegetable
cooking spray until juice bubbles.

• Add pork and ginger; cook and stir 3 minutes or
until pork is no longer pink. Remove pork from
skillet.

• Heat 3 more tablespoons juice in skillet; add
carrots, prunes and green onions. Cook and stir
3 minutes.

• Stir soy sauce and cornstarch into remaining juice;
add to carrot mixture. Stir in pork; cover and cook
2 minutes until heated through. Garnish as desired.

Makes 4 servings

Tuscan Turkey Cutlets

1 pound turkey cutlets
3/4 teaspoon salt, divided
3/4 teaspoon black pepper, divided
1 tablespoon olive oil, divided
2 cups onion, coarsely chopped
1 cup carrots, coarsely chopped
3 to 4 cloves garlic, minced
1/2 teaspoon dried oregano
1/2 teaspoon dried thyme
1 (10-ounce) bag fresh spinach leaves, stems
    removed
1 (14-1/2-ounce) can diced tomatoes, undrained
1 (15-ounce) can cannellini or white kidney
    beans, drained and rinsed
1/4 cup shredded Parmesan cheese, divided

1. Place cutlets on cutting board and sprinkle with
1/4 teaspoon salt and 1/4 teaspoon pepper. Slice
cutlets into 1/2-inch strips.

2. In 12-inch or larger non-stick skillet over medium-
high heat, sauté turkey strips in 1-1/2 teaspoons oil,
4 to 5 minutes or until no longer pink. Remove from
skillet; set aside.

3. Add remaining 1-1/2 teaspoons oil to skillet. Sauté
onion, carrots, garlic, oregano and thyme 5 minutes
or until vegetables are tender. Gradually add
spinach and stir an additional 2 minutes or until
spinach is wilted, but not quite done. Add tomatoes
and remaining 1/2 teaspoon salt and 1/2 teaspoon
pepper; cook 2 minutes.

4. Stir in turkey strips and beans. Cook until heated
through.

5. Serve topped with Parmesan cheese.

Makes 4 servings

Serving Suggestion: Serve over orzo, noodles or a
whole grain such as quinoa.

Favorite recipe from **National Turkey Federation**

Angel Hair Al Fresco

(Pictured below)

- 3/4 cup milk
- 1 tablespoon margarine or butter
- 1 package (4.8 ounces) PASTA RONI® Angel Hair Pasta with Herbs
- 1 can (6-1/8 ounces) white tuna in water, drained, flaked *or* 1-1/2 cups chopped cooked chicken
- 2 medium tomatoes, chopped
- 1/3 cup sliced green onions
- 1/4 cup dry white wine or water
- 1/4 cup slivered almonds, toasted (optional)
- 1 tablespoon chopped fresh basil *or* 1 teaspoon dried basil

1. In 3-quart saucepan, combine 1-1/3 cups water, milk and margarine. Bring just to a boil.

2. Stir in pasta, Special Seasonings, tuna, tomatoes, onions, wine, almonds and basil. Return to a boil; reduce heat to medium.

3. Boil, uncovered, stirring frequently, 6 to 8 minutes. Sauce will be thin, but will thicken upon standing.

4. Let stand 3 minutes. Stir before serving. Garnish as desired. *Makes 4 servings*

Main-Dish Pie

- 1 package (8 rolls) refrigerated crescent rolls
- 1 pound ground beef
- 1 medium onion, chopped
- 1 can (12 ounces) beef or mushroom gravy
- 1 box (10 ounces) BIRDS EYE® frozen Green Peas, thawed
- 1/2 cup shredded Swiss cheese
- 6 slices tomato

• Preheat oven to 350°F.

• Unroll dough and separate rolls. Spread to cover bottom of ungreased 9-inch pie pan. Press together to form crust. Bake 10 minutes.

• Meanwhile, in large skillet, brown beef and onion; drain.

• Stir in gravy and peas; cook until heated through.

• Pour mixture into partially baked crust. Sprinkle with cheese.

• Bake 10 to 15 minutes or until crust is brown and cheese is melted.

• Arrange tomato slices over pie; bake 2 minutes more. *Makes 6 servings*

Angel Hair Al Fresco

Down-Home Pork and Beans

(Pictured at right)

3/4 cup sliced onion
3/4 cup diced green bell pepper
  2 cloves garlic, minced
  1 can (15 ounces) white kidney or cannellini
     beans, rinsed and drained
  1 can (10-3/4 ounces) condensed tomato soup
10 ounces pork tenderloin, trimmed and cubed
1/2 cup packed brown sugar
1/4 cup barbecue sauce
1/2 teaspoon salt

Spray large saucepan with vegetable cooking spray. Add onion, bell pepper and garlic; cook and stir until tender. Add beans, soup, pork, brown sugar, barbecue sauce and salt; cover and simmer 1 hour. Serve with tomato wedges, if desired.

Makes 6 servings

Swanson® Savory Pot Roast with Harvest Vegetables

(Pictured on page 126)

  2 tablespoons vegetable oil
  3 pounds boneless beef bottom round *or* rump
     roast
  1 can (14 ounces) SWANSON® Seasoned Beef
     Broth with Onion
3/4 cup V8® 100% Vegetable Juice
  2 cups fresh *or* frozen baby carrots
  3 medium potatoes, quartered
  3 stalks celery, cut into 1-inch pieces
  2 tablespoons all-purpose flour
1/4 cup water

HEAT oil in saucepot. Add roast and cook until browned on all sides. Pour off fat.

ADD broth and vegetable juice. Heat to a boil. Cover and cook over low heat 1 hour and 45 minutes.

ADD vegetables. Cover and cook 30 minutes or until vegetables are tender. Remove roast and vegetables and keep warm.

MIX flour and water. Add to saucepot. Cook and stir until mixture boils and thickens. Serve with roast and vegetables.

Makes 6 servings

Zucchini Meat Sauce with Pasta

  1 package (12 ounces) shell macaroni pasta
  2 pounds ground beef
     Salt and pepper
  2 onions, chopped
  2 cans (26 ounces each) DEL MONTE® Chunky
     Spaghetti Sauce with Garlic & Herb
  1 can (14-1/2 ounces) DEL MONTE Diced
     Tomatoes
  2 small zucchini, thinly sliced

1. Cook pasta in 8-quart pot according to package directions; drain. Keep pasta hot.

2. Brown meat in Dutch oven over medium-high heat. Season with salt and pepper, if desired; drain. Add onions; cook until tender. Stir in spaghetti sauce and undrained tomatoes; cook 5 minutes, stirring occasionally.

3. Add zucchini; cover and cook over medium heat 7 to 10 minutes or until zucchini is tender. Serve sauce over hot pasta. Sprinkle with grated Parmesan cheese and garnish, if desired.

Makes 8 servings

Make-Ahead Brunch Bake

  1 pound bulk pork sausage
  6 eggs, beaten
  2 cups half-and-half cream
1/2 teaspoon salt
  1 teaspoon ground mustard
  1 cup (4 ounces) shredded cheddar cheese,
     divided
1-1/3 cups *French's®* French Fried Onions, divided

Crumble sausage into large skillet. Cook over medium-high heat until browned; drain well. Stir in eggs, cream, salt, mustard, *1/2 cup* cheese and *2/3 cup* French Fried Onions; mix well. Pour into greased 7×11-inch baking dish. Refrigerate, covered, 8 hours or overnight. Remove from refrigerator 30 minutes before baking. Bake, uncovered, at 350°F for 45 minutes or until knife inserted in center comes out clean. Top with remaining cheese and onions; bake, uncovered, 5 minutes or until onions are golden brown. Let stand 15 minutes before serving.

Makes 6 servings

Campbell's® Easy Chicken & Biscuits

(Pictured at right)

1 can (10-3/4 ounces) CAMPBELL'S® Condensed Cream of Celery Soup *or* 98% Fat Free Cream of Celery Soup
1 can (10-3/4 ounces) CAMPBELL'S® Condensed Cream of Potato Soup
1 cup milk
1/4 teaspoon dried thyme leaves, crushed
1/4 teaspoon pepper
4 cups cooked cut-up vegetables*
2 cups cubed cooked chicken, turkey *or* ham
1 package (7-1/2 or 10 ounces) refrigerated buttermilk biscuits (10 biscuits)

*Use a combination of broccoli flowerets, cauliflower flowerets and sliced carrots or broccoli flowerets and sliced carrots or broccoli flowerets, sliced carrots and peas.

1. In 3-quart shallow baking dish mix soups, milk, thyme, pepper, vegetables and chicken.

2. Bake at 400°F. for 15 minutes or until hot.

3. Stir. Arrange biscuits over chicken mixture. Bake 15 minutes more or until biscuits are golden.

Makes 5 servings

Tip: To microwave vegetables, in 2-quart shallow microwave-safe baking dish arrange vegetables and 1/4 cup water. Cover. Microwave on HIGH 10 minutes.

Beef Kabobs with Apricot Glaze

1 can (15-1/4 ounces) DEL MONTE® Apricot Halves
1 tablespoon cornstarch
1 teaspoon Dijon mustard
1/2 teaspoon dried basil leaves
1 pound beef sirloin steak, cut into 1-1/2-inch cubes
1 small green bell pepper, cut into 3/4-inch pieces
4 medium mushrooms, cut in half
4 to 8 skewers*

*To prevent burning of wooden skewers, soak skewers in water for 10 minutes before assembling kabobs.

1. Drain apricot syrup into small saucepan. Blend in cornstarch until dissolved. Cook over medium heat, stirring constantly, until thickened. Stir in mustard and basil. Set aside.

2. Thread meat, apricots, green pepper and mushrooms alternately onto skewers; brush with apricot syrup mixture. Grill kabobs over hot coals (or broil) about 5 minutes on each side or to desired doneness, brushing occasionally with additional syrup mixture. Garnish, if desired.

Makes 4 servings

Pork and Vegetable Stew with Noodles

2 tablespoons vegetable oil
1 pound lean boneless pork, cut into 3/4-inch cubes
3 cups beef broth
3 tablespoons chopped fresh parsley, divided
1 can (14-1/2 ounces) stewed tomatoes
1 large carrot, sliced
3 green onions, sliced
2 teaspoons Dijon mustard
1/4 teaspoon rubbed sage
1/8 teaspoon black pepper
3 cups uncooked noodles
1 teaspoon butter or margarine
2 tablespoons all-purpose flour
1/3 cup cold water
Apples and parsley for garnish

Heat vegetable oil in large saucepan over medium-high heat. Add pork; cook, stirring frequently until browned on all sides.

Carefully stir beef broth into saucepan. Stir in 1 tablespoon chopped parsley, tomatoes, carrot, onions, mustard, sage and black pepper. Bring to a boil over high heat. Reduce heat to medium-low; simmer, uncovered, 30 minutes.

Meanwhile, cook noodles according to package directions; drain. Add remaining 2 tablespoons chopped parsley and butter; toss lightly. Keep warm until ready to serve.

Combine flour and cold water in cup until smooth. Stir into stew. Cook and stir over medium heat until slightly thickened. To serve, spoon noodles onto each plate. Ladle stew over noodles. Garnish, if desired.

Makes 4 servings

Campbell's® Easy Chicken & Biscuits

Desserts

Berry Cobbler

(Pictured at left)

2-1/2 cups fresh raspberries*
2-1/2 cups fresh blueberries or strawberries,* sliced
2 tablespoons cornstarch
1/2 to 3/4 cup sugar
1 cup all-purpose flour
1-1/2 teaspoons baking powder
1/4 teaspoon salt
1/3 cup milk
1/3 cup butter or margarine, melted
2 tablespoons thawed frozen apple juice concentrate
1/4 teaspoon ground nutmeg

One (16-ounce) bag frozen raspberries and one (16-ounce) bag frozen blueberries or strawberries can be substituted for fresh berries. Thaw berries, reserving juices. Increase cornstarch to 3 tablespoons.

1. Preheat oven to 375°F.

2. Combine berries and cornstarch in medium bowl; toss lightly to coat. Add sugar to taste; mix well. Spoon into 1-1/2-quart or 8-inch square baking dish. Combine flour, baking powder and salt in medium bowl. Add milk, butter and juice concentrate; mix just until dry ingredients are moistened. Drop 6 heaping tablespoonfuls batter evenly over berries; sprinkle with nutmeg.

3. Bake, uncovered, 25 minutes or until topping is golden brown and fruit is bubbly. Cool on wire rack. Serve warm or at room temperature. *Makes 6 servings*

Tip: Cobblers are best served warm or at room temperature on the day they are made. Leftovers should be kept covered and refrigerated for up to two days. Reheat them, covered, in a 350°F oven until warm.

Clockwise from top left: *Awesome Sundae Pie (p. 194), Berry Cobbler, Blueberry Angel Food Cake Roll (p. 206) and Chocolate Peanut Butter Parfaits (p. 184)*

Country Apple Rhubarb Pie

(Pictured at right)

CRUST
9-inch Classic CRISCO® Double Crust (recipe follows)

FILLING
9 cups sliced, peeled Granny Smith apples (about 3 pounds or 6 large apples)
1-1/2 cups chopped (about 1/2 inch) fresh rhubarb, peeled if tough
3/4 cup granulated sugar
1/2 cup firmly packed light brown sugar
2 tablespoons all-purpose flour
1 tablespoon cornstarch
1 teaspoon ground cinnamon
1/4 teaspoon freshly grated nutmeg

GLAZE
1 egg, beaten
1 tablespoon water
1 tablespoon granulated sugar
1 teaspoon ground pecans or walnuts
1/8 teaspoon ground cinnamon

1. For crust, prepare dough. Roll and press bottom crust into 9- or 9-1/2-inch deep-dish pie plate. Do not bake. Heat oven to 425°F.

2. For filling, combine apples and rhubarb in large bowl. Combine 3/4 cup granulated sugar, brown sugar, flour, cornstarch, 1 teaspoon cinnamon and nutmeg in medium bowl. Sprinkle over fruit. Toss to coat. Spoon into unbaked pie crust. Moisten pastry edge with water. Cover pie with lattice top, cutting strips 1 inch wide. Flute edge high.

3. For glaze, combine egg and water in small bowl. Brush over crust. Combine remaining glaze ingredients in small bowl. Sprinkle over crust.

4. Bake at 425°F for 20 minutes. Reduce oven temperature to 350°F. Bake 30 to 40 minutes or until filling in center is bubbly and crust is golden brown. *Do not overbake.* Place sheet of foil or baking sheet under pie if it starts to bubble over. Cool to room temperature.

Makes one 9- or 9-1/2-inch deep-dish pie
(8 servings)

Classic Crisco® Double Crust

2 cups all-purpose flour
1 teaspoon salt
3/4 CRISCO® Stick or 3/4 cup CRISCO® all-vegetable shortening
5 tablespoons cold water (or more as needed)

1. Spoon flour into measuring cup and level. Combine flour and salt in medium bowl.

2. Cut in 3/4 cup shortening using pastry blender or 2 knives until all flour is blended to form pea-size chunks.

3. Sprinkle with water, 1 tablespoon at a time. Toss lightly with fork until dough forms a ball. Divide dough in half.

4. Press dough between hands to form 5- to 6-inch "pancake." Flour rolling surface and rolling pin lightly. Roll both halves of dough into circle. Trim one circle of dough 1 inch larger than upside-down pie plate. Carefully remove trimmed dough. Set aside to reroll and use for pastry cutout garnish, if desired.

5. Fold dough into quarters. Unfold and press into pie plate. Trim edge even with plate. Add desired filling to unbaked crust. Moisten pastry edge with water. Lift top crust onto filled pie. Trim 1/2 inch beyond edge of pie plate. Fold top edge under bottom crust. Flute. Cut slits in top crust to allow steam to escape. Follow baking directions given for that recipe.   *Makes 1 (9-inch) double crust*

Chocolate Peanut Butter Parfaits

(Pictured on page 182 and on back cover)

3 tablespoons milk
3 tablespoons peanut butter
1 cup thawed COOL WHIP® Whipped Topping
2 cups cold milk
1 package (4-serving size) JELL-O® Chocolate Flavor Instant Pudding & Pie Filling
1/4 cup chopped peanuts

STIR 3 tablespoons milk into peanut butter in medium bowl until smooth. Gently stir in whipped topping.

POUR 2 cups milk into medium bowl. Add pudding mix. Beat with wire whisk 2 minutes. Alternately spoon whipped topping mixture and pudding into 6 parfait glasses.

REFRIGERATE until ready to serve. Sprinkle with peanuts.   *Makes 6 servings*

Country Apple Rhubarb Pie

Fudgy Hazelnut Brownies

(Pictured at right)

1 (21-ounce) package DUNCAN HINES® Chewy
    Fudge Brownie Mix
2 eggs
1/2 cup vegetable oil
1/4 cup water
1 cup chopped toasted hazelnuts
1 cup semisweet chocolate chips
1 cup DUNCAN HINES® Dark Chocolate
    Frosting
3 squares white chocolate, melted

Preheat oven to 350°F. Grease bottom only of
13×9-inch baking pan.

Combine brownie mix, eggs, oil and water in large
bowl. Stir with spoon until well blended, about
50 strokes. Stir in nuts and chips. Spoon into
prepared pan. Bake 25 to 30 minutes or until set.
Cool completely.

Heat frosting in microwave oven at HIGH for
15 seconds or until thin; stir well. Spread over
brownies. Spoon dollops of white chocolate over
chocolate frosting; marble white chocolate through
frosting. Cool completely. Cut into bars.

Makes 24 brownies

Carrot Raisin Spice Cookies

1-1/4 cups all-purpose flour
1/2 cup CREAM OF WHEAT® Cereal (1-minute,
    2-1/2-minute or 10-minute stovetop
    cooking)
1-1/2 teaspoons ground cinnamon
1 teaspoon pumpkin pie spice
3/4 teaspoon baking soda
1/2 cup margarine or butter, softened
1/2 cup granulated sugar
1/3 cup packed light brown sugar
1 egg
1 teaspoon vanilla extract
1/2 cup finely grated carrot
1/2 cup seedless raisins
1/4 cup PLANTERS® Walnuts, finely chopped
    Powdered sugar glaze, optional

1. Mix flour, cereal, cinnamon, pumpkin pie spice
and baking soda in medium bowl; set aside.

2. Beat margarine or butter and sugars in large bowl
with mixer until creamy; beat in egg and vanilla.

3. Reduce speed to low; blend in flour mixture.

4. Stir in carrot, raisins and walnuts; let stand
10 minutes.

5. Drop by teaspoonfuls 2 inches apart onto lightly
greased baking sheets.

6. Bake at 350°F for 10 to 12 minutes or until golden
brown. Cool on wire racks. Drizzle with powdered
sugar glaze, if desired.

Makes 2-1/2 dozen cookies

Peachy Pecan Cake

1 (8-ounce) package cream cheese, softened
1 cup packed brown sugar
4 eggs, beaten
1/2 cup half-and-half cream
1-1/2 teaspoons vanilla extract
1 cup gingersnap crumbs
1 (6-ounce) package almond brickle chips
3/4 cup chopped pecans, toasted*
1/2 cup flaked coconut
1 (16-ounce) can sliced peaches, well drained
    and chopped
    Whipped cream (optional)

*To toast pecans, spread in single layer on baking sheet. Bake in
preheated 350°F oven 8 to 10 minutes or until lightly toasted, stirring
occasionally.*

1. Preheat oven to 350°F. Grease 9-inch square
baking pan.

2. Beat cream cheese and sugar in large bowl until
well blended.

3. Add eggs, one at a time, beating well after each
addition. Blend in half-and-half and vanilla. Stir in
crumbs, chips, pecans and coconut. Stir in peaches;
pour into prepared pan.

4. Bake 35 to 40 minutes or until center is firm and
edges are golden brown. Serve warm or chilled.
Garnish with whipped cream, if desired.

Makes one 9-inch cake

Rice Pudding

(Pictured at right)

1-1/4 cups water, divided
1/2 cup uncooked long-grain rice
2 cups evaporated skim milk
1/2 cup granulated sugar
1/2 cup raisins
1/2 cup MOTT'S® Natural Apple Sauce
3 tablespoons cornstarch
1 teaspoon vanilla extract
Brown sugar or ground nutmeg (optional)
Fresh raspberries (optional)
Orange peel strips (optional)

1. In medium saucepan, bring 1 cup water to a boil. Add rice. Reduce heat to low and simmer, covered, 20 minutes or until rice is tender and water is absorbed.

2. Add milk, granulated sugar, raisins and apple sauce. Bring to a boil. Reduce heat to low and simmer for 3 minutes, stirring occasionally.

3. Combine cornstarch and remaining 1/4 cup water in small bowl. Stir into rice mixture. Simmer about 20 minutes or until mixture thickens, stirring occasionally. Remove from heat; stir in vanilla. Cool 15 to 20 minutes before serving. Sprinkle each serving with brown sugar or nutmeg and garnish with raspberries and orange peel, if desired. Refrigerate leftovers.   *Makes 8 servings*

Brownie Berry Parfaits

1 box (10 ounces) BIRDS EYE® frozen
  Raspberries*
4 large prepared brownies, cut into cubes
1 pint vanilla or chocolate ice cream
4 tablespoons chocolate syrup
2 tablespoons chopped walnuts

Or, substitute Birds Eye® frozen Strawberries.

• Thaw raspberries according to package directions.

• Divide half the brownie cubes among four parfait glasses. Top with half the ice cream and raspberries. Repeat layers with remaining brownie cubes, ice cream and raspberries.

• Drizzle chocolate syrup over each dessert; sprinkle with walnuts.   *Makes 4 servings*

Chocolate Truffles

3 cups (18 ounces) semi-sweet chocolate chips
1 (14-ounce) can EAGLE® BRAND Sweetened
  Condensed Milk (NOT evaporated milk)
1 tablespoon vanilla extract
  Coatings: finely chopped toasted nuts, flaked
  coconut, chocolate sprinkles, colored sugar,
  unsweetened cocoa, powdered sugar or
  colored sprinkles

1. In heavy saucepan over low heat, melt chips with Eagle Brand. Remove from heat; stir in vanilla.

2. Chill 2 hours or until firm. Shape into 1-inch balls; roll in desired coating.

3. Chill 1 hour or until firm. Store covered at room temperature.   *Makes about 6 dozen truffles*

Microwave Directions: In 1-quart glass measure, combine chips and Eagle Brand. Microwave at HIGH (100% power) 3 minutes, stirring after 1-1/2 minutes. Stir until smooth. Proceed as directed above.

Butter Almond Classic Cookies

1 cup (2 sticks) I CAN'T BELIEVE IT'S NOT
  BUTTER!® Spread
1/2 cup confectioners' sugar
3/4 teaspoon almond extract
1-3/4 cups all-purpose flour
1/2 cup finely chopped almonds

In large bowl, with electric mixer beat I Can't Believe It's Not Butter! Spread and 1/2 cup sugar until light and fluffy, about 5 minutes. Beat in almond extract, then flour until blended. Beat in almonds. Turn dough onto plastic wrap and shape into flat circle. Cover and refrigerate at least 1 hour.

Preheat oven to 350°F. Divide dough into 8 pie-shaped wedges. On lightly floured surface, with lightly floured hands, roll each wedge into 1-inch-thick log. Cut each log into slices, each about 2 to 3 inches long. Shape each slice into crescent and arrange on ungreased baking sheets.

Bake 15 minutes or until edges are lightly golden. On wire rack, let stand 2 minutes; remove from sheets and cool completely. Before serving, sprinkle cookies with additional sugar.   *Makes 40 cookies*

Date-Nut Macaroons

(Pictured at right)

1 (8-ounce) package pitted dates, chopped
1-1/2 cups BAKER'S® Angel Flake Coconut
1 cup PLANTERS® Pecan Halves, chopped
3/4 cup sweetened condensed milk (not
   evaporated milk)
1/2 teaspoon vanilla extract

1. Preheat oven to 350°F.

2. Mix dates, coconut and nuts in medium bowl; blend in sweetened condensed milk and vanilla. Drop by rounded tablespoonfuls onto greased and floured cookie sheets. Bake 10 to 12 minutes or until light golden brown. Carefully remove from cookie sheets; cool completely on wire racks. Store in airtight container.   *Makes about 2 dozen cookies*

Classic Lemon Meringue Pie

(Pictured on front cover)

CRUST
            Classic CRISCO® Single Crust (recipe follows)
FILLING
   1-1/2 cups sugar
      1/4 cup cornstarch
         3 tablespoons all-purpose flour
      1/4 teaspoon salt
   1-1/2 cups hot water
         3 egg yolks, beaten
         2 tablespoons butter or margarine
   1-1/2 teaspoons grated lemon peel
      1/3 cup plus 1 tablespoon fresh lemon juice
MERINGUE
      1/2 cup sugar, divided
         1 tablespoon cornstarch
      1/2 cup cold water
         4 egg whites
      3/4 teaspoon vanilla extract

1. For crust, prepare and bake as directed. Cool. Heat oven to 350°F.

2. For filling, combine 1-1/2 cups sugar, 1/4 cup cornstarch, flour and salt in medium saucepan. Add 1-1/2 cups hot water gradually, stirring constantly. Cook and stir on medium heat until mixture comes to a boil and thickens. Reduce heat to low. Cook and stir constantly 8 minutes. Remove from heat. Add about one third of hot mixture slowly to egg yolks. Mix well. Return mixture to saucepan. Bring mixture

to a boil on medium-high heat. Reduce heat to low. Cook and stir 4 minutes. Remove from heat. Stir in butter and lemon peel. Add lemon juice slowly. Mix well. Spoon into baked pie crust.

3. For meringue, combine 2 tablespoons sugar, 1 tablespoon cornstarch and 1/2 cup cold water in saucepan. Stir until cornstarch dissolves. Cook and stir on medium heat until mixture is clear. Cool.

4. Mix egg whites and vanilla in large bowl. Beat at high speed of electric mixer until soft peaks form. Beat in remaining 6 tablespoons sugar, 1 tablespoon at a time. Beat well after each addition. Combine meringue with cornstarch mixture and continue beating until stiff peaks form. Spread over filling, covering completely and sealing to edge of pie.

5. Bake at 350°F for 12 to 15 minutes or until meringue is golden. *Do not overbake.* Cool to room temperature before serving. Refrigerate leftover pie.
                         Makes 1 (9-inch) pie

Classic Crisco® Single Crust

   1-1/3 cups all-purpose flour
      1/2 teaspoon salt
      1/2 CRISCO® Stick or 1/2 cup CRISCO®
         all-vegetable shortening
         3 tablespoons cold water

1. Spoon flour into measuring cup and level. Combine flour and salt in medium bowl.

2. Cut in shortening using pastry blender or 2 knives until all flour is blended to form pea-size chunks.

3. Sprinkle with water, 1 tablespoon at a time. Toss lightly with fork until dough forms a ball.

4. Press dough between hands to form 5- to 6-inch "pancake." Flour rolling surface and rolling pin lightly. Roll dough into circle. Trim circle 1 inch larger than upside-down pie plate. Carefully remove trimmed dough; set aside to reroll and use for pastry cutout garnish, if desired.

5. Fold dough into quarters. Unfold and press into pie plate. Fold edge under. Flute.

6. **For recipes using a baked pie crust,** heat oven to 425°F. Prick bottom and side thoroughly with fork (50 times) to prevent shrinkage. Bake at 425°F for 10 to 15 minutes or until lightly browned.

7. **For recipes using an unbaked pie crust,** follow directions given for that recipe.
                  Makes 1 (9-inch) single crust

Date-Nut Macaroons

Lemon Poppy Seed Cupcakes

Lemon Poppy Seed Cupcakes

(Pictured above)

CUPCAKES
    1 package DUNCAN HINES® Moist Deluxe®
      Lemon Supreme Cake Mix
    3 eggs
  1-1/3 cups water
    1/3 cup vegetable oil
    3 tablespoons poppy seeds

LEMON FROSTING
    1 container (16 ounces) DUNCAN HINES®
      Vanilla Frosting
    1 teaspoon grated lemon peel
    1/4 teaspoon lemon extract
    3 to 4 drops yellow food coloring
      Yellow and orange gumdrops, for garnish

Preheat oven to 350°F. Place 30 (2-1/2-inch) paper liners in muffin cups.

For cupcakes, combine cake mix, eggs, water, oil and poppy seeds in large bowl. Beat at medium speed of electric mixer 2 minutes. Fill paper liners about half full. Bake 18 to 21 minutes or until

toothpick inserted in center comes out clean. Cool in pans 5 minutes. Remove to cooling racks. Cool completely.

For lemon frosting, combine Vanilla frosting, lemon peel and lemon extract in small bowl. Tint with yellow food coloring to desired color. Frost cupcakes with lemon frosting. Decorate with gumdrops, if desired.   *Makes 30 cupcakes*

Double Blueberry Cheese Pie

CRUST
    Classic CRISCO® Single Crust (page 190)

FILLING
    2 packages (8 ounces each) cream cheese,
      softened
    1 cup granulated sugar
    2 tablespoons all-purpose flour
    2 eggs
    2 teaspoons vanilla extract
  1/2 cup whipping cream
    2 cups fresh blueberries

TOPPING
    2 cups whipping cream
    2 tablespoons confectioners' sugar
    1 teaspoon vanilla extract
    1 cup fresh blueberries

1. For crust, prepare as directed in 9- or 9-1/2-inch deep-dish pie plate. Do not bake. Heat oven to 350°F.

2. For filling, place cream cheese and granulated sugar in food processor bowl. Process, using steel blade, until smooth. Add flour, eggs, 2 teaspoons vanilla and 1/2 cup whipping cream through feed tube while processor is running. Process until blended. Add 2 cups blueberries. Pulse (quick on and off) twice. Pour into unbaked pie crust.

3. Bake at 350°F for 45 minutes. *Do not overbake.* Cool on wire rack for 2 hours. Refrigerate 6 hours or overnight.

4. For topping, beat 2 cups whipping cream in large bowl at high speed of electric mixer until stiff peaks form. Beat in confectioners' sugar and 1 teaspoon vanilla. Spread over top of pie. Garnish with 1 cup blueberries. Serve immediately. Refrigerate leftover pie.

Makes 1 (9- or 9-1/2-inch) deep-dish pie

Pumpkin Crunch Cake

1 package (18.25 ounces) yellow cake mix,
divided
2 large eggs
1-2/3 cups LIBBY'S® Easy Pumpkin Pie Mix
2 teaspoons pumpkin pie spice
1/3 cup flaked coconut
1/4 cup chopped nuts
3 tablespoons cold butter or margarine

PREHEAT oven to 350°F. Lightly grease 13×9-inch baking pan.

COMBINE *3 cups* yellow cake mix, eggs, pumpkin pie mix and pumpkin pie spice in large bowl. Beat on medium speed of electric mixer for 2 minutes. Pour into prepared baking pan.

COMBINE *remaining* cake mix, coconut and nuts in small bowl; cut in butter with pastry blender or two knives until mixture is crumbly. Sprinkle over batter.

BAKE for 30 to 35 minutes or until wooden pick inserted in center comes out clean. Cool in pan on wire rack. *Makes 20 servings*

Creamy Chocolate Pie

(Pictured below)

1-3/4 cups cold milk
2 packages (4-serving size) JELL-O® Chocolate or Chocolate Fudge Flavor Instant Pudding & Pie Filling
1 tub (8 ounces) COOL WHIP® Whipped Topping, thawed
1 prepared chocolate flavor crumb crust (6 ounces)

POUR milk into large bowl. Add pudding mixes. Beat with wire whisk until well mixed. (Mixture will be thick.) Immediately stir in whipped topping. Spoon into crust.

REFRIGERATE 4 hours or until set. Garnish as desired. *Makes 8 servings*

Helpful Hint

When storing pies, any type made with dairy products should always be kept refrigerated.

Creamy Chocolate Pie

Orange Glazed Pound Cake

(Pictured at right)

1 package DUNCAN HINES® Moist Deluxe®
  Butter Recipe Golden Cake Mix
4 eggs
1 cup sour cream
1/3 cup vegetable oil
1/4 cup plus 1 to 2 tablespoons orange juice
2 tablespoons grated orange peel
1 cup confectioners' sugar

Preheat oven to 375°F. Grease and flour 10-inch tube pan.

Combine cake mix, eggs, sour cream, oil, 1/4 cup orange juice and orange peel in large bowl. Beat at medium speed with electric mixer for 2 minutes. Pour into prepared pan. Bake 45 to 50 minutes or until toothpick inserted in center comes out clean. Cool in pan 25 minutes. Invert onto cooling rack. Cool completely.

Combine sugar and remaining 1 to 2 tablespoons orange juice in small bowl; stir until smooth. Drizzle over cake. Garnish as desired.

Makes 12 to 16 servings

Awesome Sundae Pie

(Pictured on page 182)

6 squares BAKER'S® Semi-Sweet Baking
  Chocolate
1 tablespoon butter
3/4 cup finely chopped nuts, toasted
3/4 cup BAKER'S® ANGEL FLAKE® Coconut
2 pints ice cream, any flavor, softened
  Thawed COOL WHIP® Whipped Topping,
  chopped nuts and maraschino cherries
  Hot Fudge Sauce (recipe follows)

LINE 9-inch pie plate with foil; lightly grease foil.

MICROWAVE chocolate and butter in large microwavable bowl on HIGH 2 minutes or until butter is melted. Stir until chocolate is completely melted. Stir in nuts and coconut. Spread evenly onto bottom and up side of prepared pie plate.

REFRIGERATE 1 hour or until firm. Lift crust out of pie plate. Carefully peel off foil. Return crust to pie plate or place on serving plate. Refrigerate until ready to use. Fill crust with scoops of ice cream and cover.

FREEZE 2 hours or until firm. Garnish with whipped topping, nuts and maraschino cherries. Serve with Hot Fudge Sauce. *Makes 8 servings*

Hot Fudge Sauce

1 package (8 squares) BAKER'S® Unsweetened
  Baking Chocolate
1/4 cup (1/2 stick) butter *or* margarine
1/2 cup milk
1/2 cup whipping (heavy) cream
2 cups sugar
1 tablespoon vanilla extract

MICROWAVE chocolate and butter in large microwavable bowl on HIGH 2 minutes or until butter is melted. Stir until chocolate is completely melted.

STIR in milk, cream and sugar until well blended. Microwave 5 minutes until mixture is thick and smooth and sugar is completely dissolved, stirring halfway through cooking time. Stir in vanilla.

Makes 3-1/2 cups

Tip: To serve pie, let stand at room temperature 10 minutes or until pie can be easily cut.

Individual Cherry Cheesecakes

12 NILLA® Wafers
2 (8-ounce) packages cream cheese, softened
3/4 cup sugar
2 eggs
  Cherry pie filling

1. Place 1 wafer in bottom of each of 12 (2-1/2-inch) paper-lined muffin-pan cups; set aside.

2. Beat cream cheese, sugar and eggs in large bowl with electric mixer at medium speed until light and fluffy. Spoon cream cheese mixture into each cup, filling about 2/3 full.

3. Bake at 350°F for 30 minutes. Turn off oven; open door slightly. Let cool in oven for 30 minutes. Remove from oven; cool completely. Top with pie filling. Refrigerate at least 1 hour.

Makes 12 servings

Orange Glazed Pound Cake

Ooey Gooey Peanut Butter and Fudge Brownies

(Pictured at right)

BATTER

PAM® No-Stick Cooking Spray
3 cups sugar
1 cup (2 sticks) butter, softened
1/2 cup WESSON® Vegetable Oil
1 tablespoon plus 1-1/2 teaspoons vanilla
6 eggs
2-1/4 cups all-purpose flour
1-1/4 cups baking cocoa
1-1/2 teaspoons baking powder
3/4 teaspoon salt
1 (10-ounce) bag peanut butter chips

FILLING

1-1/2 cups PETER PAN® Creamy Peanut Butter
1/3 cup WESSON® Vegetable Oil
1/2 cup sugar
3 tablespoons all-purpose flour
3 eggs
1 tablespoon vanilla

FROSTING

3 (1-ounce) squares unsweetened chocolate
3 tablespoons PETER PAN® Creamy Peanut Butter
2-2/3 cups powdered sugar
1/4 cup water
1 teaspoon vanilla
1/4 teaspoon salt

BATTER

Preheat oven to 350°F. Spray two 13×9×2-inch baking pans with PAM® Cooking Spray. In a large bowl, beat sugar and butter until creamy. Add Wesson® Oil and vanilla. Add eggs, one at a time, beating well after *each* addition. In a small bowl, combine flour, cocoa, baking powder and salt; blend well. While beating, gradually add flour mixture to creamed mixture; mix well. Fold in peanut butter chips. Evenly spread 1/4 of batter into 1 pan.

FILLING

In a small bowl, cream together Peter Pan® Peanut Butter and Wesson® Oil. Add sugar and flour; blend well. Add eggs and vanilla; beat until smooth. Carefully spread 1/2 of filling mixture evenly over batter in pan. Top filling with an additional 1/4 of batter and spread evenly. Gently cut through layers to create a marble effect throughout the brownies. Repeat process with *remaining* pan, *remaining* batter and *remaining* filling. Bake for 30 minutes. *Do not overbake.*

FROSTING

Meanwhile, in a medium saucepan, melt chocolate and peanut butter over low heat, stirring constantly. Remove from heat and stir in *remaining* ingredients; mix until smooth. If frosting is too thick, add an additional 1 to 3 tablespoons water. Spread frosting over brownies *immediately* after baking. Cool in pans on wire racks. *Makes 3 dozen brownies*

Dulce de Leche Frozen Dessert

3 cups half-and-half or milk
6 tablespoons KRAFT® Caramel Topping, divided
1 package (4-serving size) JELL-O® Butterscotch Flavor Instant Pudding & Pie Filling
1 package (4-serving size) JELL-O® Vanilla Flavor Instant Pudding & Pie Filling
1 tub (8 ounces) COOL WHIP® Whipped Topping, thawed

POUR half-and-half into large bowl. Stir in 2 tablespoons caramel topping until dissolved. Add pudding mixes. Beat with wire whisk 1 minute or until well blended. Gently stir in whipped topping until well mixed.

SPOON 1/2 of the pudding mixture into 8×4-inch loaf pan which has been lined with plastic wrap. Drizzle remaining caramel topping over mixture. Carefully spoon remaining pudding mixture over caramel and smooth with spatula.

FREEZE about 6 hours or overnight or until firm. Carefully invert pan onto serving platter and remove plastic wrap. Let stand at room temperature about 15 minutes before slicing.

Makes 8 servings

Variation: To prepare individual Dulce de Leche frozen pops or cups, spoon 1/2 of the pudding mixture into 10 to 12 paper-lined muffin cups. Place teaspoonful of caramel topping in center of each cup and cover with remaining pudding mixture. For pops, stick wooden popsicle sticks into each cup and freeze.

Ooey Gooey Peanut Butter and Fudge Brownies

Lemon Cheesecake

(Pictured at right)

CRUST

 35 vanilla wafers
 3/4 cup slivered almonds, toasted
 1/3 cup sugar
 1/4 cup butter, melted

FILLING

 3 packages (8 ounces each) cream cheese, softened
 3/4 cup sugar
 1/3 cup whipping cream
 1/4 cup lemon juice
 1 tablespoon grated lemon peel
 1 teaspoon vanilla extract
 4 eggs

TOPPING

 1 pint strawberries
 2 tablespoons sugar

1. Preheat oven to 375°F. For crust, combine wafers, almonds and 1/3 cup sugar in food processor; process until fine crumbs are formed. Combine crumb mixture with melted butter in medium bowl. Press mixture evenly on bottom and 1 inch up side of 9-inch springform pan. Set aside.

2. For filling, beat cream cheese and 3/4 cup sugar in large bowl on high speed of electric mixer 2 to 3 minutes or until fluffy. Add whipping cream, lemon juice, lemon peel, vanilla and eggs; beat just until blended. Pour into prepared crust. Place springform pan on baking sheet. Bake 45 to 55 minutes or until set. Cool completely on wire rack. Cover and refrigerate at least 10 hours or overnight.

3. To complete recipe, for topping, hull and slice strawberries. Combine with sugar in medium bowl. Let stand 15 minutes. Serve over cheesecake. Garnish as desired.   *Makes 16 servings*

Pepperidge Farm® Chocolate Bundles

1/2 package (17-1/4-ounce size) PEPPERIDGE FARM® Frozen Puff Pastry sheets (1 sheet)
 1 package (6 ounces) semi-sweet chocolate pieces
1/4 cup chopped walnuts
 Confectioners' sugar

1. Thaw pastry sheet at room temperature 30 minutes. Preheat oven to 400°F. Mix chocolate pieces and walnuts and set aside.

2. Unfold pastry on lightly floured surface. Roll into 12-inch square. Cut into 9 (4-inch) squares. Place about *2 tablespoons* chocolate mixture in center of each square. Brush edges of squares with water. Fold corners to center on top of filling and twist tightly to seal. Fan out corners. Place 2 inches apart on baking sheet.

3. Bake 15 minutes or until golden. Remove from baking sheet. Cool on wire rack 10 minutes. Sprinkle with confectioners' sugar.   *Makes 9 bundles*

Variation: For large bundles, cut pastry into 4 (6-inch) squares and place about 1/3 cup chocolate mixture in center of each. Proceed as in step 2. Makes 4 bundles.

Black Magic Banana Cupcakes

 2 ripe, medium DOLE® Bananas
 1 egg
1/2 cup buttermilk
1/4 cup vegetable oil
1/2 teaspoon vanilla extract
 1 cup sugar
3/4 cup plus 2 tablespoons all-purpose flour
 6 tablespoons unsweetened cocoa
 1 teaspoon baking soda
1/4 teaspoon baking powder
1/4 teaspoon salt

• Purée bananas in blender (1 cup).

• Blend bananas, egg, buttermilk, oil and vanilla in large bowl.

• Combine sugar, flour, cocoa, baking soda, baking powder and salt in medium bowl; add to banana mixture. Stir just until moistened.

• Line 12 muffin cups with paper liners; lightly spray with vegetable cooking spray. Spoon batter into cups, filling two-thirds full.

• Bake at 350°F 25 minutes or until toothpick inserted in centers comes out clean.
    Makes 12 cupcakes

Pepperidge Farm® Chocolate Mousse Napoleons with Strawberries & Cream

(Pictured at right)

1/2 package (17-1/4-ounce size) PEPPERIDGE
  FARM® Frozen Puff Pastry Sheets (1 sheet)
  1 cup heavy cream
1/4 teaspoon ground cinnamon
  1 package (6 ounces) semi-sweet chocolate
    pieces, melted and cooled
  2 cups sweetened whipped cream *or* whipped
    topping
1-1/2 cups sliced strawberries
  1 square (1 ounce) semi-sweet chocolate, melted
    (optional)
  Confectioners' sugar

1. Thaw pastry sheet at room temperature
30 minutes. Preheat oven to 400°F.

2. Unfold pastry on lightly floured surface. Cut
into 3 strips along fold marks. Cut each strip into
6 rectangles.

3. Bake 15 minutes or until golden. Remove from
baking sheet and cool on wire rack.

4. In medium bowl place cream and cinnamon. Beat
with electric mixer at high speed until stiff peaks
form. Fold in melted chocolate pieces. Split pastries
into 2 layers. Spread 12 rectangles with chocolate
cream. Top with another rectangle. Spread with
whipped cream, sliced strawberries and remaining
rectangles. Serve immediately or cover and
refrigerate up to 4 hours. Just before serving,
drizzle with melted chocolate and sprinkle with
confectioners' sugar. *Makes 12 napoleons*

Chocolate Caramel Drops

24 caramels (about 7 ounces), unwrapped
 2 tablespoons heavy (whipping) cream
 1 cup pecan halves
 4 squares BAKER'S® Semi-Sweet Baking
   Chocolate, melted

MICROWAVE caramels and cream in large
microwavable bowl on HIGH 1-1/2 minutes; stir.
Microwave 1-1/2 minutes; stir until caramels are
completely melted. Cool.

PLACE pecan halves on lightly greased cookie
sheets in clusters of 3. Spoon caramel mixture
over nuts, leaving ends showing. Spread melted
chocolate over caramel mixture. Let stand until
chocolate is set. *Makes about 2 dozen drops*

Roasted Honey Nut Sandwich Cookies

1-1/2 cups quick oats
  1/2 cup all-purpose flour
  1/2 teaspoon baking powder
  1/2 teaspoon baking soda
  1/8 teaspoon salt
  1/2 cup Roasted Honey Nut SKIPPY® Creamy
    Peanut Butter
  1/2 cup (1 stick) margarine or butter, softened
  1/2 cup granulated sugar
  1/2 cup packed brown sugar
    1 egg
  1/2 teaspoon vanilla extract
    Cookie Filling (recipe follows)

1. Preheat oven to 350°F. In medium bowl, combine
oats, flour, baking powder, baking soda and salt.

2. In large bowl, with mixer at medium speed, beat
peanut butter, margarine and sugars until well
blended. Beat in egg and vanilla. Stir in oat mixture
until well mixed.

3. Shape dough by heaping teaspoonfuls into balls;
place 2 inches apart on ungreased cookie sheets.
Flatten each ball to 2-inch round.

4. Bake 8 minutes or until golden brown. Cool
3 minutes on cookie sheets. Remove to wire racks;
cool completely.

5. Spread bottoms of half the cookies with heaping
teaspoonfuls of Cookie Filling; top with remaining
cookies.
  Makes about 2-1/2 dozen sandwich cookies

Cookie Filling: In small bowl, combine 1 cup
Roasted Honey Nut SKIPPY® Creamy Peanut Butter
and 1/2 cup confectioners' sugar; stir until smooth.

*Pepperidge Farm® Chocolate Mousse
Napoleons with Strawberries & Cream*

Lemon Crumb Bars

Lemon Crumb Bars

(Pictured above)

1 (18.25-ounce) package lemon or yellow cake
  mix
1/2 cup (1 stick) butter or margarine, softened
1 egg
2 cups finely crushed saltine cracker crumbs
3 egg yolks
1 (14-ounce) can EAGLE® BRAND Sweetened
  Condensed Milk (NOT evaporated milk)
1/2 cup lemon juice from concentrate

1. Preheat oven to 350°F. Grease 15×10×1-inch
baking pan. In large mixing bowl, combine cake mix,
butter and 1 egg; mix well (mixture will be crumbly).
Stir in cracker crumbs. Reserve 2 cups crumb
mixture. Press remaining crumb mixture firmly
on bottom of prepared pan. Bake 15 minutes.

2. Meanwhile, in medium mixing bowl, combine egg
yolks, Eagle Brand and lemon juice; mix well. Spread
evenly over baked crust.

3. Top with reserved crumb mixture. Bake
20 minutes or until firm. Cool. Cut into bars. Store
covered in refrigerator. *Makes 3 to 4 dozen bars*

Dreamy Orange Cream Puffs

Cream Puffs (recipe follows)
3/4 cup granulated sugar
3 tablespoons cornstarch
1-1/2 cups orange juice
3 egg yolks, beaten
1 cup plain yogurt
2 tablespoons butter
1/2 teaspoon almond extract
1 can (11 ounces) mandarin oranges, drained
  Powdered sugar

1. Prepare Cream Puffs.

2. Mix sugar, cornstarch and orange juice in medium
saucepan. Cook over medium heat until bubbly,
stirring often. Cook 2 minutes; remove from heat.
Gradually stir half of hot mixture into egg yolks.
Return to saucepan; bring to a boil over medium-
high heat. Reduce heat to low and cook 2 minutes;
remove from heat. Stir in yogurt, butter and extract.

3. To serve, spoon filling into bottoms of cream
puffs. Pile orange sections on top of filling. Add
cream puff tops. Lightly sift powdered sugar over
tops. *Makes 6 servings*

Cream Puffs

1 cup water
1/2 cup butter
1 cup all-purpose flour
1/2 teaspoon salt
4 eggs

1. Preheat oven to 400°F. Lightly grease baking
sheet; set aside.

2. Combine water and butter in medium saucepan;
bring to a boil, stirring until butter melts. Add flour
and salt, all at once, stirring vigorously. Cook,
stirring constantly, until mixture forms a ball that
does not separate. Remove from heat and cool
10 minutes. Add eggs, 1 at a time, beating after each
addition until mixture is smooth.

3. Drop heaping tablespoons of batter into
6 mounds, 3 inches apart, onto prepared baking
sheet. Bake about 35 minutes or until golden brown
and puffy. Cool slightly. Carefully cut off tops and
remove soft dough inside. Let puffs cool completely
on wire rack. *Makes 6 cream puffs*

Original Nestlé® Toll House® Chocolate Chip Cookies

(Pictured below)

2-1/4 cups all-purpose flour
1 teaspoon baking soda
1 teaspoon salt
1 cup (2 sticks) butter or margarine, softened
3/4 cup granulated sugar
3/4 cup packed brown sugar
1 teaspoon vanilla extract
2 large eggs
2 cups (12-ounce package) NESTLÉ® TOLL HOUSE® Semi-Sweet Chocolate Morsels
1 cup chopped nuts

PREHEAT oven to 375°F.

COMBINE flour, baking soda and salt in small bowl. Beat butter, granulated sugar, brown sugar and vanilla extract in large mixer bowl until creamy. Add eggs, one at a time, beating well after each addition. Gradually beat in flour mixture. Stir in morsels and nuts. Drop by rounded tablespoonfuls onto ungreased baking sheets.

BAKE for 9 to 11 minutes or until golden brown. Cool on baking sheets for 2 minutes; remove to wire racks to cool completely.

Makes about 5 dozen cookies

Pan Cookie Variation: GREASE 15×10-inch jelly-roll pan. Prepare dough as directed. Spread into prepared pan. Bake for 20 to 25 minutes or until golden brown. Cool in pan on wire rack. Makes 4 dozen bars.

Slice and Bake Cookie Variation: PREPARE dough as directed. Divide in half; wrap in wax paper. Refrigerate for 1 hour or until firm. Shape each half into 15-inch log; wrap in wax paper. Refrigerate for 30 minutes.* Preheat oven to 375°F. Cut into 1/2-inch-thick slices; place on ungreased baking sheets. Bake for 8 to 10 minutes or until golden brown. Cool on baking sheets for 2 minutes; remove to wire racks to cool completely. Makes about 5 dozen cookies.

May be stored in refrigerator for up to 1 week or in freezer for up to 8 weeks.

Original Nestlé® Toll House®
Chocolate Chip Cookies

Lemon Berry Pie

(Pictured at right)

1/2 package (4 ounces) PHILADELPHIA® Cream
    Cheese, cubed, softened
1 tablespoon milk
1 tablespoon sugar
1 tablespoon fresh lemon juice
2 teaspoons grated lemon peel
1 tub (8 ounces) COOL WHIP® Whipped
    Topping, thawed
1 prepared graham cracker crumb crust
    (6 ounces)
1 pint strawberries
2 cups cold milk
2 packages (4-serving size) JELL-O® Vanilla or
    Lemon Flavor Instant Pudding & Pie Filling

BEAT cream cheese, 1 tablespoon milk and sugar in medium bowl with wire whisk until smooth. Stir in lemon juice and peel. Gently stir in 1-1/2 cups of the whipped topping. Spread evenly onto bottom of crust. Reserve a few strawberries for garnish, if desired; cut remaining strawberries in half. Press strawberry halves into cream cheese layer.

POUR 2 cups milk into large bowl. Add pudding mixes. Beat with wire whisk 1 minute. Gently stir in 1 cup of the whipped topping. Spoon over strawberries in crust.

REFRIGERATE 4 hours or until set. Garnish with remaining whipped topping and reserved strawberries just before serving.

Makes 8 servings

Chocolate Orange Gems

2/3 cup butter-flavored solid vegetable shortening
3/4 cup firmly packed light brown sugar
1 large egg
1/4 cup orange juice
1 tablespoon grated orange zest
2-1/4 cups all-purpose flour
1/2 teaspoon baking powder
1/2 teaspoon baking soda
1/2 teaspoon salt
1-3/4 cups "M&M's"® Chocolate Mini Baking Bits
1 cup coarsely chopped pecans
1/3 cup orange marmalade
Vanilla Glaze (recipe follows)

Preheat oven to 350°F. In large bowl, cream shortening and sugar until light and fluffy; beat in

egg, orange juice and orange zest. In medium bowl, combine flour, baking powder, baking soda and salt; blend into creamed mixture. Stir in "M&M's"® Chocolate Mini Baking Bits and nuts. Reserve 1 cup dough; spread remaining dough into ungreased 13×9×2-inch baking pan. Spread marmalade evenly over top of dough to within 1/2 inch of edges. Drop reserved dough by teaspoonfuls randomly over marmalade. Bake 25 to 30 minutes or until light golden brown. *Do not overbake.* Cool completely; drizzle with Vanilla Glaze. Cut into bars. Store in tightly covered container. *Makes 24 bars*

Vanilla Glaze: Combine 1 cup powdered sugar and 1 to 1-1/2 tablespoons warm water until desired consistency. Place glaze in resealable plastic sandwich bag; seal bag. Cut a tiny piece off one corner of the bag (not more than 1/8 inch). Drizzle glaze over cookies.

Apple Crisp

10 Golden Delicious apples (about 5 pounds),
    peeled, cored and sliced (about 12 cups)
1 cup firmly packed brown sugar, divided
2 teaspoons ground cinnamon
3/4 cup all-purpose flour
1/2 cup (1 stick) cold IMPERIAL® Spread
3/4 cup uncooked quick or old-fashioned oats

Preheat oven to 375°F.

In large bowl, combine apples, 1/2 cup sugar and cinnamon. Turn into 13×9-inch baking pan or 3-quart shallow casserole; set aside.

In medium bowl, combine flour and remaining 1/2 cup sugar. With pastry blender or 2 knives, cut in spread until mixture is size of coarse crumbs. Stir in oats. With hands, gently squeeze mixture to form crumbs; sprinkle over apple mixture.

Bake, uncovered, 1 hour or until apples are tender and topping is golden. Serve warm or at room temperature and, if desired, with vanilla ice cream or frozen yogurt. *Makes 8 servings*

Lemon Berry Pie

Cashew Macadamia Crunch

(Pictured at right)

>   2 cups (11.5 ounce package) HERSHEY'S Milk
>   Chocolate Chips
>   3/4 cup coarsely chopped salted or unsalted
>   cashews
>   3/4 cup coarsely chopped salted or unsalted
>   macadamia nuts
>   1/2 cup (1 stick) butter, softened
>   1/2 cup sugar
>   2 tablespoons light corn syrup

1. Line 9-inch square pan with foil, extending foil over edges of pan. Butter foil. Cover bottom of prepared pan with chocolate chips.

2. Combine cashews, macadamia nuts, butter, sugar and corn syrup in large heavy skillet; cook over low heat, stirring constantly, until butter is melted and sugar is dissolved. Increase heat to medium; cook, stirring constantly, until mixture begins to cling together and turns golden brown.

3. Pour mixture over chocolate chips in pan, spreading evenly. Cool. Refrigerate until chocolate is firm. Remove from pan; peel off foil. Break into pieces. Store tightly covered in cool, dry place.

Makes about 1-1/2 pounds

Blueberry Angel Food Cake Rolls

(Pictured on page 182)

>   1 package DUNCAN HINES® Angel Food Cake
>   Mix
>   1/4 cup confectioners' sugar plus additional for
>   dusting
>   1 (21-ounce) can blueberry pie filling
>   Mint leaves for garnish (optional)

Preheat oven to 350°F. Line two 15-1/2×10-1/2×1-inch jelly-roll pans with aluminum foil.

Prepare cake mix as directed on package. Divide and spread evenly into pans. Cut through batter with knife or spatula to remove large air bubbles. Bake 15 minutes or until set. Invert cakes at once onto clean, lint-free dishtowels dusted with sugar. Remove foil carefully. Roll up each cake with towel jelly-roll fashion, starting at short end. Cool completely.

Unroll cakes. Spread about 1 cup blueberry pie filling to within 1 inch of edges on each cake. Reroll and place seam-side down on serving plate. Dust with 1/4 cup sugar. Garnish with mint leaves, if desired. *Makes 2 cakes (8 servings each)*

Tip: For a variation in flavor, substitute cherry pie filling for the blueberry pie filling.

Colonial Apple Cake

>   2-3/4 cups unsifted all-purpose flour
>   1 teaspoon baking powder
>   1 teaspoon ground cinnamon
>   3/4 teaspoon salt
>   1/2 teaspoon baking soda
>   1-3/4 cups granulated sugar
>   1-1/4 cups CRISCO® Oil* plus additional for greasing
>   2 eggs
>   1/4 cup milk
>   1 teaspoon vanilla extract
>   2 cups chopped peeled apples
>   1/2 cup chopped dates
>   1 teaspoon grated lemon peel
>   1 to 2 tablespoons confectioners' sugar

Use your favorite Crisco Oil product.

1. Heat oven to 350°F. Grease and flour 12-cup fluted tube pan.

2. Mix flour, baking powder, cinnamon, salt and baking soda in medium mixing bowl. Set aside. Combine granulated sugar, oil, eggs, milk and vanilla in large mixing bowl. Beat with electric mixer at medium speed until blended, scraping bowl constantly. Add dry ingredients. Beat at medium speed 2 minutes longer, scraping bowl frequently. Stir in apples, dates and lemon peel. Pour into prepared pan.

3. Bake at 350°F 1 hour to 1 hour 15 minutes or until toothpick inserted in center comes out clean. Do not overbake. Let stand 10 minutes. Invert onto serving plate. Cool slightly. Sift confectioners' sugar over cake. Serve warm. Top with whipped cream, if desired. *Makes 1 ring cake*

Cashew Macadamia Crunch

Easy Chocolate Cream-Filled Torte

(Pictured at right)

    1 frozen pound cake (10-3/4 ounces), thawed
1/2 cup powdered sugar
1/4 cup HERSHEY'S Cocoa
    1 cup (1/2 pint) cold whipping cream
    1 teaspoon vanilla extract
        Chocolate Glaze (recipe follows)
        Sliced almonds (optional)

1. Cut cake horizontally to make 4 layers. Stir together sugar and cocoa in medium bowl. Add whipping cream and vanilla; beat until stiff.

2. Place bottom cake layer on serving platter. Spread 1/3 of the whipped cream mixture on cake layer. Place next cake layer on top of whipped cream mixture; continue layering whipped cream mixture and cake until all have been used.

3. Prepare Chocolate Glaze; spoon over top of cake, allowing to drizzle down sides. Garnish with almonds, if desired. Refrigerate until ready to serve. Cover; refrigerate leftover torte.
Makes 8 to 10 servings

Chocolate Glaze

    2 tablespoons butter or margarine
    2 tablespoons HERSHEY'S Cocoa
    2 tablespoons water
    1 cup powdered sugar
1/4 to 1/2 teaspoon almond extract

1. Melt butter in small saucepan over low heat. Add cocoa and water. Cook, stirring constantly, until smooth and slightly thickened. Do not boil.

2. Remove from heat. Gradually add powdered sugar and almond extract, beating with whisk until smooth. *Makes about 1/2 cup glaze*

Banana Praline Sauce

1/4 cup margarine
1/4 cup packed brown sugar
    2 teaspoons lemon juice
1/2 teaspoon ground cinnamon
    1 cup sliced banana
1/4 cup PLANTERS® Walnuts, chopped

1. Heat margarine, brown sugar, lemon juice and cinnamon in saucepan over medium heat until margarine melts and mixture is smooth.

2. Stir in banana. Cook for 2 to 3 minutes or until fruit is tender. Stir in walnuts. Cool. Cover and store in refrigerator.

3. Serve sauce warm over ice cream or frozen yogurt. *Makes 1-1/2 cups*

Pineapple Mousse Torte

        Chocolate Crumb Crust (recipe follows)
    1 package (8 ounces) cream cheese, softened
1-1/4 cups sugar
    1/2 teaspoon grated lemon peel
    1 can (15-1/4 ounces) DEL MONTE® Crushed
        Pineapple In Its Own Juice, undrained
    1 can (8 ounces) DEL MONTE Pineapple Tidbits
        In Its Own Juice, undrained
    2 envelopes unflavored gelatin
2-1/4 cups whipping cream, whipped

1. Prepare crumb crust; set aside.

2. Blend cream cheese with sugar and lemon peel.

3. Drain juice from crushed pineapple and tidbits into small saucepan. Sprinkle gelatin over juice. Let stand 5 minutes. Place over low heat and stir until gelatin is completely dissolved.

4. Add crushed pineapple to cream cheese mixture; stir in gelatin mixture until blended. Thoroughly fold in whipped cream.

5. Pour filling into crust. Chill at least 5 hours or overnight. Remove sides of pan. Top with pineapple tidbits and garnish, if desired.
Makes 10 to 12 servings

Chocolate Crumb Crust

2-1/4 cups chocolate wafer crumbs
    1/2 cup butter or margarine, melted

1. Mix ingredients; press firmly onto bottom of 9-inch springform pan.

Easy Chocolate Cream-Filled Torte

Apple Oatmeal Snack Bars

(Pictured at right)

1-1/2 cups all-purpose flour
3/4 cup uncooked rolled oats
1 teaspoon baking powder
1/2 teaspoon salt
1 cup granulated sugar
2 tablespoons margarine, softened
1/2 cup MOTT'S® Cinnamon Apple Sauce
1 egg
1 teaspoon vanilla extract
1 cup MOTT'S® Chunky Apple Sauce
1/3 cup raisins
1 tablespoon firmly packed light brown sugar
1/2 teaspoon ground cinnamon

1. Preheat oven to 375°F. Spray 8-inch square baking pan with nonstick cooking spray.

2. In medium bowl, combine flour, oats, baking powder and salt.

3. In large bowl, beat granulated sugar and margarine with electric mixer at medium s, until blended. Whisk in 1/2 cup cinnamon ap. sauce, egg and vanilla.

4. Add flour mixture to apple sauce mixture; s until well blended. Spoon half of batter into prepared pan, spreading evenly.

5. In small bowl, combine 1 cup chunky apple sa raisins, brown sugar and cinnamon. Pour evenly over batter.

6. Spoon remaining batter over filling, spreading evenly.

7. Bake 30 to 35 minutes or until lightly browned. Cool on wire rack 15 minutes; cut into 16 bars.
Makes 16 servings

Rocky Road Clusters

2 cups (12-ounce package) NESTLÉ® TOLL
   HOUSE® Semi-Sweet Chocolate Morsels
1 can (14 ounces) NESTLÉ® CARNATION®
   Sweetened Condensed Milk
2-1/2 cups miniature marshmallows
1 cup coarsely chopped nuts
1 teaspoon vanilla extract

LINE baking sheets with waxed paper.

COMBINE morsels and sweetened condensed milk in large, microwave-safe bowl. Microwave on HIGH (100%) power for 1 minute; stir. Microwave at additional 10- to 20-second intervals, stirring until smooth. Stir in marshmallows, nuts and vanilla extract.

DROP by heaping tablespoonfuls in mounds onto prepared baking sheets. Refrigerate until firm.
Makes about 2 dozen candies

Cranberry Mousse Mold

1-1/2 cups boiling water
1 package (8-serving size) *or* 2 packages
   (4-serving size each) JELL-O® Brand
   Cranberry Flavor Gelatin Dessert
1 cup cold water
1 can (16 ounces) whole-berry cranberry sauce
1 tub (8 ounces) COOL WHIP® Whipped
   Topping, thawed

STIR boiling water into gelatin in large bowl 2 minutes or until completely dissolved. Stir in cold water and cranberry sauce. Spoon 2 cups gelatin mixture into 6-cup mold. Refrigerate about 30 minutes or until set but not firm (should stick to finger and mound).

MEANWHILE, refrigerate remaining gelatin mixture about 30 minutes or until slightly thickened (consistency of unbeaten egg whites).

STIR in 2 cups whipped topping with wire whisk until smooth. Pour over gelatin layer in mold.

REFRIGERATE 4 hours or until firm. Unmold. Garnish with remaining whipped topping.
Makes 12 servings

Unmolding: Dip mold in warm water for about 15 seconds. Gently pull gelatin from around edges with moist fingers. Place moistened serving plate on top of mold. Invert mold and plate; holding mold and plate together, shake slightly to loosen. Gently remove mold and center gelatin on plate.

The publisher would like to thank the companies and organizations listed below for the use of their recipes and photographs in this publication.

A.1.® Steak Sauce

Barilla America, Inc.

Birds Eye®

Bob Evans®

Butterball® Turkey Company

California Dried Plum Board

Campbell Soup Company

ConAgra Foods®

Cream of Wheat® Cereal

Del Monte Corporation

Dole Food Company, Inc.

Duncan Hines® and Moist Deluxe® are
registered trademarks of Aurora
Foods Inc.

Eagle® Brand

Egg Beaters®

Fleischmann's® Original Spread

The Fremont Company, Makers of
Frank's & SnowFloss Kraut and
Tomato Products

The Golden Grain Company®

Grey Poupon® Dijon Mustard

Heinz U.S.A.

Hershey Foods Corporation

The Hidden Valley® Food Products
Company

Hormel Foods, LLC

JOLLY TIME® Pop Corn

The Kingsford Products Company

Kraft Foods: Biscuit, Snacks and
Confections Group

Kraft Foods Holdings

Lawry's® Foods, Inc.

© Mars, Incorporated 2002

McCormick®

McIlhenny Company (TABASCO®
brand Pepper Sauce)

Minnesota Cultivated Wild Rice
Council

Mott's® is a registered trademark of
Mott's, Inc.

National Chicken Council / US
Poultry & Egg Association

National Honey Board

National Pork Board

National Turkey Federation

Nestlé USA

General Index

Alphabetical Index

METRIC CONVERSION CHART

VOLUME MEASUREMENTS (dry)

$1/8$ teaspoon = 0.5 mL
$1/4$ teaspoon = 1 mL
$1/2$ teaspoon = 2 mL
$3/4$ teaspoon = 4 mL
1 teaspoon = 5 mL
1 tablespoon = 15 mL
2 tablespoons = 30 mL
$1/4$ cup = 60 mL
$1/3$ cup = 75 mL
$1/2$ cup = 125 mL
$2/3$ cup = 150 mL
$3/4$ cup = 175 mL
1 cup = 250 mL
2 cups = 1 pint = 500 mL
3 cups = 750 mL
4 cups = 1 quart = 1 L

VOLUME MEASUREMENTS (fluid)

1 fluid ounce (2 tablespoons) = 30 mL
4 fluid ounces ($1/2$ cup) = 125 mL
8 fluid ounces (1 cup) = 250 mL
12 fluid ounces ($1 1/2$ cups) = 375 mL
16 fluid ounces (2 cups) = 500 mL

WEIGHTS (mass)

$1/2$ ounce = 15 g
1 ounce = 30 g
3 ounces = 90 g
4 ounces = 120 g
8 ounces = 225 g
10 ounces = 285 g
12 ounces = 360 g
16 ounces = 1 pound = 450 g

DIMENSIONS

$1/16$ inch = 2 mm
$1/8$ inch = 3 mm
$1/4$ inch = 6 mm
$1/2$ inch = 1.5 cm
$3/4$ inch = 2 cm
1 inch = 2.5 cm

OVEN TEMPERATURES

250°F = 120°C
275°F = 140°C
300°F = 150°C
325°F = 160°C
350°F = 180°C
375°F = 190°C
400°F = 200°C
425°F = 220°C
450°F = 230°C

BAKING PAN SIZES

Utensil	Size in Inches/Quarts	Metric Volume	Size in Centimeters
Baking or Cake Pan (square or rectangular)	$8 \times 8 \times 2$	2 L	$20 \times 20 \times 5$
	$9 \times 9 \times 2$	2.5 L	$23 \times 23 \times 5$
	$12 \times 8 \times 2$	3 L	$30 \times 20 \times 5$
	$13 \times 9 \times 2$	3.5 L	$33 \times 23 \times 5$
Loaf Pan	$8 \times 4 \times 3$	1.5 L	$20 \times 10 \times 7$
	$9 \times 5 \times 3$	2 L	$23 \times 13 \times 7$
Round Layer Cake Pan	$8 \times 1 1/2$	1.2 L	20×4
	$9 \times 1 1/2$	1.5 L	23×4
Pie Plate	$8 \times 1 1/4$	750 mL	20×3
	$9 \times 1 1/4$	1 L	23×3
Baking Dish or Casserole	1 quart	1 L	—
	$1 1/2$ quart	1.5 L	—
	2 quart	2 L	—